The civilized imagination

The civilized imagination

A study of Ann Radcliffe, Jane Austen, and Sir Walter Scott

DANIEL COTTOM
Wayne State University

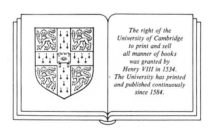

The right of the
University of Cambridge
to print and sell
all manner of books
was granted by
Henry VIII in 1534.
The University has printed
and published continuously
since 1584.

CAMBRIDGE UNIVERSITY PRESS

Cambridge
London   New York   New Rochelle
Melbourne   Sydney

For my mother and father

Published by the Press Syndicate of the University of Cambridge
The Pitt Building, Trumpington Street, Cambridge CB2 IRP
32 East 57th Street, New York, NY 10022, USA
10 Stamford Road, Oakleigh, Melbourne 3166, Australia

© Cambridge University Press 1985

First published 1985

Printed in the United States of America

Library of Congress Cataloging in Publication Data

Cottom, Daniel.
The civilized imagination.

Bibliography: p.

Includes index.

1. English fiction – 19th century – History and
criticism. 2. Aesthetics in literature. 3. Perception
in literature. 4. Social classes in literature.
5. Radcliffe, Ann Ward, 1764–1823 – Aesthetics.
6. Austen, Jane, 1775–1817 – Aesthetics. 7. Scott,
Walter, Sir, 1771–1832 – Aesthetics. I. Title.
PR778.A38C68 1985 823'.7'09 84–17002
ISBN 0 521 30172 6

Contents

∾

Acknowledgments

⌒

I would like to express my appreciation to my colleagues Nancy Armstrong, Charles Baxter, Michael Bell, John Franzosa, and Ross Pudaloff, whose comments about various parts of this work have been of great value to me.

Special thanks are due to Leonard Tennenhouse; the generosity of his encouragement and criticism have made this book far better than it would have been without his aid.

I also would like to thank the editors of *The Journal of Aesthetics and Art Criticism, Novel, ELH,* and *Studies in Romanticism,* where the original versions of chapters one, five, eight, and nine first appeared.

Abbreviations

∾

Works of Ann Radcliffe
CAD	The Castles of Athlin and Dunbayne
I	The Italian
J	A Journey
MU	The Mysteries of Udolpho
RF	The Romance of the Forest
SR	A Sicilian Romance

Works of Jane Austen
E	Emma
L	Letters
MP	Mansfield Park
NA	Northanger Abbey
P	Persuasion
PP	Pride and Prejudice
SS	Sense and Sensibility

Works of Walter Scott
Ab	The Abbott
AG	Anne of Geierstein
An	The Antiquary
B	The Betrothed
BD	The Black Dwarf
BL	The Bride of Lammermoor
CD	Castle Dangerous
CRP	Count Robert of Paris
FMP	The Fair Maid of Perth

Works of Walter Scott *(cont.)*

FN	*The Fortunes of Nigel*
GM	*Guy Mannering*
HM	*The Heart of Midlothian*
I	*Ivanhoe*
K.	*Kenilworth*
LM	*The Legend of Montrose*
M	*The Monastery*
OM	*Old Mortality*
P	*The Pirate*
PP	*Peveril of the Peak*
QD	*Quentin Durward*
R	*Redgauntlet*
RR	*Rob Roy*
SD	*The Surgeon's Daughter*
SRW	*St. Ronan's Well*
Wa	*Waverley*
Wo	*Woodstock*

1

INTRODUCTION: OF TASTE AND THE CIVILIZED IMAGINATION

∽

An unedified palate is the irrepressible cloven hoof
of the upstart.

— PARSON SWANCOURT IN THOMAS HARDY'S
A Pair of Blue Eyes

I

VIRTUALLY ALL eighteenth-century writers on aesthetics direct their arguments against certain popular proverbs: *Chacun à son goût, De gustibus non est disputandum,* and so on. In an age being nudged toward relativistic postulates by the doctrine of association in psychology, the beginnings of a modern historical consciousness, and the popularization of comparative anthropology in fictional works like *The Persian Letters* as well as in nonfictional accounts of voyages and travels, these writers find it all the more necessary to insist on a universal standard of taste. It has been noted by Bernard Bosanquet, among others, that even so notorious a skeptic as Hume is unable to believe that the perceptions of different people might be completely incommensurable in the terms of aesthetic judgment. Though Hume begins one of his essays on taste by agreeing with proverbial wisdom − "common sense, which is so often at variance with philosophy, especially with the skeptical kind, is found, in one instance at least, to agree in pronouncing the same decision" − he concludes by asserting that "amidst all the variety and caprice of taste, there are certain general principles of approbation or blame, whose influence a careful eye may trace in all operations of the mind."[1] It seems that for Hume, as for almost all other writers on this topic, there have to be universal principles of taste if there are not to be disruptions in sensation and communication that would lead to social chaos. Burke's forthright argument is typical in this regard and an interesting complement to Hume's:

> If we suffer ourselves to imagine, that their senses present to different men different images of things, this sceptical proceeding will make every sort of reasoning vain and frivolous, even that sceptical reasoning itself, which had persuaded us to entertain a doubt concerning the agreement of our perceptions.[2]

In taking this stance, writers such as Hume and Burke are certainly in accord with the prevailing tendency in their age to subsume all local differences and particulars within the universal operations of reason; and yet the topic of taste has a special significance for the study of aesthetics, the history of art, and history in general. For within eighteenth-century discourse on this topic one can see with particular clarity the extent to which the critical consciousness of that age is a defensive consciousness directed less to arguing what art is or should be than to arguing that it is not and must not be popular – a property of the common people. Like a geographical position that appears to be of relatively minor importance in itself but is known to be strategic to the defense of an entire country, the principled nature of aesthetics has to be protected in order to insure against challenges to social presumptions of much greater moment. At stake in the promotion of a universal standard of taste are the standards that order and govern eighteenth-century society.

In his important work on this subject, R. G. Saisselin has described the situation as follows:

> What mattered was not to give in to sensation but precisely to master it . . . The whole problem of taste in the eighteenth century consisted in finding an effective answer to the calls which fancy made on men, and the problem was not resolved empirically, but in terms of certain values inseparable from a concept of man and of civilization . . . The man of taste was an aristocrat in spirit if not by race, and the judgment of taste was aristocratic rather than democratic, for it was not founded upon the likes or the dislikes of a majority.[3]

What remains to be explained is the way in which the discourse of taste is not only an aristocratic discourse but a discourse *of* aristocracy; not only a discourse related to a specific social and historical environment but a discourse upon that environment; not only a response to the inconsistencies in individual tastes or in the tastes of various nations or races but even more importantly a response to inconsistencies in the tastes of different classes within society. In fact, it is only by supporting a particular social order and the repression of the lower classes within that order that eighteenth-century writers are able to maintain a universal standard of taste. Thus, the discourse of taste does not simply attempt to place perception under the power of morality – an ambition that would be unremarkable enough – but to prove that perception is and must be under this power, despite whatever signs to the contrary empirical evidence and common sense may present. Proper social attitudes are made a precondition for any experience as well as for any meaningful discourse. The law that governs criticism is that a perceptual event will not be judged to have occurred unless it can be proved to have been the result of both nature and education, which work together to form taste, which is a mechanism for discovering that the aristocracy is the universal class within the state and the state, in effect, an internal government to the body.

II

According to eighteenth-century aesthetics, uneducated perceptions are pseudo-events.[4] The assurance with which an individual may report an experience is of no consequence if that report does not defer to the social prescriptions for the senses. This is not simply a matter of denying value to certain experiences – as all educators must do to gain the attention of their students – or of denying that particular expressions of experience are true or real – as Plato did in censoring the poets – but of denying that the experience, whether one cares to call it true or imaginary, valuable or worthless, has even occurred. The individual who happens upon a work of art without an educated judgment has had no experience of that work. Whatever may have happened has not involved this object called "art," for the eighteenth-century object of art literally does not appear to anyone who does not have good taste. As Alexander Gerard writes, without the judgment of taste "we should, like per-

3

sons in a mist, see something, but could not tell what we saw."[5] Since the existence of a work of art can be established only through its educated appreciation, tasteless persons are not allowed to experience it. One has only to consider Lord Kames's wonderfully paradoxical but nonetheless representative formulation:

> Those who depend for food on bodily labor are totally void of taste; of such a taste at least as can be of use in the fine arts. This consideration bars the greater part of mankind; and of the remaining part, many by corrupted taste are unqualified for voting. The common sense of mankind must then be confined to the few that fall not under these exemptions.[6]

And looking at the situation from a slightly different angle, Hugh Blair comes to the same conclusion:

> A relish for the entertainments of taste . . . is favourable to many virtues. Whereas to be entirely devoid of relish for eloquence, poetry, or any of the fine arts, is justly construed to be an unpromising symptom of youth; and raises suspicions of their being prone to low gratifications, or destined to drudge in the more vulgar and illiberal pursuits of life.[7]

It is in response to such formulations that René Wellek has noted "the paradox of a universal audience, of a true taste confined to a very few select groups" as one of the "difficulties . . . inherent in the term 'taste.' "[8] Even though exceptions to this paradox may sometimes seem to appear, upon closer examination they are almost always found to surrender to the generality. The aesthetic doctrine of the Abbé du Bos may remain more liberal than that of most writers, for instance, but his argument in favor of sentiment as the basis for judgment does not extend the experience of art to an audience as large as one might expect. One must consider the qualifications he places upon his rejection of judgment according to formal rules, the following among them:

> I do not include the lower orders in the public capable of pronouncing upon poems or paintings so as to decide to what degree they are excellent. The word "public" here includes

only those persons who have acquired enlightenment, whether it be through reading or through the intercourse of the world.[9]

Indeed, the point is so well understood as to be completely unremarkable: Taste is a domain of the upper classes and is ultimately a property exclusive to the purest representatives of the aristocracy. As Thomas Reid notes, "We see that in matters which relate to human conduct, good taste and good breeding are the same."[10] Or, as Mandeville says of honor, in words that also convey the satiric attitude his work assumes toward taste:

> The Excellency of this Principle is, that the Vulgar are destitute of it, and it is only to be met with in People of the better Sort, as some Oranges have Kernels, and others not, tho' the out-side be the same.[11]

What is somewhat more remarkable, though, is that those who suffer from defective perceptions are even made to testify against themselves. As Lord Kames writes,

> Men, it is true, are prone to flatter themselves, by taking it for granted that their opinions and their tastes are in all respects conformable to the common standard; but there may be exceptions, and experience shows there are some: there are instances without number, of persons who are addicted to the grosser amusements of gaming, eating, drinking, without having any relish for more elegant pleasures; such, for example, as are afforded by the fine arts: yet these very persons, talking the same language with the rest of mankind, pronounce in favor of the more elegant pleasures, and they invariably approve those who have a more refined taste, being ashamed of their own as low and sensual.[12]

Such testimony in favor of aristocratic values is not only extorted from commoners throughout eighteenth-century criticism but also throughout eighteenth-century literature. One thinks, for example, of the way in which Pamela is made to regard her marriage to Mr. B. as "a happy Exception to the rule"[13] that maintains class differences – an exception that is emphatically *not* a precedent for further violations. Exceptions do occur, in literature and in critical writings – Hogarth's idiosyncratic, practical, and humorous *Analysis of Beauty* may be instanced – but the generality is overwhelming, and most exceptions are like Pamela's. For instance, when referring to the scandalous pleasures from which he hopes painting will lead the indolent gentleman, Jonathan Richardson will confess that no man "can . . . pronounce upon the pleasures of another" and thus will seem to break the rule of taste; but he quickly says of the two types of pleasures, "I know what I am recommending is so great a one, that I cannot conceive the other can be equal to it."[14] No matter what ideas may be excited by the evidence of experience or by psychological, historical, and anthropological theory and evidence, there are certain suppositions that the civilized imagination will automatically reject on the grounds that they would violate distinctions and differences that form the very basis of social order. A rapprochement between "low" and aesthetic pleasures would represent an approach of the commonalty to the aristocracy that must be rejected if the proper government of society is to be maintained – and this despite the fact that so many of these writers were not themselves aristocrats except in spirit. D'Alembert, therefore, while initially saying that it is only that vanity whereby "one praises oneself for having become difficult" which distinguishes refined from gross pleasures, will hasten to say of this vanity that "the pleasure it makes us feel is not, like so many others, the effect of a sudden and violent impression, but is more continuous, more uniform, and more durable, and allows itself to be tasted for longer stretches."[15] Similarly, despite all the qualifications he places upon the perception of beauty in his treatise on that subject, even to the point of proffering the concession that there may be no two individuals whose perceptions are exactly alike, Diderot still upholds the idea of an objective beauty and says, in his "Essay on Painting," that "neither nature nor the art which copies it says anything to the stupid or cold man, and little to the ignorant."[16]

When qualifications are placed upon aesthetic values, then, they may assume forms as varied as those employed by Samuel Richardson, d'Alembert, Jonathan Richardson, and Diderot, but they always represent similar demands for distance, subordination, and deferential service in the relations between those who are tasteful and those who are not. Aesthetic judgment is defined by a separation of classes within society, and this separation is patterned upon the traditional separation between aristocrats and commoners. Such exceptions as exist do little more than emphasize all the more powerfully the rule of taste that imprisons them within its discursive procedures just as unreason in general is isolated and overpowered within the word of reason. The prevailing attitude remains that expressed by Kames, and by Batteux:

> As a man, who has an exquisite taste, is attentive to the impression that the work of art makes upon him, as he senses distinctly, and as he consequently pronounces on it, it is scarce possible that other men should not subscribe to his judgment. They feel the same sentiment as he, if not to the same degree, at least of the same type: and whatever prejudice and bad taste there may be, they submit themselves, and secretly render homage to nature.[17]

This subscription of submission accompanies all aesthetic discourse, showing the coercion that aristocratic sensibility exercises over what might otherwise be experience.

Furthermore, the "invariable approval" thus elicited from the lower classes also foreshadows the argument in John Stuart Mill's *Utilitarianism* that enabled him to support liberal paternalism toward the lower classes because as an educated man, he could argue as one experienced in both lower and higher states of being, whereas the lower classes could not pretend to a knowledge of their superiors' experience. The fact that a prominent advocate of Reform and admirer of the poetry of Wordsworth should thus expound an essentially aristocratic eighteenth-century doctrine is indicative of the persistence with which this ideology survives not only in the mouths of unreconstructed Tories, such as Hardy's Parson Swancourt, but even in programs that seem to be expressly formulated to oppose it, such as Wordsworth's. After all, the idea of taste not only represents the aspiration to attain the status or recognition of the aristocracy but also the aspiration of the aristocracy to fulfill the idea of itself. The aristocratic attitudes used in this essay to describe taste are thus not simply those of the actual upper classes of the eighteenth century (although these are included) but also those of the aristocratic temperament as such. References to aristocratic values do more than point to the strictest definition of the aristocracy as a ruling class privileged through its inherited rank: They also encompass the broad influence wielded by values that are strictly bound, no matter at what metaphorical remove, to the idea of a blood inheritance. Although it was in the eighteenth century that the word "taste" gained massive currency as a name for judgment after having been used in this metaphorical sense since the fifteenth century, the attitudes enmeshed in its popularity reach back as far as antiquity and are still with us today.[18]

To say this is to admit to an extremely broad definition of the subject, but such a definition is necessary to an understanding of the way in which a doctrine appealing explicitly to only a minuscule minority of people could enjoy such a wide appeal. For according to the doctrine of taste, the vast majority of the population of any country, as well as the vast majority of countries throughout the development of history, must be without it. A quotation illustrating this point could be plucked from the writings of almost any eighteenth-century writer on the subject, but perhaps Voltaire puts the matter most succinctly: "Taste is then like philosophy: it belongs to a very small number of privileged spirits."[19]

III

In what state, then, do these people live, these tasteless persons who are always said to compose the majority in society? They live in an imitation of society that is permitted to survive only as long as it is prepared to admit its nonexistence. As John Donaldson comments, "to question whether an improved taste be an advantage, is in some measure to doubt whether it is better to be or not to be, to live or not to live."[20] If a laborer should claim that the pleasure he receives in getting drunk does exist and is not simply an illusory imitation of the pleasure one receives from the fine arts, he would be a criminal, a sinner, or a madman. And as the aristocracy is thus established as the universal and uniquely legitimate class within society, a further conclusion is reached: The pleasures of the aristocracy must be a secret.

Because the lower classes are made to defer to the aristocracy's judgment over their sensations, they must not only remain ignorant of the true nature of perception but must even remain ignorant of the fact that the aristocracy has pleasures different from their own. If it were not so, their deference might be a product of thought rather than one of unconscious compulsion and therefore might be open to challenge through thought. This demand that they defer to a different kind of perception while remaining unaware of its difference would seem to be contradictory, but this contradiction is a key element in eighteenth-century aesthetic discourse and cannot be resolved in the terms of that discourse.

To the vulgar, then, who are not allowed to discover art in the first place, the difference between their own perceptions and the perception that does experience art must appear to be an entirely formal limit. For persons with no taste to impute a content or significance to the senses of the aristocracy would be to presume upon a domain they have been forbidden to enter. They must appreciate the difference to which they defer even though they can recognize it only through the demand that they not violate it. It would be difficult to conceive of a more effective method of intimidation than this one, in which an object is made to appear only through its unavailability – one need only consider the strength of that literary, philosophical, and psychological theme in which the value of an object increases in direct proportion to the mysterious distance at which it stands from the spectator. And this paradox that the greatest value is attached to the object that one cannot possess represents not only the attitude toward art demanded by the doctrine of taste but also the quintessentially aristocratic attitude toward nature, property, women, and significance in general.

Furthermore, a defense against one of the upper classes' fears is erected through this belief that their unique pleasures are imperceptible to outsiders. To put the matter as simply as possible, the fear is that the lower classes might notice what they are missing. It might appear to be an unlikely mode of assurance, but this idea that the pleasures of the aristocracy are secret enjoyed such popularity in the eighteenth century as to be reiterated again and again in the critical writings of that age. As Voltaire writes, "The connoisseur in music, in painting, in architecture, in poetry, in medals, etc., experiences sensations which the vulgar don't suspect . . . The man of taste has different eyes, different ears, and a different touch than the coarse man has."[21] Montesquieu agrees, saying that "those who tastefully judge works of talent have and become used to an infinity of sensations that other men do not have."[22] Hume notes that the delicacy of taste, like that of passion, "enlarges the sphere both of our happiness and misery, and makes us sensible to pains as well as pleasures, which escape the rest of mankind."[23] According to Gerard, "the polite and knowing are chiefly touched with those delicacies which would escape the notice of a vulgar eye."[24] And, once again, Kames spells out the rule most bluntly:

> Some people, indeed, Nature's favorites, have a wonderful acuteness of sense, which to them unfolds many a delightful scene, totally hid from vulgar eyes. But if such refined pleasure be confined to a small number, it is, however, wisely ordered that others are not sensible of the defect; nor detracts it from their happiness that others secretly are more happy. With relation to the fine arts only, that qualification seems essential; and there it is termed *delicacy of taste*.[25]

Thus established, this rule is then extended to the ultimate defense of the aristocracy. In this extension, the very property of the aristocracy is made to disappear from the view of outsiders. As the object of art and aristocratic perceptions of it are hidden from the vulgar, so are all aristocratic possessions concealed.

These possessions are hidden by the way in which the eighteenth-century critic, who may be typified by Addison and Steele's Spectator, looks upon the object of art. Like the Idler and the Rambler and the other eighteenth-century figures related to them, and like all those writers in this century who occupy themselves with the topic of taste, the Spectator claims that he takes only a detached and purely speculative view of objects, so that he may be free of prejudice, rivalry, and selfish interest. It is in following this pattern, for instance, that Sir Joshua Reynolds asserts "that as a work is conducted under the influence of general ideas, or partial, it is principally to be considered as the effect of a good or a bad taste,"[26] and Francis Hutcheson remarks that "this Pleasure of Beauty . . . is distinct from that Joy which arises from Self-love upon prospect of Advantage."[27] In fact, just as in the case of the determination that art belongs exclusively to the upper classes, this claim of impartiality is so pervasive as to seem hardly worthy of notice. Even du Bos, who argues in favor of the public and against rigid rules, ends by conceding this rule as he argues that the public's opinion is, in fact, disinterested. Kant, the greatest interpreter of aesthetics in the transition between Neoclassicism and Romanticism, is especially relentless in explicating this critical stance:

Everyone must confess that a judgment on beauty in which the slightest interest interferes must be very partial and not a pure judgment of taste. One must not be in the least partial to the existence of the thing but rather remain entirely indifferent in this consideration in order to play the judge in things of taste.[28]

The consequence of this critical stance – and of the confession forced by it – is that the realities of social organization are disguised in the form of a mental principle. That is to say, the claim of disinterest is made possible only because those objects that are regarded by the Spectator can be said to already belong to him, in spirit if not in actuality. Thus, as Addison describes the role of the Polite Imagination in the service of man,

It gives him, indeed, a kind of property in every thing he sees, and makes the most rude uncultivated Parts of Nature administer to his Pleasures: so that he looks upon the World, as it were, in another Light, and discovers in it a multitude of Charms, that conceal themselves from the generality of Mankind.[29]

In other words, the aristocracy defends its property by ceding its ownership of that property to the realm of the imagination. And thus, even as it ostensibly promotes the transcendence of all "meddling with any Practical Part in Life" (Addison),[30] the conventional stance of impartiality assumed by the eighteenth-century critic practically represents the identity of the tasteful and the aristocratic man, since it is only members of the aristocracy who can afford to look upon the world with this detachment.

IV

The criterion of disinterest that upholds the doctrine of taste is analogous to the justification traditionally given by aristocrats for their rule: that those can best govern whose rank and wealth leave them with no petty desires that might taint their judgment. Aristocrats are presumed to have the best interests of their respective regions at heart precisely because they are above most interests and so can regard them from a more expansive and accurate view. This is an idea at once as old as the writings of Plato and as recent as the arguments that took place in nineteenth-century England in its various attempts to establish the amount of property one ought to own in order to deserve the vote. (Indeed, this same idea supported many of the arguments against suffragism in this century.) After all, as Richard Payne Knight comments, one need only look to the French Revolution, which "afforded such abundant instances of [the] delicate sentiments and tender affections of men, whose minds are neither exalted by situation, enlarged by science, nor refined by culture." He goes on to add, rather unnecessarily, that "narrow selfishness is, with few exceptions, the universal principle of action in such men."[31] Humphrey Repton similarly notes that the knowledge that constitutes the basis of good taste also "marks the distinction between the higher ranks of polished society and the inferior orders of mankind, whose daily labours allow no leisure for other enjoyments than those of mere sensual, individual, and personal gratification."[32]

This association between aesthetic judgment and a more general political and social judgment may be still more fully understood, however, if one considers how the doctrine of taste moves through considerations of selfishness and disinterest into that area of eighteenth-century discourse involved with the differences between need and desire, necessity and luxury, or nature and artifice. For though it is by no means limited to the eighteenth century, discussion of the difference between real and artificial wants became extremely popular during that era and always served to justify aristocratic luxury by proving its essential insignificance. Given this character, aristocratic property in general just as surely disappears from public view as it does under the gaze of the disinterested eye. Although explorations of the difference between real and factitious need in works as central to the eighteenth century as Rousseau's *Emile*, Defoe's *Robinson Crusoe*, and Johnson's *Rasselas* seem to promote the analysis and philosophical control of desire, these writings actually serve to excuse economic inequity in general and the existence of poverty in particular. They do so by raising both the aristocracy and the object of art totally above need. After all, to possess sophistication is to communicate the illusion that one has no needs, and this illusion has always provided the glamor of the aristocracy. Similarly, in order to be art, an object must finally be beyond ordinary laws, exempted by virtue of its unique genius from the demands usually placed upon human productions. It is for this reason that everything said in the eighteenth century about the work of genius transcending rules is no more a criticism of Neoclassical doctrine than the exemption of noblemen from arrest for misdemeanors in England was a criticism of the rule of the law. The exceptional status of the aristocracy and of the work of art is what most strongly supports the rules enforced in the domain beneath them.

Kant writes, "only when need is satisfied can we decide who among the many does or does not have taste."[33] This statement obviously accords with the argument that aesthetic judgment must be divorced from interest, but the introduction of need as a factor in this aesthetic discourse enables one to define more clearly the ideality that is the goal of art. This ideality is a thoroughly negative state built upon the denial of that which is not art: It is a state of defense. Aristocratic and aesthetic property is protected insofar as it is conceded to be superfluous to biological needs, and the lower classes are humiliated insofar as they aspire to rise above the most minimal conditions of satisfaction that can be imagined. On the one hand, art is declared to be beyond the perception of the lower classes; on the other, it is declared that the exclusivity of its transcendent domain cannot be criticized, because it is immaterial to the level of survival to which people can, if necessary, be reduced. As Mandeville notes, the convenience of luxury is that "in one Sense every Thing may be call'd so, and in another there is no such Thing."[34]

In eighteenth-century aesthetic discourse, therefore, Robinson Crusoe's island may be said to be a model of the place to which the lower classes are exiled – as one might guess from the end of the novel, in which Crusoe becomes a wealthy burgher after leaving a community of shipwrecked sailors to work on that island, which has become his property. The most crucial transformation in Defoe's novel is the change from the island as nature to the island as property; and it becomes not just any property, but *sovereign* property, as Crusoe builds his castle and assumes the title of its lord and master. What *Robinson Crusoe* demonstrates is not that humans can rise above artificial needs but that the nobility (or the bourgeois aping them) can rise above need altogether, assigning it to the lower orders, who fortuitously appear and are instantly made to be indebted to the lord. In short, when it is said that "custom gives the name of poverty to the want of superfluity" (Samuel Johnson),[35] the related argument that art is unnecessary enables one to prove that poverty and oppression are illusions.

v

Vital to the defenses of eighteenth-century aesthetics, then, is the argument that custom obscures or alters man's original nature so as to make it all but unrecognizable. As Aristotle wrote, "frequency creates nature";[36] or, as it was put by Rousseau, the eighteenth-century writer most prominently associated with this view, "the more we distance ourselves from the state of nature, the more we lose our natural tastes; or rather habit makes us a second nature which we substitute for the first to such an extent that no one knows that first nature anymore."[37] Though this substitution may be regarded positively, a broad view of history almost always records a progress from an initial state of simplicity to one spoiled with refinement. But whether this initial state is admitted to be a fantasy (as in the writings of Schiller and Rousseau) or is supposed to have possessed some historical actuality (as in the writings of Addison and Kames), it is used to negate the image of poverty.

This use becomes especially apparent when one considers the contradiction to which this image of history leads the writers of the eighteenth century. For even as the argument is made that history is the spoliation of nature, another argument is advanced that will not allow taste to be truly formed until the individual, country, or race with which one is concerned has undergone an extensive education that can take place only through the development of historical experience. By themselves necessary but insufficient elements in the development of taste, nature and education together are argued to be the twin bases on which it stands. The eighteenth-century conceptions of nature and education, then, support the idea of taste even as they contradict each other. Nature and education are called upon to supplement each other even though this need for a supplement violates both the image of nature and the authority of education. And the contradictory attitudes thus displayed in the ideas of nature and education are also, it may be noted, apparent within the idea of nature itself. In the eighteenth century, nature is frequently accorded the double character of *la belle nature* and "vulgar nature," just as in the aesthetic discourse that belongs more to the seventeenth century one could distinguish between aristocrats in general and *le bel esprit*. And like the contradictions in the idea of a universal class to which very few can belong and in the demand that a commoner must defer to a different kind of perception while remaining unaware of its difference, this contradictory relationship between nature and education is a tool of eighteenth-century social order. It is a part of the illogic that sustains the operations of reason, and yet it develops logically from the definition of custom as a second nature.

"Imitations," according to Plato, "if continued from youth far into life, settle down into habits and second nature in the body, the speech, and the thought."[38] It is easy to imagine that this statement was as popular an observation in Greece some three centuries before Christ as it is in eighteenth-century England when Addison notes that "there is not a Common-Saying which has a better turn of sense in it, than what we often hear in the Mouths of the Vulgar, that Custom is a second Nature."[39] It is such a vulgar statement, in fact, even in our own time, that it is extremely difficult to bring into question. It is, as it were, beneath question; and yet to understand the doctrine of taste one must raise this concept from its common level to the level of that stupendous aristocratic prominence from which it rules over the eighteenth century.

A quotation from Seran de la Tour may help to make this concept strange enough to analyze. Arguing that it is necessary for a writer to have a thorough knowledge of his language if he would write with taste, la Tour goes on to describe how one would recognize such a man:

> The profound and universal knowledge of words has given him the habit of choosing that which is unique. This habit has become a second nature which expresses itself in him more felicitously than all the art of those who have only an imperfect knowledge of the language. The term which is proper presents itself to his spirit so naturally that if he were obligated for some particular reason to use one which was not, it would be as great a trial for him to avoid the proper term as it would be for many others to discover it.[40]

It is difficult to decide what is more remarkable: this portrait of the artist or la Tour's claim that such a man would be easy to recognize. The conception of a language in which each word has a unique and singular meaning is unexceptional enough in this era, but the image of a writer so completely imbued with this language as to find it almost impossible to transgress its proprieties is Neo-classicism carried to the extreme of cyberneticism. La Tour goes on to acknowledge that any piece of writing must necessarily be inferior to the nature it imitates, but this portrait is nonetheless upheld as an attainable and practical image. In order to possess literary taste, one must be inhabited by language as by a demon.

La Tour is by no means among the best writers of the eighteenth century, and he shows signs elsewhere in his work of a general fascination with images of obsessively systematic order; and yet this bizarre description of taste is representative of his age. La Tour's quotation is so peculiarly representative because it *is* generally true in the eighteenth century that the only way to possess any knowledge is to be totally possessed by that knowledge. Since the evidence of work is totally contrary to the ideas of education and art, education must be brought to the point of artlessness just as art must be refined until it appears so natural that it aids in discovering the art of nature. One must appear to have always had one's knowledge, just as all learning must be classified as remembrance, in accordance with the Platonic doctrine that is the model of aristocratic education *par excellence*. As Thomas Mann's Felix Krull, that most perfect aristocrat, puts the matter, "One must after all be of educable stuff in order to be educated. No one grasps what he has not possessed from birth."[41] Not only must the lower classes submit to aristocrats in all their values and perceptions, but aristocrats must submit to themselves. To evince any lesser control over knowledge would be to carry that knowledge as an excrescence on one's being or as a mixture in one's blood, whereas true philosophy, as Shaftesbury remarks, "is but to carry good-breeding a step higher."[42]

Although seemingly applicable to everyone alike, then, the distinction between a first and a second nature actually serves to distinguish between genuine nobility and those who can only aspire to this class. The aristocracy inherits nature; all other classes can only try to acquire some semblance of it. Locke, therefore, while seeming to describe the necessary role of artificial custom in establishing knowledge where there is nothing innate, actually describes the way in which those born without the innate knowledge of the aristocracy may hope to imitate their epistemic appearance. It is for this reason that eighteenth-century writers find it so easy to mingle references to and accolades for Locke with similar references to and praises for Plato.[43] Despite the tendency toward subjectivity, relativity, and emotionalism that Bate so well analyzed as the ultimate legacy of Locke's thought,[44] writers in the eighteenth century do not generally understand that thought to be contrary to universal standards of taste, disinterest, and social deference. What is important to them is not that Locke denied the existence of inherited knowledge but that he still emphasized the artificial status of custom and thus contributed to the maintenance of a system that separates aristocrats and commoners. It is for this reason also that the contradiction previously remarked between the ideas of nature and education may be allowed to exist. The aristocracy has no problem with this contradiction because, for its members, education finally has the meaning of nature, even as it exerts an extremely different, secondary meaning over the rest of humanity. The idea of a second nature ostensibly refers to the customs, manners, and thoughts that result from one's education in life; but in the case of higher education, which in the eighteenth century is for all practical purposes an aristocratic education, this reference is denied. Rather than being an imposition upon their original nature resulting from the accidental circumstances peculiar to their existence, second nature is the mirror in which aristocrats can see their privilege objectively confirmed in the deference of others toward them. Even the frequent subordination of eighteenth-century art and learning to the art and learning of antiquity is a way of preserving the sovereign status of the aristocracy, since antiquity is a property of the aristocratic education.

The case of literature exemplifies this relationship between education and aristocratic values. Generally speaking, education trains students to resist language, to distance themselves from the consummative power words may exert upon Don Quixote, Madame Bovary, mobs of all types, and devotees of pornography. The distance thus produced and maintained through the influence of the pedagogue and pedagogical writings is likely to be aristocratic. It is the distance afforded to those who can afford to look without touching; who are able, in the early eighteenth-century phrase, to approve rather than to admire. As Reynolds notes, a "submission to others is a deference which we owe, and indeed are forced involuntarily to pay" in order to obtain "a true idea of what imagination is."[45] It is this distance – the distance of condescension –

Introduction

that Mr. B. violates in his attempts on Pamela's person and writings. Richardson's novel is as much concerned with the aristocrat who disgraces himself by his vulgar taste for words as it is with the commoner who elevates herself through her attention to those forms slighted by her master.

The practice of education, in other words, either tends to repress all desire felt in the act of reading or else tends to sacralize that desire as an adoration of the Word – or of the sublime. The educated are not compelled by words, because the educated are presumed to be in possession of the power of words. Reading, for the educated, is the pretense of discovering an object that is already entirely familiar to them. Ideally, the educated will not read anything that is not anticipated within the system of aristocratic values to which they subscribe, de jure or de facto. Students will not encounter anything new, because what they can encounter will be prescribed by the social conditions that allow them to be students.

The same disinterest that appears as an aesthetic requirement and as a political justification is thus, in addition, an object of knowledge. Rather than learning literature (or any other subject), the educated primarily learn this attitude; for education is, before all else, discipline. There may be other aspects to education – those phenomena called "thought," "creativity," "information," "morality," and so on – but discipline is its first character. Education is instituted as control before it is instituted as knowledge, and that control – as can be seen so well in the discourse of taste – becomes an inseparable element in whatever may be constituted as knowledge. It can be said, in fact, that traditionally education does not serve so much to communicate complex knowledge as to communicate complexity in and of itself, as d'Alembert almost admits in the quotation cited in Section II. Whatever the content or knowledge represented by ideas may be, it is generally subordinate to their significance as a kind of higher literacy that excludes the common crowd from its discourse. What the Spectator sees is less important than the fact that his position and definition as a Spectator should be affirmed. Disinterestedness is the aristocratic interest in the privilege of status, and this privilege extends to the wealth of education.

Such considerations might do much to qualify the common view of the eighteenth century as an age of critical philosophy, since art is seen to be only the secondary object of an aesthetic criticism whose primary object is to assert the independence of the philosopher and to maintain the social system in which the philosopher can enjoy this independence.[46] Rather than being great critics of authority, the *philosophes* and the other writers of this age are desperate to assert and maintain an image of their own authority and social prestige, and one can approach a full understanding of their writings only on the basis of this recognition. It is not enough, for instance, in a philosophical study of Diderot's aesthetics, to devote just one sentence to the notation that Diderot "shuddered at a theory that would justify a peasant's taste as well as his own."[47] For this shudder, so common among the writers of this age,[48] is in fact the driving motivation for the theory of a universal standard of taste.

VI

Figuratively if not literally, the word of taste dominates eighteenth-century critical discourse because it provides an iconographic context that can encompass the kinds of contradictory, illogical, repressive procedures that produce this discourse. There are two major aspects to this iconography. Even though it is the eye, the sense of sight, and the vista that are of paramount importance in the critical writings of this era, the palate is in the first place made the stage of aesthetic communication, because it is intimately connected with the need for nutrition; whereas the senses of sight, hearing, touch, and smell do not enjoy such a strong association. The demand of eighteenth-century aesthetics that taste be separated from need and even from desire only reinforces this explanation, since this theory not only demands the luxury of denying need but also the association of the palate with nutrition so as to record this denial and proclaim this luxury. One is able, in other words, to preserve imagistically the spontaneity of natural sensation while still insisting upon the need for an educational development beyond this immediacy.[49]

Second, the word of taste may be said to hold critical power because of its connection with a sanctified image of nature that allows any violation of aesthetic theory to be interpreted as an attack upon what is considered to be the most basic of human relationships. In Kames's illustration, "a child born with an aversion to its mother's milk is a wonder, no less than if born without a mouth, or with more than one."[50] He was not the only one who saw the origin of criticism in the image of a suckling child; consider the note Rousseau appended to the extensive discussion of breastfeeding at the beginning of his educational manual:

> There are occasions when a son who lacks respect for his father may in some way be excused; but if on any occasion an infant were denatured enough to lack it towards his mother, to she who had carried him in her womb, who had nourished him with her milk, who had neglected herself for years so as to occupy herself only with him, one ought to hurry to choke this wretch, like a monster unworthy to see daylight.[51]

Like Kames, Kant, and so many others, Rousseau argues that an aesthetic judgment affected by need must be inaccurate; but the image of the mouth at the breast survives as a kind of model for the critical posture which guarantees that proper reverence be paid to art even as it transforms the nursing of a child from an ostensibly biological to a formidably ideological act. It is through a recognition of this transformation that one can better understand such apparently bizarre digressions from aesthetic discussion as the following, written by Crousaz:

> If a child were to completely understand the entire constitution of his little body, the state and the needs of all his parts, and should know with the same exactitude all the bodies which surround us, he would notice an agreement of size, of shape, and of movement between the particles of his body and those of milk which would please him and determine him to want to make use of them.[52]

Similarly, one can better understand Pamela's objection to giving her child to a wet nurse because she fears that in such cases "the Child, when grown up, owes its Taste to the Coach-box, to its Nurse's being the Coachman's Wife, or the Wife of one of like Degree, who may not have a Mind or Qualities above that Degree."[53] The fact that she loses this argument to the argument of her husband's right over his wife in no way lessens its cogency – it simply emphasizes the consideration that it is men (and men who do not want their wives' figures to be spoiled) who are the final arbiters in matters of taste.

This emphasis is by no means tangential to the doctrine of taste, for one of the illusions this doctrine makes possible is that of an equality of the sexes. Just as taste may help to promote a specious cosmopolitanism when figures like Reynolds declare that the value of any custom may be ascertained by determining "whether it preserves itself when translated" from one nation to another,[54] so may it seem to support the idea that men and women are of equal understanding, if only in the area of aesthetics. Jane Austen's Henry Tilney is therefore able to say that "in every power, of which taste is the foundation, excellence is pretty fairly divided between the sexes";[55] but he is able to make this statement precisely because he is prepared to exert his power to colonize Catherine Morland's mind with his own judgments. The idea of an international crucible for the resolution of values refers only to the impression that European values may make upon other states (the case is rarely reversed to any significant extent).[56] In the same way, the idea that men and women might be equal in their appreciation of art merely signifies that women will be allowed to value men as men value themselves. Just as both the unconscious and conscious minds of the lower classes may be seen to be creations of the aristocracy within the discourse of taste, so are the minds of alien nations and of the "opposite sex" closely regulated inventions. The realities of national and sexual chauvinism are no more open to challenge within the discourse of taste than the reality of aristocratic rule is open to challenge within *Pamela*.

VII

Still, the rule of taste, like aristocratic rule, is sometimes disturbed by the very contradictions that usually give it its power. Voltaire, for instance, runs into some trouble when he considers the tastes of different countries and concludes that the image of nature may become "so different from itself" that one cannot easily "submit to general laws the arts over which custom, which is to say inconstancy, holds such empire."[57] And in an even more dizzying moment, the Abbé Trublet comes upon one of the most peculiar results of the doctrine of taste:

> To not have a taste for certain works, it is necessary to have
> a great deal of taste – a very fine taste – or to be absolutely
> devoid of it. Thus a fool and a man of great spirit, a spirit

21

cultivated and exercised by reading: these two men, I say, may appear sometimes to agree in the judgment that they make of a work; they talk of it almost in the same terms, and they say that it hasn't given them much pleasure, while a man of mediocre spirit but of correct sense judges and speaks of it entirely differently.[58]

An individual may come to have so much taste that he appears as one who has no taste at all. Just as the image of the ill-made ragout frequently appears in eighteenth-century criticism as an emblem of the improper type of art, so does this hypersensitive or jaded man sometimes appear as a figure of the illogic that threatens to destroy the discourse of taste even as it enables that discourse to be produced. Archibald Alison approaches the meeting more indirectly when he refers to fashions that attract only the unformed taste through the train of associations they provoke. "A plain man is incapable of such associations: a man of sense . . . above them."[59] But this meeting is still representative of the general convergence between the very refined and the very ignorant in eighteenth-century aesthetics. For a man whose taste is so fine as to reject almost everything to meet with a man who has so little taste as to reject the same things *in the same language* is for the aristocrat to suspect that his truth might be in the boor or – finally – for the master to glimpse his truth in the slave. In this critical moment, an unthinkable communion is fantasized: a meeting in which the perceptions of the lower and the upper classes would mingle indiscriminately, as in a ragout. This meeting comes close to occurring quite frequently in eighteenth-century writings, and it always represents such a fantastic violation of order. In this encounter one would be led, as it were, by the irresistible (il)logic of taste, to identify with the very figure which that taste was supposed to isolate and confine within the realm of illusion.

Furthermore, this meeting is emblematic of stresses within the artistic object itself. Alongside the literary tradition in which the community and the body of man are made to be reciprocally illustrative of each other is the accompanying tradition in which the text partakes of this imagery, and this latter tradition becomes particularly significant at this point. In the eighteenth century, there are textual extremes just as there are extremes denominated by the tasteful and the tasteless man; there are high and low passages in a text, refined and common parts, legitimate and illegitimate structures, and so on. In addition to releasing anxiety about discriminations and separations within the state, descriptions of agreements between the fool and the connoisseur therefore also expose doubts about the ability of texts (including that very text in which the critic has involved himself) to maintain the proper distances and divisions among their elements. These doubts, of course, can only lead to even more severe questions about the definition of these elements as such.

It is important to reemphasize, too, that the role assumed by the discourse of taste in social and textual organization extends to the organization of the entire world. Though his exuberant use of metaphor may be somewhat idiosyncratic, Cartaud de la Villate is typical of eighteenth-century writers when he concludes, after considering differences of taste according to differences in temperaments, circumstances, times, and places throughout history, that

> one could compare the different turns of a language to the telescopes which put objects at a distance or bring them closer: almost all reflections which have the heart and the spirit as their object have been made from immemorial times. They are a species of antique statue to which new draperies are given according to the time and the place. We would find among the ancients all the seeds of our thoughts about different passions, because men have had the same tastes in every age.[60]

Even as it catalogues differences, the goal of anthropology is to discern an underlying unity; just as psychology, even as it sets certain individuals and classes and sensations beyond the pale, proves by doing so that all people are finally the same; just as aesthetics establishes the aristocracy of tasteful people as a class that, despite its few members, is universal. Adam Smith is only following the discourse of his age when he says, "I cannot . . . be induced to believe that our sense of external beauty is founded altogether on custom," even though he has just been considering the practice of training one's ears to hang down upon one's shoulders – the oft-remarked deformity of a fair complexion "upon the coast of Guinea"[61] – and the equally popular art practiced by some Indian tribes of tying boards about the heads of their children so as to squeeze their crania into the shape of a square. After all, as Blair asks, is there anyone "who will seriously maintain that the taste of a Hottentot or a Laplander is as delicate and as correct as that of a Longinus or an Addison?"[62]

VIII

All of the preceding reflections may be summarized without too much distortion by saying that according to eighteenth-century aesthetics, the primary telos of the work of art is its effect in over-awing the vulgar and keeping them at a distance. It is not by accident that Hutcheson uses the impression made by noble hospitality as an example in support of his argument for a moral sense related to the sense of beauty, adding that such external shows

> may possibly be a great, if not the only Cause of what some count *miraculous, viz.* That *Civil Governors* of no greater Ca-pacity than their Neighbors, by some inexpressible *Awe,* and *Authority,* quell the very Spirits of the *Vulgar,* and keep them in subjection by such small Guards.[63]

Even as the displays of the aristocracy must be alluring to all, they must be overawing to those individuals of inferior rank who come to regard them. The same is true of the work of art, which is definitively aristocratic in this similarity. Desire and intimidation are inseparably allied within this system of values by the fact that all objects of desire, like the object of art, can appear as such only through their representation of masterly power. Consequently, for anyone who is not a complete aristocrat (and even those who are aristocrats are never completely so), to experience desire can only be to experience an overwhelming act of aggression against one's self. What is important to note is that the very habit of mind that would put the ideology of art "above" such considerations of desire and its effects merely serves to confirm the strategic role art has played in justifying social, political, and economic oppression.

In the eighteenth century, then, "taste" is a metaphorical as well as an alphabetical anagram of "state." As Schiller writes, "taste alone brings harmony into society, because it gives harmony to the in-dividual . . . only communication of the beautiful unites society, because it refers to that which is common to all."[64] Not only does a political vocabulary permeate aesthetic discussion, and not only are the subjects of communication and social organization believed to be vitally implicated within the subject of aesthetics, but even those writings that seem to occupy themselves "purely" with matters of art encode, if only through this attitude of purity, a host of assumptions and demands based upon aristocratic values. In addition to being the stage on which beauty is judged, and as an extension of this judgment, the palate is the stage on which the ability of society to survive is tested. Every demand made upon beauty ultimately derives from a demand for civil order. Thus, when la Tour speaks of "the always present and always imperceptible thread of economy," he is directly referring to art but implicitly addressing the concerns of a nation. Economy, he writes,

> is that which austerely compels the choice of order, which exactly places each thing in its appropriate location, and which finally arranges its general and particular dispositions so perfectly that even one who is not a connoisseur is satisfied at first glance of the necessity of that arrangement, so that he doesn't imagine that what is presented to him, whether it be in Painting, Poetry, Rhetoric, or History, could have been otherwise disposed.[65]

The demonic man of taste is in this passage the demonic economy of taste, but the significance of the drive toward an appearance of necessity is the same. Taste has to be made compelling so as to ensure the maintenance of the successful communications that in their turn ensure the dominance of aristocratic values. La Tour's book on aesthetics therefore quite understandably includes a chapter on the education of princes in which the economy regulating art is explicitly connected with the government of countries, world government, and the course of time. Similarly, Trublet compares "a man of genius without taste" to "a rich man who knows nothing of the art of expenditure";[66] the penultimate chapter in la Villate's *Essai historique et philosophique sur le goût,* which proves that the taste for luxury is in the interest of the state, is followed by a chapter that is a paean to royal rule; Crousaz defines the beautiful as "recognizing to what one is truly called and knowing how to fulfill that vocation,"[67] which will of course be in accordance with the order of society; and, as Kames remarks, "the same uniformity of taste is equally necessary to perfect the art of music, sculpture, and painting, and to support the expense they require after they are brought to perfection."[68]

It is worth noting, too, that the economy discussed in writings such as these is never a mercantile economy involving the notion of expenditure made in the hope of a profitable return; it is rather an aristocratic economy involving the demand for display that at once manifests and confirms one's rank and influence. The same holds true, of course, of the notions of government and polity raised in the discourse of taste: They are always fundamentally aristocratic.

Taste is thus a massive metaphorical tool presented as aesthetic truth, devoted to aristocratic values, overtly justified by appeals to the conditions necessary to rational communication, and covertly appealing to fears about the social disorder that would result if the lower classes were to emerge from their ideological imprisonment and "communicate with" their superiors. The discourse of taste is a drama of social and political intrigue enacted in the form of an investigation of perception.

To be sure, the massive rule of this discourse is to some extent supported by a network of common texts and citations. Pamela and Rousseau as well as the Earl of Chesterfield read Locke's *Treatise on Education;* Gerard refers in his work to Baillie, Hogarth, Crousaz, Hutcheson, and du Bos, among others, and includes essays by Voltaire, d'Alembert, and Montesquieu as appendixes to its second edition; Moses Mendelssohn refers to Rousseau, Montesquieu, and Hutcheson in his essay "The Relationship between the Beautiful and the Good"; and further examples could easily be listed. The rule of taste is more significantly supported, however, by the entire history of aristocratic values – a heritage so extensive and so pervasive as very often to be all but invisible to the eye that cannot fix its gaze upon "the ordinary."

IX

Changes occur in the relations among aesthetic theory, literature, and society as one moves out of the eighteenth century and into the nineteenth – and it is the purpose of this study to analyze such changes as they appear in the works of Ann Radcliffe, Jane Austen, and Sir Walter Scott – but the changes have at times been overstated. The attitudes represented by the literature of sensibility, Romanticism, and novelistic realism did not put an end to the kinds of social attitudes that both supported and were maintained by the idea of taste. There were changes, and some of them quite dramatic; but many of the same attitudes toward society discussed up to this point still persisted within these changes. In any event, the process of changing literary and social values was so gradual and complex that a writer like Scott, who has often been seen as either a full-blown Romantic or a middle-class rationalist, can still be seen to be attached to many of the same aristocratic values that both Romanticism and middle-class rationalism are popularly supposed to have rebelled against. Generally speaking, one can say that in Ann Radcliffe's works middle-class values are just beginning to emerge within a governing aristocratic context; in Jane Austen's these newer values are precariously balanced against the old; and in Scott's they have become victorious, at least superficially. But there is no simple line of development, and no point at which one can say that the ideology of taste has died and been replaced by a brand new one. Historians of the nineteenth century – as opposed to many writers on the literature of the period – are well aware of how strongly aristocratic values continued to affect the life of all segments of society until the First World War; and, indeed, one need not read far in the literature and criticism of our own day to see that various versions of aristocratic values, often specifically oriented to the idea of taste or "quality," still survive. Society and its values do not change as quickly or as simply as the labels we customarily affix to literary and historical periods might seem to imply.

It is true that Radcliffe's novels, like all the eighteenth-century literature that at once reflected and fostered the values of middle-class sentimentality, do represent an important modification of the premises developed in the mainstream of eighteenth-century aesthetic theory. Art is conceived of on a more democratic basis, as are social relations in general. A refinement of manners, natural or learned, is urged against the coarseness that is portrayed to be all too characteristic of manners before this period. The lower classes are represented with – to use the all-important word of the new values – sympathy. Nature in its unrestrained wildness becomes the model for beauty of all sorts, and corresponding to this change in the artificial model of Neoclassical values there runs the idea that since uncultivated nature is open to all, all can appreciate its beauties, even if the observer should be unlettered and unsophisticated. More emphasis is laid upon the fineness of feeling than upon the fineness of one's birth and rank; less credit is given to prescriptive statements about the nature of beauty and aesthetic response, more to the emotional intensity of the response itself. Attention is shifted from the outward sheen of the aesthetic object and the social status of its observer to the inward processes of the observer's sensibilities as they form an intimate, individual relation with the object.

All of this is a familiar characterization of the changes occurring in the late eighteenth and early nineteenth centuries, and rightly so. It is familiar because it makes up the overt ideology of a great deal of the literature gaining popularity in this period – of Ann Radcliffe's novels, for instance, as well as of Wordsworth's poems. However, two points need to be made at the outset about this apparent change.

The first is that the new values are not coherent even in their overt expression. In the very same works in which middle-class values take on a prominent expression one may also find contradictory aristocratic values being given an equal voice. To identify the former set of values with the text while dismissing or ignoring the latter is to read retrospectively, applying to these works an image of historical development that did not even become conceivable, much less actual, until quite late in the nineteenth century. During the period in which the works of Radcliffe, Austen, and Scott were written, there was nothing in the consciousness of these writers or in the historical situation of the time to suggest that all the values associated with the aristocratic dominance of English society would be superseded in the way that they eventually were. To assert that there was such a triumph of the middle classes evident during this period is to stretch the course of events in the nineteenth century upon the framework of an idealist teleology when, in fact, each step of the shifting of power away from the upper classes and toward the middle and lower was bitterly contested, of moot significance at the time of its achievement, and quite often counterbalanced by other steps that now appear to have been retrograde. It is for this reason that even the novels of a man like Scott, who seemed to admit the ascendancy of the middle classes, remain problematic in their expression of values: first, because this ascendancy did not assume for his imagination the shape that it eventually assumed in history; and, second, because even as he proclaimed this ascen-

dancy he did so unsystematically. That is, he could only imagine
the triumph of middle-class values within the context of the discourse peculiar to his class and his time; and since this discourse
was still as strongly tied to eighteenth-century practices as it was
leaning toward figures and themes responsive to the ongoing changes
in society, it is far from being ideologically coherent in any ideal
sense of the term. Like the writings of Radcliffe and Austen, Scott's
writings record much more of tension between opposed values than
they do of resolution, and they do so because a culturally effective
form of resolution – such as that achieved in the full-blown sentimentality so popular in the mid-nineteenth century – was as yet
inconceivable. This resolution itself was precarious even when it
was strongest and quickly came to be criticized and undermined,
but even a resolution so precarious was stronger than those achieved
in the novels of these three writers. All of their resolutions turn
upon contradictions that are not only blatant but that are also, in
one way or another, formally repressed, forbidden utterance – as
opposed to the situation in Victorian novels like Dickens's, which
take such contradictions as their starting point. In the work of Radcliffe, Austen, and Scott, the shifting relations between two orders
of value can be openly recorded; but the historical significance of
this shift has not been clarified sufficiently so that they could admit
that there is an irremediable conflict between these two orders. The
results are writings rent by the same kinds of uncertainty, duplicity, and tension as were at work in the radically changing society
of this period.

    The second point that it is necessary to make about this period
of literary change is that even if one disregards, for a moment, the
overt contradictions in these works, a consideration of what is overtly
expressed does not constitute a sufficient reading of the work. In
saying this I am not referring to hidden, occult, disguised, or repressed meanings "beneath the surface" of the work but rather to
all the other elements that are as much a part of that surface as those
quotable sentiments and ideas that too often are taken alone to constitute or summarize it. Phrases like Austen's description of the
transition from "the alarms of romance to the anxieties of common
life" cannot be taken to have an independent and self-contained
meaning, for to understand the meaning of such a phrase one must
consider its nature as a literary utterance. In other words, one must
consider not only its reference in its immediate narrative context,

but the systematic conditions of the appearance of any such phrase in a novel, the social and cultural conditions within which such a phrase can have meaning, and the range of utterances that such a phrase encodes, disguises, or excludes from the realm of meaning. Such an approach is necessary to take literature out of the ideal realms of the civilized imagination and to replace it in the social and historical context in which it found meaning.

Despite these considerations, though, it still might seem odd to take the work of Radcliffe, Austen, and Scott as the subject of a single study of "the civilized imagination." The images clash: Ann Radcliffe, the author of hysterical Gothic novels; Jane Austen, the author of exquisitely composed domestic dramas; Sir Walter Scott, the self-proclaimed master of the "bow-wow" strain of adventure and historical incident. Or again: Radcliffe, the obscure author of pulp melodramas that, if read at all today, can only seem unintentionally hilarious or dreadfully boring; Austen, Henry James's "dear Jane," a writer revered within academe for her delicacy of perception, social and psychological insight, biting wit, and aesthetic grace; Scott, a writer as famous as Austen among academics but one who is now read mostly because of his historical role in legitimizing the novel and establishing the subgenre of the historical novel. Radcliffe is read only by a few scholars who often read nothing but *The Mysteries of Udolpho;* all of Austen's novels remain in print and are still read by a popular audience; some few undergraduate and graduate students may be introduced to *Waverley* or *The Heart of Midlothian* or one or two other works by Scott. In terms of the scale of taste that reigns in universities today, Austen is a "major author" and Scott a novelist who is important but not on the same scale as Austen (who has ever heard of a seminar devoted wholly to Scott?), whereas Radcliffe is a negligible historical curiosity except to a few feminists and specialists in the eighteenth century. Still other categorizations clash: Scott is popularly known as a Romantic, Radcliffe as the author of a sentimental sort of fiction, Austen as something of an anomaly in the "Age of Romanticism," a writer difficult to speak of in the same language that one uses with the likes of Wordsworth, say, or Sir Walter Scott.

To be sure, there are superficial affiliations among these writers. Austen read Radcliffe (along with other Gothic novelists) and satirized her work in *Northanger Abbey;* Scott read both Radcliffe and Austen and wrote his own Gothic novels (such as *Anne of Geier-*

stein) as well as one novel in imitation of Austen *(St. Ronan's Well)*. Moreover, these authors did live in the late eighteenth and early nineteenth centuries and so may be said to have written their works in a common cultural environment that compelled all of them to deal with the question of conflicting social values in this time of transition. Yet there is a still more important reason for analyzing these writers in each other's company.

These three novelists were chosen not only because they all appeared at the time of shifting class values that I have described, but also *because* they are almost always treated as novelists who might have come from different planets as far as canons of taste, genre, style, and theme are concerned. My argument is that these canons keep one from seeing how the works of these authors are preoccupied with the same cultural problem: the problem of finding an aesthetic solution to the conflicting values environing their creation. Radcliffe, Austen, and Scott do not come up with the same solution – hence the many differences that do distinguish them from each other – but still they share this *donnée*. Furthermore, my approach is based upon the conviction that this type of reading may yield an understanding of the individual work of these authors that changes – and, I think, corrects – assumptions about it that are bound to appear if one approaches it within the standard categories.

This is not to say that I have tried to reduce the works of these writers to a common denominator. On the contrary, I have tried to achieve a fuller understanding of the differences as well as the similarities between their works by analyzing the way conflicting values shape the smallest details as well as the more prominent forms and figures of these works. If one is to study literary history from the ground up, as it were, instead of inventing it on the basis of a library of texts that just happen to be valued according to contemporary standards of taste, then it is necessary to transgress canonical boundaries and to seek historical standards of a different order. Just as one gets a different picture of eighteenth-century aesthetics if one considers the concerns and assumptions that unite writers otherwise as diverse as Hume, Richardson, Rousseau, Voltaire, Addison, and so on, so too does this approach make available an understanding of Radcliffe, Austen, and Scott that differs in important particulars from the readings they are more commonly given. Such an approach is all the more important in light of the fact that "the novel" during this period was not the solidly institutionalized genre that it was to be by the end of the nineteenth century, but rather the site of conflicting formal approaches and definitions, no one of which could be said to have gained the ascendancy that is now given to Austen and, to a lesser extent, to Scott. Of course, this is not to deny the value of the work that has been done on these authors, which I have drawn upon extensively. Nor is it to claim that the authors I have chosen to study remain more than a narrow sampling of the writers active in this period. Despite the other writers to which I refer in the course of my analyses, this study is limited by this choice, as it is by my concentration upon one aesthetic issue: the problem of articulating a relationship between conflicting schemes of value. However, I believe this issue to be an important and a relatively neglected one, especially in terms of the type of analysis that this grouping of authors enables me to pursue.

The question I have sought to follow, then, is this: Given the relation between class values and aesthetic values that I have analyzed in the discourse of taste in the eighteenth century, what are some of the forms that this relation takes in the novel at the end of the eighteenth and the beginning of the nineteenth centuries, when aristocratic ideology would seem no longer to be as powerful as it had been? A study of literature in relation to society need not be reductive, wrapping artistic creativity in a straightjacket of theory, if one thus looks to understand different forms of literary response instead of assuming that culture at any point in history is monolithic in its nature, walled off from historical conflict and historical possibility.

PART I

ANN RADCLIFFE

∾

"Oh! I am delighted with the book! I should like
to spend my whole life in reading it."
– CATHERINE MORLAND ON *The Mysteries of
Udolpho*,
IN JANE AUSTEN'S *Northanger Abbey*

2

THE FIGURE IN THE LANDSCAPE

∾

It is difficult to spread varied pictures of such scenes
before the imagination. A repetition of the same images of rock, wood and water, and the same epithets
of grand, vast and sublime, which necessarily occur,
must appear tautologous, on paper, though their ar-
chetypes in nature, ever varying in outline, or arrangement, exhibit new visions to the eye, and produce new shades of effect upon the mind.

      – ANN RADCLIFFE, *A Journey*

LANDSCAPE HAS a talismanic importance in Ann Radcliffe's novels. Not only can one judge the character of people by the style of their estates or by their responses to
natural scenery, but one also finds parallels such as those in the first
meeting of Emily St. Aubert and Valancourt, "whose ideas were
simple and grand, like the landscapes among which they moved"
(*MU,* 49).[1] Characters often seem nothing but reflections of those
landscapes, over which their various psychological states may be
displayed on a larger scale. They journey across this background as
through the fears, limitations, contradictions, and desires of the
cultural topography in which Radcliffe wrote her novels.[2] Landscape comes to appear as the central character of her novels, or her
individual characters as fragments of a general human nature that
cannot be fully revealed unless one makes a tour of the variety of
nature, discovering character through cartography. In fact, this
parallel between landscape and character may become so close that
at times Radcliffe's characters themselves experience difficulty in
distinguishing between them. Witness further the meeting of Emily and Valancourt in *The Mysteries of Udolpho:* "The grandeur and
sublimity of the scenes, amidst which they had first met, had fascinated her fancy, and had imperceptibly contributed to render Valancourt more interesting by seeming to communicate to him
somewhat of their own character" (*MU,* 89).[3]

This kind of passage shows Radcliffe's awareness that the representation of landscape in her novels bears reference to much greater concerns than the mere depiction of natural scenery. In these novels landscape is an element of such privileged representational power that it may appear as the textual equivalent to any other element in her fiction. People, sounds, scenes, feelings, states of being may all be translated into the terms of landscape because Radcliffe – both following and helping to fashion the taste of her age – gives it a unique aesthetic status. Not only does its variety afford her with images to represent any aspect of experience, but it also is invested with a moral significance that ties aesthetic perception to the perception and dramatization of virtue. Throughout Radcliffe's novels, the transcendent status of landscape as art images forth the Providential structure of her own art and thereby keys the progress of her narratives to their final resolutions. Just as human life is variable, so is landscape; but it is so only within the limits of that Providential structure displayed in the most sublime manifestations of nature and surviving in nature even when obscured in one's personal experience. As Robert Kiely has written, "Human beings may become wild, confused, and unbalanced, but nature, if seen from the proper perspective, does not."[4] It is because it is a talisman of Providence that landscape can appear as a summary code to all the textual figurations of Radcliffe's novels. Thus Emily may be found, after listening to some minstrels,

> sunk in that pensive tranquility which soft music leaves on the mind – a state like that produced by the view of a beautiful landscape by moon-light, or by the recollection of scenes marked with the tenderness of friends lost for ever, and with sorrows, which time has mellowed into mild regret. (*MU,* 177–8)

And thus it is that one finds Emily remembering her father's estate:

> The ideal scenes were dearer, and more soothing to her heart, than all the splendour of gay assemblies; they were a kind of talisman that expelled all the poison of temporary evils, and supported her hopes of happy days: they appeared like a beautiful landscape, lighted up by a gleam of sun-shine, and seen through a perspective of dark and rugged rocks. (*MU,* 191)

Because it is so important an element in her fiction, Radcliffe's representation of landscape is marked by great complexity. First of all, as she herself indicated, one must consider the fact that her descriptions of landscape are not simple descriptions of nature. They are conceived of as attempts to draw natural scenes and the mind that perceives them out of deadening linguistic conventions. In effect, then, Radcliffe's labor in describing landscape in these novels is a moral exercise akin to that struggle to rescue virtue from vice so insistently portrayed on the dramatic level of her narratives. Moreover, as her frequent recourse to the ineffable as the terminus of her descriptions serves to indicate, this exercise may seem as daunting to her as the effort to overcome evil may seem to her heroines. Nevertheless, it is an imperative exercise if the style of her writing, like her heroines, is to end on the side of the angels.

One finds scenes of writing within these novels that show how the process of describing landscape epitomizes the drama within the novels as well as their composition as a moral whole. For instance, when one sees the hero of Radcliffe's first novel, *The Castles of Athlin and Dunbayne,* imprisoned and seeking to communicate with two ladies on the terrace beneath his cell by composing a sonnet in praise of the landscape spread out before the three of them and then dropping this poem down to the terrace, the importance of the representation of landscape as a medium for liberation from evil is clear. Eventually, as this talismanic communication indicates, these three will find their freedom together. Here as throughout Radcliffe's novels, the perception of landscape as art serves to bring into focus the relationships, values, and overall structure of her own art. Landscape is a kind of universal code that can be used to compare and evaluate any other elements in her fiction, and it is so because for Radcliffe it has a privileged value as the archetypal art of Providence, infused with moral and spiritual truth. A character of the right sort can perceive and communicate landscape as art spontaneously – unconsciously, as it were[5] – because the art that defines his own virtuous nature is also figured in the landscape to which he is responding. To see the precise significance of this parallel between landscape and character, however, what need to be analyzed are the problems that Radcliffe faces in using landscape to deliver the truth of her fiction.

Of course, it is evident to a post-Romantic age that what counted as nature to Radcliffe was itself a convention. What she considered to be the archetypal reality of nature was actually the product of a particular style of representation and of an invention of subjects for that representation. Her nature, like all natures, was a cultural fashion − a consideration emphasized by the fact that she lacked first-hand knowledge of most of the landscapes she described and drew upon others' descriptions in developing her own.[6] It is only to be expected, then, that in her account of her own travels one should witness the exposure of a landscape as a network of aesthetic allusions:

> To the west, under the glow of sun-set, the landscape melted into the horizon in tints so soft, so clear, so delicately roseate as Claude only could have painted. Viewed, as we then saw it, beyond a deep and dark arch of the ruin, its effect was enchanting; it was to the eye, what the finest strains of Paisiello are to the heart, or the poetry of Collins is to the fancy. (*J* 1: 242)

Or, in *The Mysteries of Udolpho,* there is this self-conscious scene painting:

> St. Foix stopped to observe the picture, which the party in the cave presented, where the elegant form of Blanche was finely contrasted by the majestic figure of the Count, who was seated by her on a rude stone, and each was rendered more impressive by the grotesque habits and strong features of the guides and other attendants, who were in the back ground of the piece. The effect of the light, too, was interesting; on the surrounding figures it threw a strong, though pale gleam, and glittered on their bright arms; while upon the foliage of a gigantic larch, that impended its shade over the cliff above, it appeared as a red, dusky tint, deepening almost imperceptibly into the blackness of night. (*MU,* 601)

But to see this conventionality in the nature of Radcliffe's fiction is only to take the first step toward understanding the significance of landscape in her novels. Of greater interest are the questions of how exactly Radcliffe used her attachment to nature and how this usage reveals problems in the design of her work as a whole.

As is to be expected, given the time at which these novels were written, a dominant aspect of landscape's all-encompassing importance in Radcliffe's work is the way that it is used to display or to test the delicacy of one's taste. In this respect, Radcliffe generally follows the tradition of eighteenth-century aesthetics. Only a vulgar woman like Mme. Cheron will venture to assert that "there's no accounting for tastes" (*MU,* 111),[7] while a proper character like M. St. Aubert will argue that virtue and taste "are nearly the same, for virtue is little more than active taste, and the most delicate affections of each continue in real love" (*MU,* 49–50). A universal standard of aesthetic judgment is assumed to be inseparable from proper moral, social, and even political and religious attitudes;[8] and so the most general use of landscape is as a touchstone for virtually every aspect of human character as it was defined in Radcliffe's time. This same usage was later elaborated, though in a considerably attenuated form, in the novels of Jane Austen and Sir Walter Scott. For all three writers, the truth of one's character may be revealed in one's attitude toward the scenes of nature.

Of course, this use of landscape was already complicated in Radcliffe's novels by the entrance of the more contemporary value of sentimentality into the discourse of taste. So one finds that while St. Aubert had made some "very tasteful improvements" on his family estate, "such was his attachment to objects that he remembered from his boyhood days, that he had in some instances sacrificed taste to sentiment" (*MU,* 4). Finally, however, there is no real conflict between the claims of taste and those of sentiment, at least as far as these novels are concerned. The former critical term is made an adjunct to or is absorbed within the latter, as when Radcliffe gives a recipe for sentimental conversation:

> To good sense, lively feeling, and natural delicacy of taste, must be united an expansion of mind, and a refinement of thought, which is the result of high cultivation . . . Here fancy flourishes, – the sensibilities expand – and wit, guided by delicacy and embellished by taste – points to the heart. (*SR* 1: 16)[9]

Taste and sentiment work together to draw the truth of nature into social intercourse, and through this accommodation the use of landscape as a basis for the articulation of character is preserved.

A more vexing problem does arise, though, from the fact that

Radcliffe can so easily harmonize terms that commonly are seen as marking the transition between the end of Neoclassicism and the advent of Romanticism. The problem is that Radcliffe's writing shows the semantic flexibility of these terms; and in doing so it shows a continuity between these periods that is so important that it requires a major refocusing in the way changes in literary practice, such as those that mark Romanticism, usually are regarded. Rather than making style, or even style along with subject and theme, the major grounds for a historical understanding of literature, this problem necessitates a consideration of literary history that concentrates as much upon the persistence of ideological contradictions, exclusions, and repressions in the structure of the particular work as upon superficial changes in ideological expression and literary form. For despite the way that Wordsworth, say, would anathematize the received idea of taste in the 1815 Essay supplementing the Preface to the *Lyrical Ballads,* and despite the differences in the kinds of nature that his writing and Radcliffe's helped to make fashionable, one can see their work as sharing a central conflict in its aestheticization of nature. This is a conflict related to the position from which one regards a landscape, and it ultimately developed from assumptions about class differences. One cannot approach a full understanding of Radcliffe's novels (or of Wordsworth's poetry) without seeing the importance of this conflict in their composition.

On the one hand, Radcliffe can differ from most eighteenth-century writers on taste by conceiving it as a quality that is not exclusively identified with the upper classes. As Emily considers poverty in *The Mysteries of Udolpho,*

> "It cannot deaden our taste for the grand, and the beautiful,
> or deny us the means for indulging it; for the scenes of nature
> – those sublime spectacles, so infinitely superior to all artificial luxuries! are open for the enjoyment of the poor, as well
> as the rich." (*MU*, 60)

One presumes that this passage would have raised no argument from a poet who saw the lower classes as poetry incarnate, and that this poet might have sympathized when Emily "almost wished to become a peasant of Piedmont, to inhabit one of the pleasant embowered cottages which she saw peeping beneath the cliffs, and to pass her careless hours among these romantic landscapes" (*MU*, 167–8). Elsewhere, however, Emily finds that she "had again to lament the irresistible force of circumstances over the taste and powers of the mind; and that it requires a spirit at ease to be sensible even to the abstract pleasures of pure intellect" (*MU*, 383).[10] This recognition of the privilege inherent in aesthetic appreciation also raises questions in the work of a writer who approvingly quoted Sir Joshua Reynolds' dictum on taste – that it is "an *acquired* talent, which can only be produced by thought and a long-continued intercourse with the best models of composition" – in both the Advertisement and the Preface to the Second Edition of the *Lyrical Ballads*.[11] Wordsworth's emphasis upon the acquired nature of this talent does overturn the priority characteristically given by the eighteenth century to inborn nature and thus is superficially more democratic, but the education he demands was generally a privilege of birth and thus de facto still a property of the nonlaboring classes. It is for this reason that nature – that is, nature as liberating art – was *not* open to all. Consequently, Wordsworth's as well as Radcliffe's writings show consciousness of the fact that a condition of leisured detachment was necessary to constitute the individual as an aesthetic observer, and the work of both writers further shows an awareness that this requirement posed a problem for their art.

In Radcliffe's novels as in Wordsworth's poetry there is a great tension between the aesthetic enjoyment of landscape and the consciousness of landscape as inhabited rather than observed nature. The problem is that inhabitation raises questions that privileged observers literally cannot perceive, much less enjoy, if they are to continue to see landscape as art. This tension arises especially in relation to the lower classes, because it is so clear that they can be included within the demands of this art only as objects or as the voices of nature, not in terms of their own consciousness; but it finally involves all of the characters in Radcliffe's novels. Since the exclusion of this type of inhabiting consciousness becomes a problem whenever anyone is placed in a position in which ease and leisurely thought are impossible, all the toils and tribulations of Radcliffe's characters come to serve as the genteel equivalent to the labors of the lower classes. They are the preoccupations that remove one from the art of nature as they place one within nature.

Given this recognition, the problem of describing nature without sinking under tautologous language may be restated as a problem of conflicting ideological attitudes appearing as an aesthetic dilemma. The more particular one's description of a landscape becomes – the more one's description confronts the socialized, personalized, worldly existence of the landscape – the harder it becomes to maintain nature as a coherent aesthetic object. One can be a detached observer with a universal language that inevitably comes to sound repetitious and empty, or one can observe landscape as an inhabitant, in which case discursive demands arise that are too full of worldly significance to be encompassed by this aesthetic mode of perception keyed to transcendent truth. And though the mainstream of eighteenth-century aesthetic theory could escape this conflict by accepting – indeed, demanding – a separation between the cultured and the uncultured drawn along the lines of social class, this conflict cannot be avoided within any aesthetics, such as those of Radcliffe and Wordsworth, that advances the claim that nature is the liberating archetype of all art and in this role is available to all.

One could open any of Radcliffe's novels almost at random and find a passage illustrative of this conflict, but one scene from *The Italian* may serve as a representative example. The first position, that of the privileged observer, is shown when Ellena Rosalba is imprisoned in a convent but is allowed to look out a turret window:

> Hither she would come, and her soul, refreshed by the views it afforded, would acquire strength to bear her, with equanimity, thro' the persecutions that might await her. Here . . . looking, as it were, beyond the awful veil which obscures the features of the Deity . . . how insignificant would appear to her the transactions, and the sufferings of this world! . . . Thus man, the giant who now held her in captivity, would shrink to the diminutiveness of a fairy. (*I*, 90–1)

And with, perhaps, unintentional humor on Radcliffe's part, the position conflicting with this one is illustrated by the fact that immediately after Ellena has thus meditated, she is deprived of the right to look out this window by one of the nuns imprisoning her. Here as throughout Radcliffe's novels, one sees how evanescent is that liberating nature supposedly available even to the poorest of men. As soon as the imaginary omnipotence of solitude is interrupted, it is liable to disappear. Occasionally, these two moments may even occur together, as when Blanche de Villefort in *The Mysteries of Udolpho* looks out from an endangered boat at sea: "As she silently surveyed the vast horizon, bending around the distant verge of the ocean, an emotion of sublimest rapture struggled to overcome a sense of personal danger" (*MU*, 480). However it is dramatized, though, the conflict between these two positions makes it clear that the talismanic significance of landscape in Radcliffe's novels can exist only as a textual and not as an existential reality. The rhetoric of landscape loses its meaning or at least is threatened with this loss when, unlike the solitary reader of a book, one no longer has the apparently unlimited power to decide on a frame for the text or even to ignore it entirely. Literally, therefore, in that Radcliffe's image of nature was fashioned according to the cultural environment of her time, and figuratively, in this tension apparent in her writing, one can see that Radcliffe was not really drawing nature into language but rather was trying to inscribe the language of her art into the appearance of nature. The extent to which she has difficulty in this task measures the extent of her awareness that her books, even if their didactic intent should be realized, might not succeed in refashioning the world as easily as they may impress the reader. For her novels show that the perceptions one enjoys in a privileged position – such as that of the reader – may not easily be transferred to the labor of living. Or, to put it another way, the trials of her novels are the trials of an aesthetics in transition, one tilted toward those values of middle-class sentimentality that would make nature a democratic form of art but suffering its dependence upon aristocratic values that restrict the audience capable of appreciating art to a very small number.

A comparable example of this problem in Wordsworth may be taken from "Resolution and Independence." This poem deals with a confrontation between an observer who is in but not of a landscape – "a Traveller then upon the moor" – and an old man who is so decidedly a part of the landscape that the poet first distinguishes him "unawares" and compares him to "a large stone," "a sea-beast crawled forth," and "a cloud." From the old man's first appearance, then, he is denied a consciousness of nature like that held by the poet and even like that held by nature itself, as the similes he calls forth are distinctly insentient in comparison to the visions of humanized nature that open the poem: a dove brooding "over his own sweet voice," a sky that "rejoices," and a hare "running races in her mirth." It might seem that the leech gatherer is brought into consciousness when the poet sees him stirring the waters of a pond "as if he had been reading in a book" – taking nature as a text in the manner of the poet – but the "as if" in this phrase is crucial, as one sees when the old man responds to the poet's question about his occupation. His voice soon becomes "like a stream / Scarce heard," his words no longer intelligible words, his very body like that of a man "in a dream" or "from a far region sent." In other words, the poet can attend to his voice only if it is detached from the leech gatherer as an independent figure and also from all reference to the occupation that was the ostensible subject of the inquiry. It is thus that the reader finds the poet's question stupidly reiterated – "How is it that you live, and what is it you do?" – and the leech gatherer's discourse renewed not only a second but a third time. For the poet is not conversing with the leech gatherer but rather rejecting his immediate appearance in favor of a fantasy of the old man wandering the moor: "I these thoughts within myself pursued." And the lesson he learns from the old man – "I'll think of the leech-gatherer on the lonely moor" – while presumably reinforcing the doubt expressed in stanza VI that one's "life's business" should be as "a summer mood," still does not remove the distance between the poet and this figure in the landscape. What impresses the poet is that the leech gatherer has "so firm a mind," not "the matter" of his speech as it is recorded in the poem. The leech gatherer can be perceived by the poet as various natural objects, or as a fantasy, or as a mind that is all surface and no content, but not as the laborer of his own description. Working, speaking, even living as a man, he would not be art. And yet the poem includes a description of his labor, unsettlingly, since the reader follows it only to learn that the poet is disregarding it. As in Radcliffe's novels, then, included in the very text that tries to maintain a privileged mode of perception is a tension that raises doubts about that privilege.[12]

Furthermore, this example may serve to illustrate an important result of the conflict within the aesthetics of Radcliffe's novels. This is the recognition that even when one seems apart from such a scene, one is a part of it. That is, although the aesthetic perception of nature is predicated upon a privileged transcendence, this transcendence can be saved from tautologous abstraction only through an immediate contrast with an imprisoned, darkened, threatened mode of perception. Thus it is that the poet's fantasy is not only contrasted to the old man's words but also to the example of Chatterton, and that the redemptive topography of Radcliffe's nature is always approached by way of demonic darknesses, caves, wastelands, and castles.[13] This is not a question of the writer finding a greater harmony that transcends the appearance of discord, but rather of a structural paradox at the heart of this mode of aesthetic perception. Harmony and transcendence are defined in terms of disharmony and oppression; the former cannot appear without the latter; their triumph appears unimaginable apart from their destruction because of a fundamental incoherence in the development of this new, sentimental aesthetics. One can only assert a vision of nature as art through a contradiction in terms. Without this discordant strain within the harmony of the aesthetic viewpoint, the art of nature appears empty and unreal – an outmoded fashion – and even with this necessary discordance the art of nature appears as a fashion that has triumphed prematurely, in advance of any coherent ideological underpinnings.

In effect, then, this conflicting mode of perception is structurally internal to the aesthetic mode even though it is thematically excluded by it. It is necessary to the articulation of landscape-as-art in Radcliffe's novels just as it is in a great deal of Romantic poetry. What is conceived of as transcendence is, at the same time, nontranscendence; and this contradiction or "untruth" is vital to every articulation of truth in these novels. Transcendence must include nontranscendence as a mark of its universality, even though this inclusion threatens to violate the purity of transcendence. And if this description sounds like an abstract of the predicament of Radcliffe's heroines, it is justly so. They embody this contradiction in their lives. The suspenseful course of their existence from the beginning to the end of her novels illustrates this irresoluble tension between the demands of artistic perception and those of social life – or, as Radcliffe put it in the epigraph to this chapter, between the perception of nature and its communication to others.

Of course, this tension exists only because aesthetic perception is conceived of as something apart from communication and a social life. It is not thought of as a learned rhetoric of responses inextricably allied to social traditions, productions, and transfigurations, but as an immediate, individual, natural, and yet tasteful process that one strives to reproduce in art. And that is just the point: that the conflict herein described is not just a matter of dramatic necessity but of a structural necessity that can be seen to tie Radcliffe's writing to a basic contradiction in the society of her time. Specifically, this contradiction lies in the fact that in this period of aesthetic transition a status both transcendent and democratically universal was demanded for art, even though the idea of transcendence necessarily required the repression of those aspects of society that were without privilege. As a result, when the rhetoric of landscape-as-art came into a dramatic conjunction with the demands of worldly life, as it would whenever one was faced with the problem of a landscape inhabited by people other than the aesthetic observer, some means had to be found to mark these demands as simultaneously being included in and excluded from the domain of art.

One such means is that conflation of fear and attraction that so frequently structures the perception of romantic scenes in Radcliffe's novels. For example, as she approaches the ruined remains of an abbey, "Adeline, who had hitherto remained silent, now uttered an exclamation of mingled admiration and fear. A kind of pleasing dread thrilled her bosom, and filled all her soul. Tears started to her eyes: – she wished, yet feared to go on" (*RF* 1: 38–9). In passages such as this one, the ambivalent feelings aroused by the scene indicate that a character is standing on the boundary between a transcendent and a nontranscendent viewpoint. As Adeline discovers, once one comes to inhabit the abbey, all admiration may be engulfed by fear; yet it also is clear that a retreat from this position may leave one with a sense of admiration unalloyed by any sense of personal danger. The fact that this boundary is so frequently touched upon in Radcliffe's novels, moreover, indicates what a distinct importance it has in itself, as compared to the importance of the two perspectives it divides. The existence of this boundary is so insistently dramatized because its spatial location in any particular landscape is just one manifestation of its structural omnipresence in Radcliffe's world. The contradiction intrinsic to the aesthetics of the Gothic as practiced by Radcliffe – which may be summarized by the sight of "the ruins of monasteries and convents, which, though reason rejoices that they no longer exist, the eye may be allowed to regret" (*J* 2:250) – makes this boundary within the landscape of her fiction, in effect, the circumference of her fiction. It seems that art can exist only on the verge of its own destruction if it is to be preserved from tautology, on the one hand, and vulgarity, on the other. Because of the shifting values in the society reflected in Radcliffe's novels, her aesthetics *is* this perilous balance between the idealism of the preceding period, which was tending to appear exhausted of meaning, and the sentimental middle-class values that became dominant in the nineteenth century but in which Radcliffe saw as much to fear as to embrace, since their more democratic basis could also imply a debasement of disinterested, transcendent truth.[14] So characters hesitate on this boundary or are continually driven from one side to the other, thereby preserving the contradiction necessary to the deliverance of truth in Radcliffe's novels. This is the line where the inhabitant and the observer of nature meet and fail to communicate; but this failure, because it is continually reiterated and thus developed into the substance of a plot, allows the illusion of transcendent closure to appear in Radcliffe's novels just as it does in "Resolution and Independence."[15]

For the same reason, Radcliffe's heroines are continually finding their world bifurcated into extremes related to each other by a boundary so fine that these extremes almost meet. Characteristic of such passages is the following description of Adeline in *The Romance of the Forest:*

> She contemplated the past, and viewed the present; and, when she compared them, the contrast struck her with astonishment. The whole appeared like one of those sudden transitions so frequent in dreams, in which we pass from grief and despair, we know not how, to comfort and delight. (*RF* 3: 45)

Here, as in the sensation of "pleasing dread," diametrically opposed feelings are virtually fused in the heroine's experience, because the boundary between them is so unaccountable – which is to say, so unreasonable in transcendent terms and yet so necessary to sustain those terms. It is also for this reason that Radcliffe's lovers so often fantasize each other's suffering and death. Precisely because the feeling of love is categorically transcendent, it can be fully articulated in these novels only on the basis of its utter destruction in death. Thus, when Vivaldi in *The Italian* is told by a mysterious monk that "death is in the house" in which his beloved lives with her elderly guardian, the following description ensues:

An indifferent person would probably have understood the words of the monk to allude to Signora Bianchi, whose infirm state of health rendered her death, though sudden, not improbable; but to the affrighted fancy of Vivaldi, the dying Ellena only appeared. His fears, however probabilities might sanction, or the event justify them, were natural to ardent affection; but they were accompanied by a presentiment as extraordinary as it was horrible; – it occurred to him more than once, that Ellena was murdered. He saw her wounded, and bleeding to death; saw her ashy countenance, and her wasting eyes, from which the spirit of life was fast departing, turned piteously on himself, as if imploring him to save her from the fate that was dragging her to the grave. (*I, 41*)

Not only must Vivaldi himself be described as falling from a moment of "eternity, rendering him independent of all others . . . into the region of time and suffering" (*I, 31*), but Ellena must suffer the same fate in his imagination so as to include her death within the very transcendence of love that excludes it. As in Wordsworth's Lucy poems, the voluptuous elaboration of this character's vision of death is precisely what defines him as a lover. The pleasing nature of that dreadful occurrence is not as openly admitted by Radcliffe's various lovers as it is by the narrator of Wordsworth's poems, but still it is clearly evident in the luxuriance of the vision. Here, again, opposite states of being and feeling are fused so that the Providential pattern of Radcliffe's art may be defined and maintained.

The case remains similar when one considers the way Radcliffe emphasizes the element of obscurity in the appearance of sublime landscapes. As she comments in the *Journey*, "perhaps a sudden display of the sublimest scenery, however full, imparts less emotion, than a gradually increasing view of it; when expectation takes the highest tone, and imagination finishes the sketch" (*J* 2: 301). Obscurity allows a free perceptual detachment on the part of the observer, and as long as such observers can be detached from the scene, they may be in it but not of it. Many problems in natural as well as social landscape, then, may be absorbed and neutralized in the imagination. Thus, the "distant note of a torrent, the weak trembling of the breeze among the woods, or the far-off sound of a human voice, now lost and heard again, are circumstances which

wonderfully heighten the enthusiastic tone of the mind" (*MU*, 599).
And even if this heightening is one of terror, even such terror as
"overwhelmed" Mme. de Menon in one scene in *A Sicilian Romance* when "the terrific aspect of the objects" that Fancy presented
to her "was heightened by the obscurity that involved them" (*SR*,
1 : 239–40), this obscurity preserves that liminal suspense that signifies the transcendent assurance of artistic control in Radcliffe's
novels. Emily, then, will remember with terror the veiled picture
in *The Mysteries of Udolpho;* but "a terror of this nature, as it occupies and expands the mind, and elevates it to high expectation, is
purely sublime, and leads us, by a kind of fascination, to seek even
the object, from which we appear to shrink" (*MU*, 248). Here as
elsewhere, what characterizes the fascination of the Gothic is that it
allows a commingling of detachment and absorption, a "pleasing
dread," and thus symbolically resolves the contradiction in the nature of Radcliffe's art – a contradiction that can be resolved only
symbolically, since it masks divisions between social classes and
political ideologies that cannot be acknowledged in this art.[16]

The same purpose is served by Radcliffe's elevation of the feeling
of melancholy to such a high status in these novels – "that delicious
melancholy, which no person, who had felt it once, would resign
for the gayest pleasure" (*MU*, 46). For melancholy, as Radcliffe
conceives it, is above all else a "complacent" (*RF* 1: 183) and "luxurious" (*I*, 65) feeling, so delicious because it, too, exists on the
boundary of transcendence and nontranscendence. One feels some
kind of pain or loss, and to that extent is absorbed within social life;
but this feeling is resolved into pleasure through its internalization
– that is, its solitary, detached enjoyment – or through its attenuation by the distance of time. So one finds M. La Luc in *The
Romance of the Forest* going off into the country to remember his
late wife:

> This was the secret luxury to which he withdrew from temporary disappointment – the solitary enjoyment which dissipated the cloud of care, and blunted the sting of vexation –
> which elevated his mind above the world, and opened to his
> view the sublimity of another. (*RF* 3: 51–2)

Melancholy at once preserves and transcends worldly darkness and
oppression. It captures better than any other feeling the boundary

that Radcliffe's art must draw between observed and inhabited nature, for it includes the problems of social life and yet excludes them by assigning them to memory and using this memory as a launching pad for futurity.[17]

It is only to be expected, then, that this privileged feeling should be related to a privileged appearance in Radcliffe's women: one in which features gain from distress "an expression of captivating sweetness" (*RF* 1: 13) or in which "the vivid glow of health" is "succeeded by a languid delicacy, less beautiful, but more interesting" (*SR* 1: 145–6). This idealization of the neurasthenic character in women is the logical consequence of the need to find a symbolic resolution for an aesthetics suffering such a severe internal conflict. The heroine must be victimized but made transcendent through this victimization; no wonder, then, if she must shed "tears which she would not have exchanged for mirth and joy" (*RF* 3: 151) and appear most interesting when her beauty is touched with suffering.[18] In such a character, Radcliffe's heroines *are* the landscape of her art, as their bodies as well as their perceptions are designed to deny conflict by making a virtue of suffering.

3

THE LABYRINTH OF DECORUM

⟳

It is painful to know, that we are operated upon by
objects whose impressions are variable as they are
indefinable.
— ANN RADCLIFFE, *A Sicilian Romance*

. . . I was lost in a labyrinth of conjecture.
— ADELINE DE MONTALT IN ANN RADCLIFFE'S
Romance of the Forest

WITH ITS DRAMATIC FOCUS upon the Inquisi-
tion and the tortured villainy of Schedoni, *The Italian* is
the only novel in which Ann Radcliffe went appreciably
beyond a schematic psychology that divided characters into the
simple categories of the innocent and the corrupted. However, this
is not to say that the psychology of her other novels is entirely
without depth. Rather, one may look for and find considerable
psychological complexity in aspects of her work other than the depiction of character. In these other novels – and also in *The Italian,*
in addition to its more subtle characterizations – psychological
meaning is dramatized through a vocabulary of repeated situations
rather than analyzed through narrative exposition. Moreover, in
considering the most prominent among these repeated situations –
the appearance of "speaking bodies," of cryptic figures and sounds,
and of heroines lost in labyrinths – one sees how such a dramatization of psychological meaning is significant in itself.

It seems appropriate to begin with the body; for when Gothic
fiction has been satirized, from the time of *Northanger Abbey* to our
own day, the role of the female body is always among the major
topics of this satire. And, indeed, the swoons, syncopes, and trances
that so frequently seize Radcliffe's heroines do make them ludi-
crous in terms of the style of realism that Austen helped to develop.
Nevertheless, as Austen showed even as she satirized it,[1] such be-

havior does have meaning. It dramatically expresses a great problem that these heroines face in controlling themselves and in controlling the way they appear to others. In this respect, Radcliffe's novels are not so much Austen's target as they are the material that she interprets and shows in a new light by converting it to a different style of literary representation. To a great extent, Austen's descriptions of the characters of her heroines are related to the way that the bodies of Radcliffe's heroines behave. Both varieties of women face similar problems, however differently they may be expressed. In both cases it is proper behavior that is at stake, even though the heroines of Radcliffe's novels are so extremely alienated from the behavior of their own bodies.

Even when they are not paralyzed, unconscious, or physically abducted and confined by others, these heroines frequently find their bodies beyond their control. As Laura is confronted by her lover in *The Castles of Athlin and Dunbayne,* her case is typical: "Laura was silent; she wished to speak her gratitude, yet feared to tell her love; but the soft timidity of her eye, and the tender glow of her cheek, revealed the secret that trembled on her lips" (*CAD*, 167). Over and over, Radcliffe's heroines find their bodies betraying them in this manner, speaking for them when they desire to be secretive or, in the more extreme situations of paralysis and unconsciousness, stealing from them all power of response. In fact, not only is the body generally given such power as a means of responding to others, but it actually is given value as a more eloquent medium of communication than words or deliberate actions:

> Ellena, still weeping, and agitated by various considerations, spoke not, but withdrawing the handkerchief from her face, she looked at him through her tears, with a smile so meek, so affectionate, so timid, yet so confiding, as expressed all the mingled emotions of her heart, and appealed more eloquently to his, than the most energetic language could have done. (*I*, 39)

That this should be a characteristic situation in Radcliffe's novels is not simply a matter of unthinking literary convention. By considering the strictures placed upon the behavior of women in these novels, one can see why the body of the heroine should and even must rebel against her and take control over communication, whether that communication be desired or undesired. For throughout these novels one finds a pressure for decorous behavior so immense that it can only eventuate in this rebellion of the body.

To judge the extent of this pressure, one need only consider that heroine, abducted by a marquis who wants her as his mistress and confined by him in a house staffed by lewd women, who yet can think that though her purpose in saving herself through dissimulation would be good, "she scarcely believed that end could justify the means" (*RF* 2: 111). In these novels, the opportunity for error is so great and Radcliffe's heroines always so "anxious to avoid every opportunity of erring" (*MU*, 126) that their bodies *must* rebel if they are to be able to act at all. Their bodies come to betray their meaning, but that meaning can be expressed only through betrayal, because it is so probable that any open and voluntary communication might be judged indecorous at best, sinful at worst.[2]

The "speaking body," in other words, is the result of an otherwise insurmountable conflict between the desire for expression and the fear of impropriety. The paradox of a world as strictly governed as Radcliffe's is that the only communication that one can be certain is properly controlled is communication over which one has no control. Consequently, hysteria is decorum in these novels, though it is only in *The Italian* that there is any explicit approach to this recognition, as when Ellena Rosalba begins to consider that her virtues, "now that they were carried to excess, seemed to border upon vices" (*I*, 181).

Given this behavioral dilemma, one can see why Osbert in *The Castles of Athlin and Dunbayne* should first be able to press Laura's hand to his breast, and she to yield her hand, when she has not yet recovered from a swoon. Such a scene of unconscious communication may be said to be paradigmatic for the heroines of Radcliffe's novels. From this perspective one also can see the physical abductions and confinements of these heroines as a related representation of this conflict between desire and decorum. Instead of having the body breaking into symptomatic speech to resolve this conflict, villains carry away the heroine and thereby relieve her of responsibility for her actions. These incidents, of course, lead to new dramas that revive the problem; but in themselves these kidnappings and imprisonments appear as dramatic corollaries to the way the heroines of these novels are kidnapped or confined by their own bodies. Just as the quality of one's sensibility is established by one's liability to insensibility, so is "this existence of endless persecution"[3] further confirmation of one's delicacy. The fineness of one's character is measured by how rude the world appears in contrast to it. A further corollary to this rebellious behavior of the body appears in the role accidents play in Radcliffe's novels. Just as Laura's swoon serves to communicate an affection that otherwise might be impossible to express, and just as "the negligence of her dress" that results from one of Adeline's swoons serves to reveal "those glowing charms, which her auburn tresses, that fell in profusion over her bosom, shaded, but could not conceal" (*RF* 1: 193), so do accidental meetings and revelations allow communications to take place that a reserved, responsible, decorous order of behavior would prohibit. Thus, when Julia in *A Sicilian Romance* accidentally overhears Count Hippolitus confessing his love for her to her brother and then is accidentally discovered as an interested auditor to this scene, the logic that takes priority in her admission of affection is highly significant. "If I wished even to deny the partiality I feel," she says, "it would now be useless; and since I no longer wish this, it would also be painful" (*SR* 1: 117). Events must divest the heroine of the possibility of concealment before a deliberate admission can be made, just as the heroine must be abducted by a villain or by her own body to allow communication in other circumstances. These related means of communication may even appear redundantly, as when her lover accidentally discovers Ellena expressing her affection for him, and when he breaks in upon her soliloquy, obtains the following response: " 'I cannot be detained Signor,' interrupted Ellena, still more embarrassed, 'or forgive myself for having permitted such a conversation;' but as she spoke the last words, an involuntary smile seemed to contradict their meaning" (*I,* 27). All important communications involving desire must take place in the mode of unconsciousness, and thus one need not be surprised to find that a character like Adeline may permit someone to be mistaken about a particular circumstance in her behavior as long as she need not actively lie but only passively submit to his mistaken supposition. She is not entirely happy even with this kind of dissimulation, but passivity is close enough to unconsciousness to allow her to accept it.

Three major factors are responsible for the fact that this conflict between desire and decorum should be so strong in Radcliffe's novels as to necessitate communication through these varieties of unconsciousness, thereby showing the extent of the paranoia that could be generated by the pressures placed upon female behavior in the society to which these novels responded and in which they proved so popular. The first relates to the moral tradition of thinking in absolutes that was so much a part of the culture of Radcliffe's time. As previously noted, it was not until the writing of *The Italian* that Radcliffe came anywhere near Austen's idea that there is "a general though unequal mixture of good and bad" in people;[4] and even in that novel this recognition is developed through dramatic situations and juxtapositions more than it is through an explicit narrative consciousness. (One finds, for instance, that *The Italian*'s version of the moral with which Radcliffe habitually ends her novels does not differ significantly from those concluding the other novels.) The result is that the slightest deviation from the absolutes of goodness and propriety is felt to contain, in embryo, *all* deviations, great and small. "Sister! beware of the first indulgence of the passions; beware of the first!" Sister Agnes tells Emily (*MU*, 646); and though this nun's senses are somewhat unbalanced in other respects, the reader of Radcliffe's novels knows that this demand is not part of her insanity. Within these novels, one need only take a single step away from absolute propriety to find oneself drawn toward disaster. This same moral is illustrated, for example, in the history of Pierre de la Motte: "He had been led on by slow gradations from folly to vice, till he now saw before him an abyss of guilt which startled even the conscience that so long had slumbered. The means of retreating were desperate – to proceed was equally so" (*RF* 3: 6). There are those who take a step over the edge and still manage to find their way back – Valancourt in *The Mysteries of Udolpho* is a notable example – but by and large the rule is that the slightest moral infraction, if left unreproved, is liable to become a virulent infection that destroys one's character entirely. And even though the tendency to think in such extremes might often reflect a more purely literary than a social consciousness, so that the habit of mind evident in these novels might exaggerate the consciousness that people of Radcliffe's sort actually applied to judgments in everyday life, this literary consciousness interprets the forces at work within the shaping of individuals in Radcliffe's society with a perspicacity evidenced by the novels' popularity. The extreme interpretation that rules these novels would not always have ruled the actual consciousness of people in the society of Radcliffe's time, but it ruled often enough so that these novels made good sense to their readers.

The second reason for the extremity of this conflict is the unsettled disposition in these novels of the conflict between traditional aristocratic and sentimental middle-class orders of value. As in Austen's novels and those of Sir Walter Scott, there is a great tension between the emphases upon individual merit, sensibility, and the dignity of common labor, which were growing throughout Radcliffe's era, and the continuing though gradually waning strength of the aristocratic emphases upon family character, rank, fortune, and heritage. (It is irrelevant in this regard that Radcliffe's novels generally are set in centuries before and countries other than her own, for in terms of manners and sentiments they are quite blithely anachronistic.) In such an unsettled state of affairs, it is only to be expected that propriety should become an empty concept that can be maintained only through unconsciousness or passivity, because the individual is trapped between two quite different and yet equally imperative orders of value. Although Radcliffe's novels do not illustrate this problem through a depiction of manners as precise as Austen's, her heroines do find just as frequently as do Austen's that it is one thing to desire to behave with propriety and quite another to know just what proper behavior in any particular circumstances might be.

Furthermore, one can see the severity of this conflict between two orders of value when one considers the division between the sentiments accorded approbation in these novels and the formal resolutions to their plots. For instance, Ellena is first discovered in *The Italian* living as a dependent orphan, helping to support her aunt by embroidering silks, and feeling that this work is virtuous. Yet she is able to marry her lover at the end of the novel only because she has been discovered to be the daughter of a count and so is of a background sufficiently elevated to satisfy the pride of Vivaldi's father, the marchese. Similarly, although Radcliffe's first novel expresses regret that the authority of ancient prejudice should keep the earl who is its hero from approving the affection between his sister and Alleyn, a noble spirit but a commoner, the problem is resolved at the end of the novel by the discovery that Alleyn in reality is nobly born. And this discovery, of course, explains how Alleyn *can* be so heroic – because he is not really a commoner. In this respect, Radcliffe's novels are based upon the same division of values as are Scott's and show this division in the same way. In these novels, a resolution that would cut across the lines of birth is unimaginable. All the sentiments marked with Radcliffe's approval are on the side of middle-class values, but the dramatic structures of her novels tend to contradict or at least weaken that approval by showing it to have no force in the practical course of life. Their dramatic structures, in other words, tend to empty the narrative moralizing of its meaning; and so it is not surprising that a similar irresolution should appear as a characteristic behavior of Radcliffe's heroines.

It is also significant that in these novels as in Austen's and Scott's, it is primarily through such structural constraints that aristocratic values find expression, whereas middle-class values are more explicitly voiced. This unvoiced, structural modification of the superficial ideology of these works perfectly reflects the way the middle classes of this time would consciously assert a new standard of values while frequently emulating and imitating the aristocracy in ways that did not reach an explicit consciousness. Similarly, in showing the power that her various noblemen enjoy over her heroines and her other characters, Radcliffe shows the power that the order of values represented by such characters could still have over those who tried to adhere to the newer standards.

Finally, this extreme conflict between desire and decorum also has a source in the general subordination of women to the power of men in these novels, as in Radcliffe's time. The various rapes with which Radcliffe's heroines are threatened, and the close conjunction between them and threats of other physical abuse – even of murder – testify sufficiently that women, in these novels as in Richardson's and even Austen's and Scott's,[5] might literally have no other refuge except unconsciousness if they wished to resist the power of men.

The mysterious figures that appear in these novels can also be seen to have a connection with the behavior of their heroines, for these figures bring another psychological dimension to Radcliffe's work. Such figures appear so frequently that their effect is that of one recurring character, "the mysterious figure," who suddenly appears out of the obscurity of forests or shadows and then, when pursued, just as suddenly disappears. And even though the true identities of all such figures are always sorted out by the ends of these novels, it is not fanciful to speak of all of them as a single character; for the function of the mysterious figure is always the same, however various the people may be who eventually are identified as the player of this role. Not only does this figure help to bring a general atmosphere of mystery and suspense to these novels, but it specifically brings mystery to the attempt to fathom human character. However simple and unmixed Radcliffe's characters may be in her descriptions of their personalities and moral natures, this figure appears in her novels to upset this simplicity and to introduce a radical uncertainty even to judgments that would seem unquestionable.

Although it might seem too impressionistic, then, to say that Radcliffe's characters are continually passing into and out of blindness, or appearing as fitful illuminations against a background of impenetrable and terrifying darkness, her novels actually develop this impression in very specific ways. It is not so much that the mysterious figure creates disorder in the realm of appearances, because its unaccountable identity leads one to suspect the identities of others (although it does have this effect to some extent[6]), but more importantly, that it appears in these novels as the dramatic symbol of a general potential for misconception in one's perception of other people. Radcliffe's characters may be described in relatively simple terms, but they do not appear to each other, and especially not to the heroines of these novels, in the state of simplicity presented to the reader. Not only is the mysterious figure in these novels frequently accompanied by a flickering torch, but it is figuratively a representation of the limits of the enlightenment Radcliffe employs to dispel all doubt, superstition, and terror at the ends of her tales.

The image that arises when Julia tries to understand her lover, then, is not at all accidental: "Julia sought with eager anxiety to discover the sentiments of Vereza towards her; she revolved each circumstance of the day, but they afforded her little satisfaction; they reflected only a glimmering and uncertain light, which instead of guiding, served only to perplex her" (*SR* 1: 20). At such a moment, the inability to judge behavior accurately results in an inability to understand other people; and both problems are connected, here as throughout these novels, to a primitive and labyrinthine darkness that repeatedly threatens to engulf the lives as well as the thoughts of Radcliffe's characters.[7] Parents and friends and enemies as well as lovers are all liable to develop such a doubtful appearance, perplexing and sickening the heroines of these novels and even causing one – Emily in *The Mysteries of Udolpho* – to believe quite firmly that her erstwhile lover would be better off dead than different in character from what she initially had supposed him to be.[8] This difficulty in knowing the truth of another is so important to these novels that it may even appear as the psychological matrix to the entire novelistic macrocosm, as when Emily regards Montoni and, in doing so, can be seen to summarize in her thoughts the dramatic substance of Radcliffe's art: " 'O could I know,' said she to herself, 'what passes in that mind; could I know the thoughts, that are known there, I should no longer be condemned to this torturing suspense!' " (*MU*, 243).

Just as decorum and hysteria are, in effect, identical, so is the appearance of others, in effect, one with the darkness of the shadow and the night that provide the scenic background to the trials of Radcliffe's heroines. The literal and metaphorical darkness with which these heroines so frequently are environed and in which they so often are bewildered corresponds to the darkness that the human countenance presents to those who have become aware that it is a mystery, a legend of suspense, not a clear and readily comprehensible text. And, as in the case of decorum, the final result is that the heroine is led into uncertainty about her own identity, as Adeline finds after reading a suspenseful manuscript that she has discovered in the apartment in which she has been confined:

> While she sat musing, her fancy, which now wandered in the regions of terror, gradually subdued reason. There was a glass before her upon the table, and she feared to raise her looks towards it, lest some other face than her own should meet her eyes; other dreadful ideas and strange images of fantastic thought now crossed her mind. (*RF* 2: 52)

It is only to be expected that soon after these musings she should glimpse a mysterious figure in the darkness of her room.

A further dramatic corollary to this kind of uncertainty is found in the difficulty Radcliffe's heroines face in determining their true origins or in dealing with those substitute guardians who represent in a dramatic form the mixed identities that Radcliffe's novels, like many fairy tales, are unable to comprehend within a single character. Thus does Emilia, for example, regard her stepmother:

In reviewing the events of the last few weeks, she saw those most dear to her banished, or imprisoned by the secret influence of a woman, every feature of whose character was exactly opposite to that of the amiable mother she had been appointed to succeed. (*SR* 2: 25–6)

The circumstances that lead Emily in *The Mysteries of Udolpho* to believe "that there was a mystery in her birth dishonourable to her parents" (*MU*, 650) – even though this mystery is finally dispelled, following the general rule of Radcliffe's novels[9] – is entirely parallel to Emilia's situation in all important respects except the manner of representation. The role played by two different characters in *The Sicilian Romance* is played in *The Mysteries of Udolpho* by one set of parents and the confusions that arise in regard to their identities – although Emily also has a malign substitute family in Mme. Cheron and Montoni, which makes apparent the correspondence between these two modes of representation.

At the beginning of her first novel, this whole problem of uncertainty was described by Radcliffe, conventionally enough, as the problem of passing from innocence to experience. Despite its conventionality, however, the passage is worth quoting at some length, as its imagery epitomizes the dramatic problems of all of Radcliffe's fiction:

> When first we enter on the theatre of the world, and begin to notice the objects that surround us, young imagination heightens every scene, and the warm heart expands to all around it . . . As we advance in life, imagination is compelled to relinquish a part of her sweet delirium; we are led reluctantly to truth through the path of experience; and the objects of our fond attention are viewed with a severer eye. Here an altered scene appears; – frowns where late were smiles; deep shades where late was sunshine: mean passions, or disgusting apathy, stain the features of the principal figures . . . The fine touch of moral susceptibility, by frequent irritation, becomes callous; and too frequently we mingle with the world, till we are added to the number of its votaries. (*CAD*, 4–6)

This passage makes it clear that the skepticism and cynicism of the votaries of the world are seen by Radcliffe as unnecessary, unnatural, and reprehensible results of intercourse with the world; but this perception does not alleviate the problem of perceiving character. Just because Radcliffe's novels show that enlightenment will finally come to virtue does not mean that the trials undergone by virtue before that end are inconsequential. Rather – again as in Richardson's novels and as in the traditions of Puritan literature – it is only by encountering these trials and accepting the suffering they bring that virtue proves itself to be such. In fact, suffering is shown to be as much a positive value as an unfortunate necessity. As Adeline exclaims immediately after noticing that she has been "betrayed by the very persons . . . whom she had loved as her protectors, and revered as her parents":

> "How has my imagination deceived me! . . . what a picture did it draw of the goodness of the world! And must I then believe that every body is cruel and deceitful? No – let me still be deceived, and still suffer, rather than be condemned to a state of such wretched suspicion!" (*RF* 2: 88–9)

Suffering is not simply the necessary result of a heroine finding herself in bewildered and evil circumstances, but the means by which she expels the potential for evil from within herself. The function of hysterical seizures in proving the delicacy of one's sensibility is seen still more fully in the light of such a passage, which shows the aspect of unconsciousness in these novels that is a willed ignorance rather than the only possible response to an intolerable dilemma. The negative desire to avoid an unwholesome state of being takes precedence over a positive desire for truth. It becomes clear that enlightenment is not necessarily bliss in Radcliffe's novels, and this realization does much to qualify the optimism generated by the novels' conclusions, which seems to radiate back and infuse all the mysteries of the preceding pages. There are some countenances and some kinds of identities that one *wants* to disappear into obscurity, however terrifying that obscurity may be as a result of its use as a locus of repression.

Mysterious figures often are accompanied in these novels by mysterious sounds as well as by flickering lights; and here, again, one finds a corollary psychological representation. There are two basic varieties of such sounds – music (generally played on a lute) and hollow groans, sighs, or voices – but all such sounds have the same narrative function. As long as their source remains unknown, they call into question all expressions of meaning, auditory and otherwise, that environ Radcliffe's characters. Sometimes this challenge is direct, as when a mysterious voice interrupts Montoni as he attempts to explain the fate of the previous owner of Udolpho, but more often the challenge is indirect and therefore all the more powerful. Sounds appear in conjunction with certain situations but without any clear relationship to them, and the result is that a labyrinthine darkness is made to suffuse all of one's perceptions. Because these sounds seem to be assertions of significance and yet assertions without any specific content, any thought becomes possible, and there seems to be no way of putting an end to such thoughts. One of the most frequent positions in which one finds Radcliffe's characters is, as Adeline says, "lost in a labyrinth of conjecture"; and when they are in this position there is little difference between the metaphorical and the physical experience of bewilderment. It becomes a meaningless question as to whether a character is wandering in a mental or a physical landscape, for the dividing lines between thought and reality disappear. And thus, again, one may find a kind of solipsistic and paranoid self-doubt developing, as when Ferdinand, marquis of Mazzini, returning from an unsuccessful pursuit of a figure so mysterious "that he scarcely knew whether it bore the impression of a human form," hears the echoes of his own footsteps as "uncertain sounds of strange and fearful import" (*SR* 1: 103, 105).[10]

Again as in the case of mysterious figures, Radcliffe often characterizes the reactions of her characters to mysterious sounds in terms of an unfortunate tendency toward superstition. As she writes in reference to a noise that Emily hears at night, reason "cannot establish her laws on subjects, lost in the obscurity of imagination, any more than the eye can ascertain the form of objects, that only glimmer through the dimness of night" (*MU*, 330). Such is the moral lesson she tries to draw from such occurrences: that one must resist the multiplicity of conjectures that may throng one's mind in such moments and instead wait in the patience of virtue, confident that the end of the novel will come and illuminate all such perplexities. As she writes in describing why one should not despair at the variability of impressions, "Happiness has this essential difference from what is called pleasure, that virtue forms its basis, and virtue being the offspring of reason, may be expected to produce uniformity of effect" (*SR* 1: 45). So, for instance, one will find that the mysterious figures, lights, and sounds in the castle in *The Sicilian Romance* are explained by the confinement of the marquis's first wife in an apartment there. The mystery, it seems, is dispelled; but still a vexing problem remains in regard to mysterious sounds.

Just as the appearance of mysterious figures is related to a more general recognition that even the most clearly illuminated figures may actually be shrouded in darkness, so do mysterious sounds develop the broad impression that sound in general and the human voice in particular are not securely fixed to individual identities. That is to say, the way sounds are continually startling Radcliffe's characters, breaking into their world as incomprehensible events, creates the impression that sound as such is a profoundly alien phenomenon; that it arises, as it were, out of that darkness in which Radcliffe's heroines so frequently find themselves or the figures of others being lost; that it is as independent of control as are the bodies of the heroines of these novels. The dramatic emphasis in these novels upon the immaterial nature of sound contributes to their general emphasis upon the lack of substantial signs, guarantees, and protections in the world of experience so as to make all of reality, in one of Radcliffe's favorite tropes, "like a dream." This emphasis, of course, is finally subsumed in the even broader dedication of these novels to the sublime providence of God and enlightened Reason; but still one finds this dreamlike problem as inescapable a reality as the eventual triumph of virtue. It may be temporary, but at the moment of its occurrence it cannot help but seem eternal. It is no wonder that heroines should so frequently fall into trances, fits, and faints when one considers that at any moment their world may be transformed by the effect of a mysterious figure or sound into an immaterial darkness of the understanding. With such moments to drain experience of its substantial reality, it is only appropriate that one should respond by becoming disembodied in one's own person.

Even when the startling sound is entirely trivial, as when characters in *The Romance of the Forest* are made to hesitate by a sound they soon realize was made by owls, the very triviality of such alarms shows how pervasively sound is experienced as an alien phenomenon. It may make an impression exactly opposite to its true significance, as when Adeline first hears the voice of a servant who comes to help her as a terrifying threat, or even more frequently, it suggests an impersonal background to experience in which all individual identities and histories become, not so much mysterious, but insignificant. This is the case, for instance, with all those unidentifiable groans and sighs that are heard behind tapestries, casements, or walls. One gets the impression of a general environment of suffering and, consequently, of suffering as an experience in which the individual victim has no significance in comparison to the primitive reality of suffering in and of itself.[11]

Given this consideration, the schematic nature of most of Radcliffe's characters need not be seen only as the result of conventional, moralized allegory. Their simple natures and their similar experiences also can be seen as the appropriate means for concentrating art upon aspects of experience that are neither individual nor social but bestially impersonal: fear, suffering, and terror.[12] After all, it is in its fascination with such primitive experiences that popular, formulaic, melodramatic art approaches the concerns of myth and mythical habits of thinking, often – as in Radcliffe's case – approaching these concerns all the more closely because of its lack of stylistic sophistication. Although the distance between problems of decorum and the mythical representation of suffering may seem great, it is the virtue of popular fiction like Radcliffe's that it may bring one to see just how intimate the connection is between speaking and acting politely and falling into a realm of primordial incoherence. One is reminded of Lionel Trilling's description of Jane Austen's social world as one of terror with a capital "T."[13]

This disappearance of physical security into a darkness of endless conjecture is found in all of the alarms that upset Radcliffe's heroines, whether or not they are specifically related to mysterious voices or music. Nothing in Radcliffe's fiction seems more mechanical and unrealistic than the way her characters are continually being scared and then quickly relieved of their fright in an apparently pointless way – as Emily, for instance, is scared by the approach of her dog in a darkened room. And yet these moments of fright indicate the extent to which the security of Radcliffe's heroines is strictly circumscribed by immediacy. Nothing but the present moment, the present situation, and the environment immediately within one's view can be depended upon. Beyond all is darkness, no matter what one's actual location and the actual time of day may be. The transcendent security afforded by God is not found incarnated in any earthly form to which one can cling for security, and the result is that the sense of place, like those of sound and of identity, is drained of its materiality. The world of Radcliffe's heroines is, in effect, no more extensive than their immediate environment. They live and move through the world as in a spotlighted circle of consciousness surrounded by a night in which memory and knowledge have no real power. As soon as a particular area is not within one's view, there is no assurance that it remains the same. The paradigm for this sense of place may be found in those apartments in which secret doors are always being discovered: doors that may lead one to regions completely unknown just as they may allow the entrance of that terrifying unknown into one's immediate sphere of consciousness. Such, for instance, is the secret door by which Schedoni enters into the apartment in which he has had Ellena confined. Having found herself locked into this room, she had thought herself secure at least in that small space; but even this tightly limited security proves evanescent.

In describing this concern of Radcliffe's novels with primitive terrors, though, it is important to remember the specific reference of those terrors. When entering a literary environment as extreme as that of Radcliffe's novels, it is easy to forget its grounding in historical life – and yet such an understanding is essential if one is to grasp the significance of this literature. It is important to remember that, as Marc Bloch has noted, "it was not only in the novels of Mrs. Radcliffe that castles, whether large or small, had their *oub-liettes.*"[14] In emphasizing the psychological meaning of Radcliffe's style of representation, it is always necessary to keep in mind that there was a historical, material reality to the sufferings she describes. The transition Austen effected from the alarms of romance to the anxieties of common life may be generally perceived as having produced a fiction more closely mirroring the surface of social life, but this change from the representation of physical to mental distress resulted in a fiction as limited in its own way as was Radcliffe's. Despite Henry Tilney's forceful reminder to Catherine Morland that she is in England and not in the realm of Italian banditti, one need not be an especially profound student of history to realize that suffering and terrors on a Gothic scale were as much a part of Austen's England as they were a part of past history, however peripheral they may be to her fiction. These contemporary sufferings and terrors are the stuff of Radcliffe's fiction, however they may be mediated – as they were in her culture generally –

through the demands of taste, morality, and decorum. Her melodramatic situations are distillations of the fears and dangers uppermost in the society of her time, especially as that society appeared to women.[15] The average English girl in the late eighteenth century may not have had to face a kidnapping by banditti if she did not behave in society as she had ought to, but she could very well face consequences that are hardly exaggerated in the image of the marauding band of outlaws, as Austen was so intent upon demonstrating in *Sense and Sensibility*. So however allegorically schematic Radcliffe's fiction may be – "Emily might now have appeared, like an angel of light, encompassed by fiends" (*MU*, 317) – it is at least arguable that the peculiarities of its style are more profoundly touched by a historical consciousness than the more measured control of Austen's writing.

Of course, one need not use either writer to knock the other over the head. Certainly Austen appreciated Radcliffe even as she satirized her, and Scott, similarly, was able to appreciate both. In any event, it is important to note that even though Radcliffe's style may seem as hysterical as the bodies of her heroines, that hysteria is not simply the result of a fad in literary taste or of an immature stage in the rise of the novel as a genre. The style and the structure of her novels reflect the urgent themes of her writing.

The recurrent situation that encompasses all the foregoing considerations is that in which one finds Radcliffe's heroines in a labyrinth, whether of the mind or of natural landscape or of a building. Thus, for instance, one finds Emily in *The Mysteries of Udolpho*:

> As she returned towards her chamber, Emily began to fear, that she might again lose herself in the intricacies of the castle, and again be shocked by some mysterious spectacle; and, though she was already perplexed by the numerous turnings, she feared to open one of the many doors that offered. (*MU*, 258)

Or Julia in *The Sicilian Romance:*

> Julia, whose fears conspired with the gloom of night to magnify every object around her, imagined at each step that she took, she perceived the figures of men, and fancied every whisper of the breeze the sound of pursuit. (*SR* 2: 100–1)

Such situations easily become the stage of farce – as in Austen's juvenilia and *Northanger Abbey* – because they occur on the very edge of dramatic coherence. As previously noted, in all the moments related to these in Radcliffe's novels, the scope of conjecture tends to become so limitless that the logic, continuity, and form of drama are threatened with a complete dissolution of meaning. If all objects are put into question and if anything at all can happen, then the distinctions among characters, actions, and scenes break down; and the easiest way to make sense of this possibility is to transform the situation into a comedy in which this threatened anarchy may provoke laughter rather than fearful bewilderment. This, in fact, is the transformation that has been made by disenchanted readers of the Gothic novel from the time of Clara Reeve to the present day.[16] And, of course, it must be kept in mind that this reaction to the extremes of Radcliffe's fiction is in accord with its governing morality, even if Radcliffe intended her readers to wait until the end of the novels, when all mysteries are explained, to smile at the terrors represented in them. After all, these labyrinthine situations are represented so often rather than elaborated at any length because through repetition they gain the status and security of convention. To imagine the labyrinth as the dominant setting of these novels rather than a repeated interruption to their overall progress would be to imagine a fiction that does not belong to the late eighteenth century but rather to the twentieth, when a writer such as Kafka could so conflate farce and terror as to make them indistinguishable from each other. Nevertheless, even though the modern reader is likely to find the style of Radcliffe's terrors so dated that they will appear farcical even without Austen's intervention, they are evidence of social and psychological conflicts that are no less real for being alien in their substance and in their manner of representation to modern society and psychology. The taste for Radcliffe's style of writing may already have largely passed by the time *Northanger Abbey* was published, as Austen felt compelled to note at the beginning of that novel, but this does not mean that this style was only a matter of taste. As Austen indicated when she had Catherine Morland speak to Miss Tilney of a shocking event in London – a literary reference that Miss Tilney mistakes as a report of riots among the lower classes – it was not only Gothic castles that had their *oubliettes*.

PART II

JANE AUSTEN

∽

They belong to a class of fictions which has arisen
almost in our own times, and which draws the characters and incidents introduced more immediately
from the current of ordinary life than was permitted
by the former rules of the novel.

– SIR WALTER SCOTT ON JANE AUSTEN'S
NOVELS IN A REVIEW OF *Emma*

4

THE CONTROL OF MEANING

~

What dire Offence from Am'rous Causes springs,
What mighty contests rise from trivial Things.
ALEXANDER POPE, *"The Rape of the Lock"*

IN "SENSE AND SENSIBILITY" Edward Ferrars arrives at one of his visits to the Dashwoods wearing a ring made of hair. Naturally, the Dashwood sisters wonder at its significance. In fact, they apply this ring to Edward's intentions just as the lock of Marianne Dashwood's hair that is cut by Willoughby comes to be applied to that gentleman's rather more culpable designs. In both cases the hair is understood to be a sign of attachment, but in both cases it is an ambiguous sign. Though Willoughby's action strongly suggests his affection for Marianne, it does not guarantee it; and Edward's ring at best seems only to resemble Elinor's hair and eventually is found to have been taken from a very unexpected head. In other words, these locks of hair spring up in the plot of the novel to trap Elinor and Marianne in embarrassing misunderstandings.

All the signs offered to the interpretation of women in Austen's novels are of a similar nature. There are no guarantees in their world. Whether they know it or not, women in these novels are always trapped in uncertainty even as they are called upon to make certain decisions about their own behavior and the behavior of others. To appreciate the significance of their words and actions, then, especially when those words and actions are related to the all-important topic of marriage, one first must analyze the nature of this entrapment and the psychology it forces upon these women.

71

As in "The Rape of the Lock," the locks of hair in *Sense and Sensibility* are not just signs of romantic attachment but also barely disguised emblems of sexual intercourse, and as such they play the same role in this novel as Colonel Brandon's cautionary tale of the two Elizas.[1] They point at that scandalous fate which may be skirted more narrowly by Marianne than Elinor but which is potential to them both. For as even Elinor is unable to restrain herself from wondering about the significance of Edward's ring, that ring serves to criticize the character of this most cautious of women, drawing forth the susceptibility to seduction from which even Elinor is not free. Her incautious speculation shows that her virtue is not impregnable.[2] In short, the plot woven around these locks of hair serves to show that scandalous fate is not just in the outside world, either in the person of the seducer or else in that terrible impersonality with which society calculates honor and dishonor, but also within these two sisters. As far as the society portrayed in these novels is concerned, these sisters are at fault for their misunderstandings even though the signs with which they dealt were so ambiguous; and thus these locks of hair are like the cabinet locks that embarrass Catherine Morland in *Northanger Abbey* even after she discovers that the cabinet itself holds no great mysteries:

> Why the locks should have been so difficult to open, however, was still something remarkable, for she could now manage them with perfect ease. In this there was surely something mysterious, and she indulged in the flattering suggestion for half a minute, till the possibility of the door's having been at first unlocked, and of being herself its fastener, darted into her head, and cost her another blush. (*NA*, 173)[3]

Like the locks of the cabinet, the locks of hair in *Sense and Sensibility* serve to catch the unconscious desires of the Dashwoods for those very mysteries they are supposed to fear and avoid and not even dream about. Austen thus is no kinder to Marianne and Elinor than Pope was to Arabella Fermor when he made her guardian sylph surrender its powers as it detected within her an element of desire for her assailant. In Austen's work as in Pope's, however, these unconscious desires have nothing to do with the modern psychoanalytic theories that would refer such desires to a powerfully irrational substratum of the psychic life common to everyone. Whatever one may think of Freud's work, the unconsciousness of Austen's women is not one that is found in the psychology of women but rather one that is imposed upon them as a result of the way in which their words and actions are interpreted in society. It derives from the fact that in these novels women do not have the power of interpretation that men have, even when that interpretation applies to their own psychological condition. Generally speaking, then, when a man's judgment runs contrary to a woman's, he has the power to presume that his judgment finds confirmation within her, even if he must allow that confirmation to be unconscious. Consequently, the minds of women may be said to be colonized by an unconsciousness that is always agreeable to men and that will be forced into consciousness by the power of men if the women should ever seem to differ from their judgment. This overruling of the minds of women is so powerful that even when a woman simply makes a mistake in judgment or comes to be threatened by an ambiguity or an actual danger in the world around her, she may be held responsible for her situation if she has not been perfectly passive, projecting an image of total unconsciousness, ceding all interpretation to those men who have the authority in her world. If she cannot refrain from all speculation and the self-assertion it entails, as Elinor and Marianne and even humble little Fanny Price in *Mansfield Park* cannot, then she has no one but herself to blame. Such is the rule of Austen's novels, and of course no woman is perfect enough to escape it. And although it may seem an extravagant rule, there are ample precedents for it in the eighteenth-century literature with which Austen was imbued and in the actual practices of the society of her time.[4]

In Richardson's *Sir Charles Grandison,* for instance, a book Austen reportedly read and reread, one finds a clear precedent for this rule in a scene that follows Harriet Byron's rescue from a seducer. Sir Charles impresses upon Harriet her own culpability in this matter as he musters his reasons against seeking to prosecute the man who had kidnapped her from a dance: "Masquerades . . . are not creditable places for young Ladies to be known to be *insulted* at them. They are diversions that fall not in with the genius of the English commonalty. Scandal will have something to say from that circumstance, however causeless."[5] However causeless the judgment may be, it appears that Harriet must be judged, in effect, to have kidnapped herself. In this case as in all of Austen's novels, women are not allowed to be innocent of the abuses, even though they be physical abuses, that are directed against them. The Dashwood sisters may be trapped by the equivocal nature of the signs offered to them by their friends, but to a certain extent they offer themselves to this mistreatment, and there is no practical way that they could entirely restrain this offering of themselves. Thus, a definitive aspect of the condition of women in Austen's world is that they must suffer more uncertainty than men and still act in the midst of that uncertainty, and yet this condition does not excuse the notation of weakness in the lives of the individual heroines. Austen does not show her women to be any better than they are allowed to be within their social circumstances. As has been noted by Stuart M. Tave, among others, "Jane Austen's characters do not have the option of solving their problems by going some place else."[6] Like the society in which Austen lived, the society of these novels does not take account of the cultural circumstances that shape the condition of women but rather considers them to be a natural state of affairs of which women ought to be aware and for which they will be held responsible.

Austen's women are never pure, then, as one might surmise from her comment to Fanny Knight that "pictures of perfection as you know make me sick & wicked" (*L* 2: 486–7). Her women are locked into a scheme of interpretation in which the power of articulation assigned to men extracts from women an unconscious submission. Perhaps all women do not surrender themselves as outrageously as does *Pride and Prejudice*'s Lydia Bennet, but all women must surrender to this unconsciousness. Women simply are not allowed to be in control of their own psychological condition: They can only learn to live with it. What Austen does, in effect, is to dramatize through the inner lives of her more complex characters and through her more detailed analysis of social interaction the significance in the fact that Radcliffe's characters should be so continuously driven into one variety of unconsciousness or another.

As previously noted, this situation is very reminiscent of Richardson's work; and even though Richardson's influence upon Austen's writing often has been commented upon in modern criticism,[7] little attention has been given to considering how thoroughly her writing is based upon the kind of extreme formulas that he developed at such length. In *Pamela* and *Clarissa*, for instance, Richardson had repeatedly referred to the Old Testament law that holds that the word of a woman often may be judged to have no binding force; and in Austen's fiction as in Richardson's (and as in Sir Walter Scott's[8]) the threat represented by this law enforces upon women a responsibility for whatever reactions men may have to them. That is to say, at any moment women in these novels may be judged not to know their own meaning. Their opinion of what they think, of what they know, and even of what they feel may be overruled by the opinion of men. To be sure, Fanny Price may seem to be rebelling against this rule when she says in *Mansfield Park*, "Let him have all the perfection in the world, I think it ought not to be set down as certain, that a man must be acceptable to every woman he may happen to like himself" (*MP*, 353); but the narrator is careful to tell us that it is only Fanny's secret affection for Edmund Bertram that enables her to resist Henry Crawford, and this secret is a dramatic concession to the rule.[9]

Fanny's situation finally does not differ greatly, then, from the drama in which Clarissa finds that it is only through a marriage with another man that she can prove she is not attracted to Lovelace. So ineffectual is her word, so powerful the presumption of unconsciousness entrapping her, that we arrive at that great paradox which rules over all of *Clarissa:* that the only sufficient proof of virtue is its violation. This rule by which men can control the meaning of women is clearly dramatized, for instance, when Clarissa is made to say of Lovelace, *"If I had never valued him, he never would have found it in his power to insult me."*[10] She accepts this scheme of interpretation that finds blame for the actions of men within the minds of women, and she has no choice but to give this acceptance, because it is only through such admissions that Richardson's women are allowed any choice at all. Fanny Burney is another writer who followed Richardson in descriptions of this situation, as in *Camilla* when Mr. Tyrold writes to his daughter to say that when she is allowed "only a negative choice" it is in her best interest "to combat against a positive wish."[11] For as *Clarissa* shows, and as Camilla often finds in a somewhat less drastic way, women frequently are not even allowed the negative.

It is upon examples like these that Austen is drawing when she establishes the rule in her novels that no virtue exists without violation. Her women cannot help but ask to be misled, betrayed, and seduced as soon as they assert themselves in the slightest way. As soon as they surrender that appearance of absolute unconsciousness conveyed by the strictest reserve imaginable, they are guilty. This is an extreme statement of the case, but no other suffices to explain the severe pressure for reticence, reserve, and secrecy exerted throughout all her novels – and the invariable failure, at one time or another, of such defenses.

Marianne's and Elinor's confusion over the locks of hair, then, not only relates them to Catherine Morland's confusion over the locked chest but also to her position in John Thorpe's carriage, when that obstreperous young man allows his vehicle to run away with her. Thorpe's driving away with Catherine despite her frantic remonstrances is a simulated rape, but a rape for which she must bear some guilt as a result of her submission to the romantic prospect of Blaize Castle, which had lured her into the carriage in the first place. She is carried away against her will, but she has shown her will to be less than adamant, and nothing less than adamantine resistance will do in Austen's world. This is a world in which substantial disasters are always liable to result from "trivial Things." As David Daiches has written, "One false step can be fatal."[12] For a woman to accept anyone's word, behavior, or appearance in any way is to make herself liable to violation and to a complete loss of character. Though one must act and so must make judgments on a practical and circumstantial basis, there is no way to discipline one's actions according to general principles so as to make oneself secure. Though women in Austen's world may be born into a position of dependency and uncertainty, they are allowed no excuses on that basis, for the world actually blames them for this position by describing their character as one ruled over by weakness and inconstancy. To put it simply, the threats they face in the world are described as the faults of their minds. Even though they have no secure basis for making judgments about anyone or anything – no book, as Burney's Evelina would have it, "of the laws and customs *à-la-mode,* presented to all young people, upon their first introduction into public company"[13] – they still are held completely responsible for those judgments. Even though such handbooks were, in fact, very popular in Austen's age, there can be no such book in her fiction, because the nature of society, as she views it, makes them as farcically useless as *The Mysteries of Udolpho* is to Catherine Morland while she tries to make her way into the world.

To understand this situation is to understand that the "sense" of

Austen's world is hardly an uncomplicated thing, despite the many critics who have followed the famous judgment of C. S. Lewis:

> The great abstract nouns of the classical English moralists are unblushingly and uncompromisingly used; *good sense, courage, contentment* . . . These are the concepts by which Jane Austen grasps the world. In her we still breathe the air of the *Rambler* and *Idler*. All is hard, clear, definable; by some modern standards, even naively so.[14]

Actually, the only sense Austen's women can gain is a sense of how vulnerable their position is in this scheme of interpretation with which they must live. The guilt in the aforementioned scene from *Northanger Abbey* may be primarily Thorpe's, as in *Sense and Sensibility* it is primarily Willoughby's and, to a lesser degree, Edward's; but this guilt ultimately is inconsequential in terms of that responsibility which has less to do with the improper actions of men than with the insufficient attention that the women involved with these men have paid to the vulnerability society gives to their characters. It is the women, after all, who suffer for the faults of the men as well as for their own. What these women must learn is that to be a woman is to be environed by uncertainty,

> for if it be true, as a celebrated writer has maintained, that no young lady can be justified in falling in love before the gentleman's love is declared, it must be very improper that a young lady should dream of a gentleman before the gentleman is first known to have dreamt of her. (*NA*, 29–30)

Such are the extreme considerations that enter the mind of a woman as a result of the power of articulation assigned to men. These considerations may appear as satire, but Austen's is not a satire that exaggerates reality. She may mock Richardson in the foregoing passage just as she mocks Radcliffe in *Northanger Abbey*, but her novels assume that every reader of Richardson ought to be aware of his perils within her own mind, and that every girl should be a reader of Richardson, just as they assume that the foolishness of Radcliffe's novels is also a serious matter. After all, was it not

Lovelace himself who asked, in a satirical but perceptive moment of self-justification, "Are not cautions against the perfidy of our Sex, a necessary part of the Female Education?"[15]

In Austen's fiction as in "The Rape of the Lock" and literary tradition generally, this psychological entrapment of women is summarized in their characterization as creatures of vanity. Vanity is not confined exclusively to the women of these novels, of course – one immediately thinks of Sir Walter Elliot in *Persuasion* – but still it applies to men only as individuals, whereas it applies to women as a sex. Mr. Elliot may be ridiculous, and Darcy in *Pride and Prejudice* may be led into error as the result of an excess of aristocratic self-regard; but when women are brought to acknowledge and recant their vanity, they are not allowed to exchange it for enlightenment but rather for submission to the word of men. Thus it is that we see epitomized in Emma's case how vanity in Austen's novels is not so much a presumption of superiority over other people as it is a presumption of control over the means of interpretation. And one sees, further, that in women this presumption can never be warranted.

Emma's vanity is represented in her belief that "a lucky guess is never merely luck" because "there is always some talent in it" (*E*, 13). While her sense of social superiority is never really criticized in the novel – indeed, Knightley's fear is that she is lowering herself by her action – Emma's disillusionment instead turns upon the fact that she begins her story bearing the socially contradictory qualities of being at once rich, attractive, unmarried, and without desire to marry.[16] Her vanity is the independence she gains through her confidence in her own understanding, and it is this *intellectual* presumption – not her casual snobbery – that must be humiliated. She must learn that she has been made "totally ignorant of her own heart" by her refusal to take Knightley's word as her own:

> With insufferable vanity had she believed herself in the secret of everybody's feelings; with unpardonable arrogance proposed to arrange everybody's destiny. She was proved to have been universally mistaken; and she had not quite done nothing – for she had done mischief. She had brought evil on Harriet, on herself, and she too much feared, on Mr. Knightley. (*E*, 412–13)

So runs Emma's lesson. Ironically, Austen's novels make it only too easy to understand how a critic could so thoroughly ignore the structure of social pressures in these novels as to argue, as does Joseph Wiesenfarth, that Austen's description of Emma's development "does not present the triumph of male society" but rather "celebrates the education of a woman who has become the equal of the good and intelligent man who has been anxious for her."[17] Like most of those who write about Austen, Wiesenfarth has simply adopted the ruling ideology of the society portrayed in these novels and has ignored all the signs that Austen may not be in agreement with that ideology – even as Austen's novels themselves explain how easy it is for interpreters in positions of power to attribute their own feelings to the minds of others.

Because Emma is so superlatively vain, though, her lesson might be thought to have no general significance, or at least not as much significance as has been claimed here. Consider, then, the relationship between Isabella Thorpe and Catherine Morland in *Northanger Abbey*. For even though the characters of these two young women seem to be almost diametrically opposed – the one manipulative and the other passive, the one flirtatious and the other unassuming, the one false and the other true, and so on – the novel shows that these apparent dissimilarities respond to the same psychological order.

At one point in the novel, Isabella claims, "I never think of myself" (*NA*, 136); and of course the reader is instantly made aware that Miss Thorpe in fact does little else. This awareness not only comes from a comparison of her other speeches and actions to this moment, but also from the way in which the entire novel focuses upon the contradiction within this particular speech. To deny attention to oneself is to proclaim it, if only grammatically; and thus Isabella's insincerity is forced upon her, as it were, by the nature of language as that nature is ideologically reinforced by the reader's awareness of traditional characterizations of female vanity. A woman cannot make a neutral reference to herself, even if that reference should be to deny an interest in herself, because women are not allowed to control their own meaning. Isabella is in the same linguistic position occupied by Catherine when that hapless creature says that she "cannot speak well enough to be unintelligible" (*NA*, 133). This speech is usually taken by critics to be a sign of Catherine's innocence, but they fail to note that Catherine *never* learns how to speak unintelligibly. Like Isabella, she cannot hide herself within her language as can those men, such as Henry Tilney, who have the power to judge "incorrectness of language" (*NA*, 107) in women. She cannot identify with linguistic practice in terms of an impersonal rule of correctness because she is the subject of that rule over which men hold mastery. And though Elinor Dashwood, for example, may be an expert liar, or Elizabeth Bennet a sophisticated talker, or Anne Elliot a study in desolate silence, all of Austen's women remain fundamentally innocent in this respect, and only in this respect. They are innocent of their own meaning. They cannot know themselves in any complete sense, for they are not allowed to be complete persons apart from men and the scheme of interpretation that belongs to them.

So when Isabella says, "The men think us incapable of real friendship you know, and I am determined to show them the difference" (*NA*, 40), this statement eventually takes on the same significance as her claim that she never thinks of herself. It proves that the attempts of women to overcome male characterizations of themselves must actually serve to confirm those characterizations, which therefore become all the more convincing as a result of the resistance they have temporarily aroused and then defeated. The character of women is generally so positioned that statements by women will be discounted – by rules of grammar, history, religion, law, and literary tradition all together – if they do not bear the stamp of subordination and frailty. So Elinor must bear the distresses of others while seeming unconscious of her own, Elizabeth must be brought to a point where she demands that her sister and Darcy should forget the words that had earlier passed between them in order that the words she now speaks might have meaning, Anne must allow the changing fortunes of her face to speak for her, and Catherine must be shown to be significantly similar to Isabella.

When Isabella says that in her modesty Catherine is "fishing for compliments" (*NA*, 144), she exhibits her own vulgarity by making such an accusation but also correctly evaluates the practical significance of Catherine's attitude. Just as certain as the fact that to be a woman is to be environed by uncertainty is the fact that to be modest is to solicit attention, whether one likes it or not, since such an attitude is so much at odds with the traditional characterization of women that it simply cannot be ignored. Although Catherine may not find any seductiveness within her conscious intentions, her modesty nonetheless can only be interpreted as a calculated self-assertion within its social context. Like all of Austen's heroines, then, she is forced to be at fault. What Catherine has to learn is that even though they are to be chastised for it, women can only be vain. Her modesty is only allowed to be that unconscious species of vanity which finally becomes conscious and receives the reproach due it when Catherine makes a fool of herself at Northanger Abbey by showing that she thinks herself as important as a heroine in a novel. What she has to learn is that, like women, books may be loved; but, like women, they are not to be taken seriously. And thus, like Emma and all of Austen's other heroines, Catherine has offered herself to violation at the hands of the world through that power of interpretation she has so inappropriately arrogated to herself. In other words, her fault is not so much the quixotic mistake of interpreting the world on the basis of literature as it is the mistake of trying to interpret it at all. She has to learn to accept Henry Tilney's word instead of trying to devise her own.

Another way of describing Catherine's education, then, is to say that she not only must learn to recognize Isabella's dissimulation but also the consequences which that recognition holds for her image of herself. Catherine is more attractive than Isabella because her vanity is more unconscious, but this unconsciousness still serves to affiliate her with Isabella's vulgarity. This consideration becomes especially important if one sees how Isabella is related to Henry Tilney as well as to Catherine. For insofar as she tries to assume the power of consciousness by proclaiming her sincerity, Isabella is being mannish; and thus it is not surprising that Henry's claim to understand Catherine "perfectly well" (*NA*, 132) should be anticipated by Isabella's statement, "I know you better than you know yourself" (*NA*, 71). Both statements are presumptuous, but Henry's presumption is accompanied by actual social power and therefore is qualitatively different. Just as Catherine is an unconscious Isabella, so is Isabella, in effect, an unnatural Henry. One might even say that Catherine and Isabella cannot be true friends because Catherine is to marry Henry and not Isabella.

So women in Austen's novels are entrapped in a world of meaning beyond their control, and they have to learn to live with it, all the while maneuvering around the central institution of marriage. Fortunately, there is one place in Austen's world where they have a chance to learn how to live with their fate without needing to fear the extreme consequences that generally will lie in wait for their mistakes. This unique place is the dance floor.

The famous discussion between Henry Tilney and Catherine Morland on the analogies that can be wrought between marriage and dancing makes explicit the considerations implicit in all of Austen's dances. These gatherings open the restricted households of her novels to the exogamous community, and they do more. With their arrangement of formal movements within a context of informal doubts and anxieties, they provide a relatively safe stage upon which desire can be stimulated, attraction exerted, and possession displayed. As it takes Austen's heroines at last slightly outside the restricted acquaintance ordinarily available to them, the dance floor becomes a realm in which experiments with an intimacy neither familial nor familiar may be sanctioned. It is for this reason that such strangers as Darcy and Bingley and Tilney make their first appearances on this floor; and one of Frank Churchill's first acts upon his arrival at Highbury is to encourage the arrangement of a greater ball than those small parties to which the locals had been accustomed.

It is true that this realm of experiment may become distasteful, as if recalling the unfortunate experience of Harriet Byron. For instance, it is at a dance that Marianne encounters Willoughby with his new fiancée, and Catherine Morland finds in the Upper Rooms at Bath that she grows tired "of being continually pressed against by people, the generality of whose faces possessed nothing to interest" (*NA*, 21–2). Such imperfections, however, can be borne with relative ease, as even so emotional a character as Marianne is able to retain some semblance of dignity as long as she is out in public on the dance floor. Located between the tightly structured family, with its claustrophobic responsibilities, and society at large, which possesses a code of manners so ambiguous that it might be said to encourage the very scandal that it certainly will condemn, the dance floor allows the uncertainties of interpretation to be explored with more pleasure and fewer harmful consequences than is possible in any other realm in these novels. The dance floor acts as an intermediary between the boredom potential to the fastness of country life and the danger potential to the exhilarating openness of society. Of course, if one tries to take the dance off the formal confines of the floor – as Louisa Musgrove does when she insists on repeatedly jumping down off the Cobb into Captain Wentworth's arms, or as Marianne does when she gets carried away while running downhill in a rainstorm – the result can only be injury. The dance floor is the place, and virtually the only place, where young ladies are allowed to move at a faster pace than that involved in walking or in riding in a carriage.[18]

Moreover, in addition to thus regulating the proper appearance of novelty and of female behavior, the dance floor also regulates speech. Conversation holds at least as many pitfalls for Austen's women as does inordinate activity, but on the dance floor these dangers are lessened by the conventionality of the topics appropriate to it, which is exploited even as it is mocked by Henry Tilney in his first meeting with Catherine. Conversation is almost always a matter of aggression and appeasement in Austen's novels – in the contemporary colloquialism, characters are always being "talked down" – but one is less likely to be drastically overpowered as long as one is on the dance floor. It is when she is away from the dance floor, for instance, that Catherine is verbally subdued by John Thorpe in a scene that anticipates his physical abduction of her in the runaway carriage. Similarly, Elizabeth Bennet may be wounded as she overhears a bit of Darcy's conversation on the dance floor, but the regulated character of that floor allows her the power to disguise this injury. The unique nature of the dance floor stems from the fact that on it nothing can go too far, whether in the range of acquaintance, the amplitude of physical activity, or the force of conversation. If the floor is unquestionably public, it also provides room for private shifts and retreats. If the psychology imposed upon women there is the same as that which obtains elsewhere, at least there is not so much at stake in the restricted experience of dancing. Such violence as may be offered on the dance floor through look, word, action, or neglect of the same must seek its consummation elsewhere. And, finally, if nothing else, the dance floor is always endurable – a quality not to be slighted in the austere environment inhabited by Austen's heroines.[19]

But the dance floor is, after all, unique. Apart from this floor, action in general and actions oriented toward marriage in particular become more dangerous. In this regard, matchmaking is especially to be condemned. Like those theatricals at Mansfield Park that represent in a scandalous way the actual tensions, amorous rivalries, and indecisions at work among the actors, matchmaking appears in Austen's novels as an improper version of the dance, and for reasons that conform to all the foregoing considerations about the control of meaning. Thus, in addition to all the other reasons that condemn Emma's interference in the lives of others, there is the fact that her actions try to control processes that are supposed to take an unconscious or at least an unspoken form. The same is true of Mrs. Bennet's actions in *Pride and Prejudice:* They are a form of interpretation by prediction and manipulation, and women are not allowed such power. Matchmaking can only be a vulgar activity, because in it women play too openly with those calculations involving pedigree, rank, fortune, property, and appearance that are so abhorrent to the sentimental version of love developed by the novelistic heirs of Richardson. It is not that these calculations were not still important in Austen's time or might not be predictable or manipulable by individuals, despite all their emotional talk of sentimental values, but that the activity of matchmaking violates the tasteful reserve in which these calculations were supposed to be wrought in the modern world. Matchmaking is vulgar in these novels because it represents an arrogant self-assertion on the part of the matchmaker and because it is inevitably associated with that type of vulnerable credulity in which "to wish was to hope, and to hope was to expect" (*SS,* 21).

It would probably be possible to list still further reasons against matchmaking, but it should be noted that one such reason is not that engagements are supposed to be spontaneous and artless and hence totally mysterious affairs between lovers, as in some versions of the sentimental romance developed in later Victorian literature. Middle-class sentimentality may provide an alternative to the traditional aristocratic order that included planned marriages based on impersonal considerations of pedigree, rank, and so on, but in Austen's novels marriage still compels regard as an economic relationship before it may be enjoyed in any personal way. Unlike Radcliffe, Austen looks to the disposition of power in society before she looks to the niceness of sentiments, and so her novels display social contradictions in a more explicit way than do Radcliffe's. Rather than being a correct response to the vulgarity of matchmaking, then, Catherine Morland's disgust at the idea of "one great

fortune looking out for another" (*NA*, 124) is a sign of her innocence and, in fact, is itself a rather indelicate statement. If it were
merely sententious or formulaic, such a reproach might be allowed,
just as formulaic reproaches against the overevaluation of rank were
traditionally allowed even among aristocrats. As a result of the degree of personal emotion in it, however, Catherine's statement becomes significant only of an ignorant desire for an unattainable purity – a purity that Austen's women are not allowed in their society.
Similarly, a paradox that may be said to doom Emma's matchmaking efforts from their beginning is that she maintains her high regard for rank even as she engages in this activity, which is not only
inappropriate because it is traditionally maternal but also because it
is inimical to those standards of gentility that she is so concerned to
uphold. Her realization that she has thus been working against her
own social interests is almost simultaneous with her realization toward the end of the novel that she loves Knightley; and, indeed,
the latter understanding is little more than a conventional sign for
the former.

It is for all these reasons that persuasions against marriage in Austen's novels not only occur more frequently but also evoke less cen-
sure than encouragements toward marriage. Such persuasions may
be foolish – as in Emma's advice that Harriet Smith should reject
Robert Martin – but such foolishness is not to be compared to the
vulgarity pursuant to the activity of matchmaking. Darcy works to
separate Bingley and Jane Bennet, General Tilney to separate Henry
and Catherine, the Bertrams to separate Fanny and Edmund (by
bringing them closer together, paradoxically enough), and Mrs.
Russell and Sir Walter to separate Anne and Captain Wentworth;
and even though these attempts prove to be of no avail against the
marriages that conclude the novels in which they take place, they
nonetheless take a respectable and even a necessary part in the course
of these narratives. For resistance toward marriage is not simply
the activity opposed to matchmaking: It is the proper way of
bringing about marriages, whereas matchmaking is improper. If it
were not for the appearance of such resistance to the engagements
of Austen's heroines, there would be no way that their love could
appear virtuous. The possibility that marriages could take place
without such resistance would imply that women could too freely
and easily know their own minds in such affairs. In order to be

sanctioned by society, romantic engagements must suffer a significant resistance.

Richardson's version of this rule said that it was only by great adversity, even to the point of defilement and death, that a girl's purity could be established. Austen directly satirizes this rule in *Northanger Abbey* – "to wear the appearance of infamy while her heart is all purity . . . is one of the circumstances which peculiarly belong to the heroine's life" (*NA*, 53) – and yet the somewhat more indirect satire conveyed by this need to legitimate marriages through the formal employment of adversity might well be considered to be even more telling. A great distance is traversed as one follows the militant Christian belief that virtue must struggle against temptation into the history of the novel. Richardson reduces it to the idea that women must struggle against the temptations of men, and Austen reduces it to the dramatic necessity that the propriety of engagements be encoded through the temporary obstructions placed in their way. Divinity has become decorum: Such is the history encapsulated in Austen's novels.

In the final analysis, the issue in all the romantic circumstances of Austen's novels is one of trust: women trusting too much in their own power of interpretation and therefore trusting too much the men who actually have the power to determine which interpretations are allowed to be legitimate. Austen's major theme in all of her novels is the argument that women must learn distrust not only of the apparent sureties of the world around them, but also of themselves. For the world will treat them as deserving of such distrust no matter what the women do; and therefore the only security a woman can have is in being aware of the uncertainty of her situation. If one is attentive to this psychology impressed upon the women of Austen's novels, one does begin to see how profoundly inaccurate is that long tradition of Austen criticism which, as Susan Morgan has said, assumes "that Jane Austen's was a conclusive vision, a sort of apotheosis of the optimism of premodern fiction."[20] Austen does indeed write within severe limits, as critics have noted from the time her work first appeared; and these limits certainly are those of a rigid propriety and morality, as has also been described in many works; but this does not mean that her novels are themselves conservative. After all, it is just as possible to give instruction in the realities of power, its organization, and its probable effects without being in agreement with those realities as it is possible to employ disguises if one is a woman who has "the misfortune of knowing any thing" (*NA*, 111). An accurate reading of Austen demands that fewer assumptions be made about her personal psychology and more attention paid to the disguises, silences, and submissions demanded by the society she portrayed in her novels.

5

ATTACHMENTS AND SUPPLANTMENTS

∽

> . . . the most charming young man in the world is
> instantly before the imagination of us all.
> — JANE AUSTEN, *Northanger Abbey*

> Elinor well knew that the sweetest girls in the world
> were to be met with in every part of England, under
> every possible variation of form, face, temper, and
> understanding.
> — JANE AUSTEN, *Sense and Sensibility*

FROM HER JUVENILIA to the drama of *Persuasion* and *Sanditon,* Jane Austen shows a persistent fascination with the variability of objects for love. Throughout Austen's fiction love is dramatized as an essentially unfocused emotional disposition that happens to be turned to a particular end only through the chance disposition of circumstances. As has been observed from the time of Sir Walter Scott's review of her work in 1815, hers is an extremely unsentimental version of love. The power of circumstances in her work has also been observed quite often.[1] Less noted, however, has been the close connection between Austen's lack of sentimentality and her general emphasis upon the power of casual circumstances in determining the success or failure of communication between individuals. That is to say, love's object is variable in Austen's world because her people can never understand each other completely, only partially and provisionally. The lack of sentimentality in her work is due to this lack of understanding and the need to protect oneself against it, and the ultimate cause of this lack of understanding is an absence of stability and wholeness in the society she describes. She shows that society plays a dominant role in the formation of personal desires and yet fails to provide a coherent background for those desires, and so as a result all the attachments of Austen's fiction fall far short of the ideal. By examining the topic of love in these novels along with the related topics of the family and education, one can see how and why the instability of society wields such power over all the circumstances of communication.

One of the scenes in *Emma* is virtually a parable of the general situation of love in these novels. At one point in the narrative, the Reverend Elton writes a charade intended for Emma that Emma thinks is meant for Harriet Smith, her orphan protégé. So as to maintain propriety, Emma instructs Harriet that she may copy the charade into her commonplace book only after she removes the concluding couplet that directs this flattering puzzle to a specific object. In giving this instruction, however, Emma's punctiliousness unintentionally serves to dramatize the puzzling nature of love's object throughout the novel. Misdirected from the beginning, the poem is cut off from any direction by this abridgment and is left as an emblem of unfocused love while Emma, Harriet, and Elton wind themselves ever tighter in their mutual incomprehension.[2] The idea that romantic attraction results from distinct affinities between people finds itself undercut by this demonstration of the inept fantasies and assumptions that contribute so much to everyone's "knowledge" of each other. The idea of love as an unadulterated and spontaneous passion survives only as a cipher cut off from any specific persons; in reality love is shown to be a sort of haphazard and therefore impersonal attachment between people.

Through these confusions in their relationships with each other, then, the characters in *Emma* may be said to be related to that "extraordinary fate" (*SS,* 378) by which Marianne Dashwood discovers how ordinary her love for Willoughby had been; to the indiscriminate flirtatiousness of Isabella Thorpe; to Mr. Collins, who changes his attachment from Jane to Elizabeth Bennet "while Mrs. Bennet was stirring the fire" (*PP,* 71); to the scandalous romance of Mrs. Rushworth and Henry Crawford at Mansfield Park; and to Captain Benwick, who proposes to Louisa Musgrove and gives her the miniature originally intended for his late wife because he has "an affectionate heart" that "must love somebody" (*P,* 167). Innocent, ignorant, foolish, fatuous, or desperately reckless, these characters all serve to demonstrate the rule that all attachments are fragile and subject to displacement. To be sure, the questionable value of first loves is not a topic unique to Austen's writing – Richardson and Edgeworth may be mentioned as being among the other novelists in whose work it occurs[3] – but in Austen's novels first impressions are shown to be so completely unreliable as to be of no value whatsoever. Rather than simply being a topic for pious admonition and thus a danger that is only one possible fate for first loves, this unreliability is so extreme as to form a thematic principle in her work. In effect, there is no such thing as an original love in Austen's novels. One need only consider how Lucy Steele intervenes between Elinor Dashwood and Edward Ferrars, Willoughby between Marianne and Colonel Brandon, Mary Crawford between Fanny Price and Edmund Bertram, Frank Churchill between Emma Woodhouse and Mr. Knightley, and a great length of time between Anne Elliot and Captain Wentworth – such a long time that when they meet again they are almost like entirely different people. According to these novels, love is by its nature imaginary and secondary, spurred variously by misleading expectations, chance locations and dislocations, and a great variety of inequitable circumstances, among them the fact that "single women have a dreadful propensity for being poor" (*L* 2: 483). Furthermore, these novels show that nothing but error can be expected to result from such an origin.

As Fanny Price realizes when she learns of the elopement of Mrs. Rushworth and Crawford, such a state of affairs is barbaric in its disorganization:

> The event was so shocking, that there were moments even when her heart revolted from it as impossible – when she thought it could not be. A woman married only six months ago, a man professing himelf devoted, even *engaged,* to another – that other her near relation – the whole family, both families connected as they were by tie upon tie, all friends, all intimate together – it was too horrible a confusion of guilt, too gross a complication of evil, for human nature, not in a state of utter barbarism, to be capable of! – yet her judgment told her it was so. (*MP,* 441)

But even though this scandal appears almost unthinkable to Fanny – and absolutely incomprehensible to at least one modern critic of the novel[4] – what Austen consistently shows is that it is sentimental love that is unthinkable. If she had been content to direct her writing to the traditional characterization of passion as a mystery, this thesis certainly would not be extraordinary, since the scandal of desire would then be brought within a sacred attitude of wonder and awe; but this is not what she did.

Rather than showing love to be a mystery, Austen's writing shows love to be unthinkable because it seeks to end mystery. Love is an aspiration to truth, certainty, and satisfying communication that Austen shows as inevitably resulting in the disclosure of lies, vacillation, and frustration. Again, Austen's drama would not be extraordinary if this failure took place on the scale of tragedy, but in these novels it takes place on the most commonplace scale imaginable. As far as Austen is concerned, love is neither mysterious nor tragic. In fact, the only persons liable to be ruined by love are those who are ashamed of how essentially impersonal and insignificant it is and who therefore try to exaggerate it into some realm of sublime transcendence. Love is the most ordinary thing in the world, and those who attempt to overcome its commonness can only succeed in amplifying the uncertainty of all communication.

Thus it is that Marianne Dashwood's favorite maxim, that "no one can ever be in love more than once in their life" (*SS*, 93), can only be a defensive statement destined to be proved wrong. As it converts chance attachments into romantic fates, this maxim represses those wandering inflections of desire evident in her own experience as in the experiences represented throughout Austen's novels. Such a love becomes a virtual mania, directed to a particular object only so that it may be directed against the instability of all the circumstances of society. By her extreme particularity, this sentimental lover tries to prove her love impartial: fated, unique, independent of all qualifying conditions. Such a love is profoundly conservative, and Austen shows this conservatism to be laughably weak in comparison to the instability of society – and therefore to be destined to catastrophe.

Moreover, this failure of love to transcend variable circumstances is evident in the very signs by which love is communicated. In the diction Austen inherited from the eighteenth century, actions and relationships were either "marked" or "unmarked" as they either did or did not display a meaning that went beyond formalities. The only way to distinguish the attentions of a lover from those of a man who was merely being polite or flirtatious was by determining whether or not his behavior was thus marked, but Austen's writing shows this distinction between empty formalities and meaningful signs to be insupportable. One can decide to which side of this dichotomy actions belong only after their significance has already been determined by events, as Emma decides that Elton's manners "must have been unmarked, wavering, dubious" (*E*, 134) precisely because she has discovered that her opinion of his intentions was wrong. These classificatory orders supposed to predict events are, in fact, subject to events. Thus, at one point in *Persuasion*, "every thing now marked out Louisa for Captain Wentworth" (*P*, 90); but this totality is re-marked by events into a completely different order of meaning that nonetheless is taken to be foreordained. Similarly, Emma can think of Jane Fairfax and Harriet at the end of her story and conclude, "Birth, abilities, and education, had been equally marking out one as an associate for her, to be received with gratitude; and the other – what was she?" (*E*, 421); but this realization is maintained only by the discovery that Emma had misread the signs of Harriet's origin. As the narrator remarks when the truth of Harriet's birth is revealed, the "stain of illegitimacy, unbleached by nobility or wealth, would have been a stain indeed" (*E*, 482).

The communication of meaning, in other words, cannot be ordered according to a rigid distinction between conventional formalities and individual expressions. Individuals are marked within social forms that never match their meaning, and the power of individual meaning is nothing to the power of these forms.[5] Although almost all critics of Austen assume, in Howard S. Babb's phrase, that Austen's world is "stabilized by public agreement on certain concepts,"[6] this assumption becomes inadequate when they fail to see that these concepts – such as "marked behavior" – are never manifested in any indisputable way. It is precisely the elusive significance of such ideal concepts that provides all the complications that move Austen's novels. It is only by a kind of retrospective fantasy that the social forms of life can be interpreted with any certainty.[7] Such a fantasy does provide the comedic plots of Austen's novels, as their misapprehensions and vagrant signs are gathered into the order of an ending; but this concluding order is not immanent in the course of the narratives. The dramatic conclusions of Austen's novels are not sustained by the events that lead up to those conclusions. The formal order of her endings does not resolve the problems that move the novels. In other words, Austen's novels leave her readers in the same uneasy position between empty formality and meaningful expression that is occupied by her characters.

In Austen's world, therefore, one learns that only circumstantial judgments have any chance of protecting one from disaster. The object of love is always uncertain in Austen's novels because it cannot appear within social forms without being marked by the conventional formality and unpredictable eventuality of those forms.[8] Austen's novels thus set a formal end to the Providential scheme of history that directed the plots of eighteenth-century English novels such as Radcliffe's, and they do so in a very sophisticated way. They preserve the basic plot of those novels while diverting the significance of the narrative from the resolution of the plot to the complications preceding that formal resolution. As opposed to the Providential pattern of communication that proceeds from a loss of truth through various confusions and errors to a final reclamation of that original truth, communication in Austen's novels generally proceeds by half-measures and half-truths.

Lloyd W. Brown has noted that "the most crucial exchanges between Jane Austen's characters are based on conflict and misunderstanding, rather than on the positive transmission of personal interests and values,"[9] and the author herself commented upon this aspect of her fictional world. "Seldom, very seldom," the narrator of *Emma* remarks, "does complete truth belong to any human disclosure; seldom can it happen that something is not a little disguised, or a little mistaken" (*E,* 431). Communication has this character in Austen's world because the maintenance of social forms demands that considerations of propriety outweigh considerations of truth. Only those seduced by "the alarms of romance" believe that any actions are absolutely true or false to one's meaning, while those who have succeeded to "the anxieties of common life" (*NA,* 209) know that they can be appropriate or inappropriate only according to the prevailing circumstances.

This situation is epitomized in *Sense and Sensibility:* "Marianne was silent; it was impossible for her to say what she did not feel, however trivial the occasion; and upon Elinor therefore the whole task of telling lies when politeness required it, always fell" (*SS,* 122). Not only does Marianne's sentimental disposition impose upon Elinor, but the very basis of that disposition in the distinction between the expression of true feelings and the forms of politeness is a false one. Instead of revealing one's feelings to others, expressions that do not take account of social forms betray those feelings because they are controlled by those forms, whether one likes it or not, and so leave one exposed to the kinds of misunderstandings that literally bring Marianne to the point of death.

So whereas circumstances traditionally are thought of by writers like Radcliffe as a kind of second nature that may modify but cannot wholly erase the original expression of meaning, Austen's novels show them to be the primary category for thinking about communication. Emma, for instance, is one who considers them in the traditional way when she asks herself, fearing that Knightley might be attracted to Harriet, "Was it new for any thing in this world to be unequal, inconsistent, incongruous – or for chance and circumstance (as second causes) to direct the human fate?" (*E*, 413). But though Emma's parenthetical curtsy to the primacy of Providence might seem to be rewarded by Knightley marrying her, her admission that she doubted this conclusion eliminates its representative authority. The same is true of all of Austen's conclusions: They never rise into the realm of symbolic authority. Instead, they are repressively formal or deliberately deflationary. At the end of *Pride and Prejudice*, for instance, when Elizabeth speaks of Darcy to Jane, she follows the general rule of these conclusions: "Perhaps I did not always love him so well as I do now. But in such cases as these, a good memory is unpardonable" (*PP*, 373). Critics traditionally have wanted to see these conclusions as integrating the individual sense of truth with social forms, but they represent nothing but an acknowledgment of the power those forms maintain over individual expression and variant circumstances.[10] Thus, although critics often cite it as a description of Emma's maturation, it is hard to imagine a conclusion more satirically disruptive than the following:

> She saw that there never had been a time when she did not consider Mr. Knightley as infinitely the superior, or when his regard for her had not been infinitely the most dear. She saw, that in persuading herself, in fancying, in acting to the contrary, she had been entirely under a delusion, totally ignorant of her own heart – and, in short, that she had never really cared for Frank Churchill at all! (*E*, 412)

Austen's conclusions might have more authority if all the social forms of her fictional world rose into a social wholeness, but her novels do not show this to happen. The power of circumstance overwhelms the power of such conclusions because of an absence of order and wholeness in the society portrayed in her fiction. The society of Austen's time was in the midst of a long period of transition from aristocratic to middle-class values, and one sees in her novels the social instability that resulted from this transition. Marvin Mudrick is among those who have asserted that Austen's novels are primarily middle class – "For Jane Austen, the accepted reality was the middle-class society of her time"[11] – but this judgment simply is not true of the novels or of her society. Jane Austen's novels are no more middle-class than are Scott's.[12] The aristocracy is not the major topic of her work, but it is still the dominant class in her work as it was in her time, although it is a class beset by the various challenges to and criticisms of its power that finally would lead to middle-class dominance in the latter half of the nineteenth century. What helps to account for the vexed situation of communication in these works is that the aristocracy still dominates social values in her novels and yet lacks the ideal purity that was supposed to justify its rule. The aristocracy is supposed to guarantee the order of taste, decorum, and truth, but it fails to do so; and the order of middle-class values, especially middle-class sentimentality, is unable effectively to take its place.

One sees the lingering power of the aristocracy, for instance, in one of Elinor Dashwood's meditations: "Every qualification is raised at times, by the circumstances of the moment, to more than its real value; and she was sometimes worried down by officious condolence to rate good-breeding as more indispensable to comfort than good nature" (*SS*, 215). In the eighteenth-century diction that permeates so much of Austen's work, "good-breeding" is the biological metaphor that stands at the apex of all social forms – and yet it is not just a metaphor. Although its immediate reference is to the behavioral grace and civility that are to be acquired through a proper education, it originates in the concept of an aristocracy that is an exclusive hereditary class. Even though the English nobility lost its last chance to gain some semblance of legal purity with the failure of the Peerage Bill of 1719, it is the idea of this purity, at once biological and metaphorical, that regulated the values of social intercourse. Good breeding is the ideal form of social forms: the definition that would unite the appearance and the reality of value in a single line of descent. According to this definition the aristocracy would reproduce itself without the contamination of marriages outside itself and without invasions into itself by those who gain influence through business, finance, the military, or government. The aristocracy would become independent of variable circumstances and thus would ensure that all social circumstances should be as clearly marked as the boundaries of those noble estates that, as F. M. L. Thompson has pointed out, symbolized the influence and power of the aristocracy even when those qualities might be lacking in actuality:

> It could happen that the titular head and apparent owner of a great estate had command over the spending of only a tithe of its revenues. What was kept intact, therefore, was essentially the land itself, the territorial unit, and it did not necessarily follow that its wealth was preserved mainly at the disposal of a single individual. To the outside world, however, the unbroken shell of a landed estate, even if in reality it was empty within, was the object which conferred position, authority, and responsibility on the owner for the time being.[13]

Of such a nature is the aristocratic ideal: a shell that, however empty within, still represents a very real power. To see this power, one need only recall Elizabeth Bennet's first impression of Pemberley. To follow Alistair Duckworth in seeing this estate as representing "the good and true in life" that "resists the perversions of the individual viewpoint" is to miss the social reality of such estates in Austen's fiction and in her time. Duckworth's argument that "the estate is a saving structure of great permanence in her thought"[14] misreads as a positive metaphor something that was a social *donné* in her thought. This is the same sort of idealistic misreading that occurs when one reads these novels in terms of an abstract schema of psychological development instead of analyzing the specific relationship between character and society.[15] The estate in Austen's novels is a traditional reality, indeed, but one in danger of usurpation, as when Anne Elliot admits in *Persuasion* "that Kellynch-hall had passed into better hands than its owners" (*P,* 125). Moreover, it is a reality that must be approached all the more circumspectly because its power is partial and unpredictable in a society that is not securely anchored by ideal values. Aristocrats and the higher gentry certainly would have one regard their estates as representing the good and the true in life rather than a mere preeminence in wealth and power, but all of Austen's writing goes to show that this representation cannot be wholly sustained even as it cannot be wholly disdained.

The aristocratic estate, then, is a source of confusion and dissonance rather than a means of transcending the errancies of communication and romantic attachment. It does not represent a stable organization of relationships among people, although it may have the power to stifle aberrant expressions and actions, bringing that amnesia which Elizabeth demands when she is talking to Jane or to Darcy: "But think no more of the letter. The feelings of the person who wrote, and the person who received it, are now so widely different from what they were then, that every unpleasant circumstance attending it, ought to be forgotten" (*PP,* 368). Because such power does not bear the stamp of wholeness or impartiality, though, individuals in Austen's fiction must always remain in a condition of formal detachment from themselves that is never completely overcome through love, no matter how fortunate one may be in one's marriage. A significant part of their personal identity must be ceded to the impersonality and incalculability of society.[16] And as with romantic relationships, so with familial relationships.

One of Austen's brothers, Edward, was taken from his family to be cared for by one that was wealthier; and the way this example is echoed in the cases of Frank Churchill and Fanny Price emphasizes the fragility of family attachments in Austen's world. Family ties in these novels have no necessary relationship to personal identity: A simple comparison of different families may suffice to efface one's biological attachment to a particular home. As Fanny comes to realize, "Portsmouth was Portsmouth; Mansfield was home." And even this extreme reversal of identities is further complicated by Fanny's realization that the delicacy with which she had kept her feelings from her parents was unnecessary, since "they were perfectly free from any jealousy of Mansfield" (*MP,* 431). Individuals in Austen's novels are always possessed of a familial identity, but this is purely a matter of conventional classification. Just as the vicissitudes in the choice of objects for love evidence the fortuitous nature of those objects, so does the negligence with which children may be excerpted from their families and transferred to others reveal the absence of any sympathy or meaning intrinsic to genealogical attachments. In effect, Austen's children are always changelings, their connection to parents and siblings as much a matter of chance and circumstance as their connections to persons outside of the family. Thus, in the Elliots' domestic circle, "Anne, with an elegance of mind and sweetness of character, which must have placed her high with any people of real understanding, was nothing" (*P*, 5); and Elinor Dashwood is similarly displaced into an inappropriate context.[17]

And yet, despite all these dissonances, one does belong to a family. In fact, families are always the dominant characters in Austen's novels. More than a formal set of relationships, they are living entities, which no individual can stand outside of. One belongs to a family as features and arms and legs belong to a body, and one finds as little agreement between its component parts as people generally find between the formal reality of their bodies and their desired appearance. Rather than finding security or satisfaction in familial attachments, one belongs to a family as one lives in a house that can be "made over to others; all the precious rooms and furniture, beginning to own other eyes and other limbs" (*P*, 47–8). Consequently, since individuals in Austen's novels can always be detached from families or can find their families detached from them, families are liable to become objects of anxiety and even of dread.

Just as the formal signs that seem to provide the security of society also lead to the insecurity of individuals within that society, so is the very source of the power of families in Austen's fiction also the source of their insecurity. For families are shown by Austen to be subject to wills, and wills are subject not only to the unpredictable element of emotional caprice but also to the predictable inequality conveyed by entails onto male heirs.[18] Families are social forms, not personal havens. Before they are anything else, families are agents acting in the interests of fortune, rank, and decorum; and any attempt to slight these powers provokes a devastating social reaction – if one is lucky. If one is unlucky, the family is like Fanny's in *Mansfield Park* and does not even notice the state of its members.

Still, even in a degenerate position, the family dominates. One must be completely inattentive to Austen's fiction and to the society with which it deals in order to argue that the question of family importance and rank in her writing is "a shadow, a pure and meaningless abstraction."[19] One cannot ignore the fact, for instance, that the significance of marriage as a relationship between individuals in these novels is always subordinate to its significance as a relationship between families. Although this precedence may be contested – and Austen's dramas always depend upon the course of such contests – it can never be ignored. Families are the central characters in these novels just as they are in Sir Walter Elliot's "book of books" (*P, 7*) and, in fact, as they were in eighteenth-century society. As H. J. Habakkuk has written of the aristocracy and gentry of that age:

> The basis of this class was the family estate, which provided the family not only with its revenue and its residence, but with its sense of identity from generation to generation . . . What a landowner did with his land was determined by a complex of decisions, in origin reaching far back into the family history, in effect stretching forward to his grandchildren yet unborn.[20]

Families are dominant, then, and they also are pervasive. There are no solitaries in Austen's novels. Harriet Smith may be a bastard, Jane Fairfax an orphan, and Mr. Knightley a bachelor; but they still are attached to families. And while there may be some temporary sanctuary to be found in Mr. Bennet's library or in Fanny Price's schoolroom, no one ever comes close to being entirely alone in these novels.[21] Families and their concerns are everywhere. The family places a duty upon every act and thought an individual may have; and though payment may be delayed, as in the case of Marianne Dashwood's improprieties, or transferred to someone other than the offender, as in the case of Lydia Bennet's, it always must be paid.

So one is always in a family in Austen's fiction, but this attachment is as basically impersonal, as controlled by chance and circumstance, as the attachments of romantic love. As Austen describes them, the relations of the individuals within families are as formal as or more formal than their relations with others outside the family. Conversation among family members, for example, is either calculated and distant or irresponsible and loose. She shows virtually no range between these extremes, and both extremes tend to be baneful. Since emotional display of all sorts follows the same pattern, one looks in vain for an intimacy – conversational, intellectual, emotional, or otherwise – peculiar to the family. There is

simply no such sentimental justification for the exactions it demands of the individual. Emma may have a patronizing fondness
for her father; Mr. Bennet may have an imperfectly manifested affection for one or two of his daughters; Mrs. Bennet may have
hysterical outbursts of emotion for her offspring; but there is nothing truly personal about such feelings. The quiddity of the family
instead lies in its social and legal disposition, and this explains why
individuals should not have any relations with other family members that are different from those they have with friends or more
distant relatives and acquaintances. The family in Austen's novels
is not gathered together by emotion or destiny or common experience, but by money, pedigree, and power – or the lack thereof.
A special affection for such impersonal and readily alienable bonds
is not to be expected; and failing to understand this consideration,
one fails to understand an essential aspect of all of these novels.[22]

So there is no interior to the family in Austen's novels, just as
there is no interior to marital relations. As Austen describes the
various individuals in a family, each may have a greater or lesser
personal reserve; but families and marriages do not shelter any aspect of individual identity within themselves, away from the world,
as do the families and marriages in Dickens's novels, for instance.
They are not havens for values or feelings that may oppose the
impersonal powers of money, birth, and rank, which run the world
outside them. As far as Austen's novels are concerned, what the
outside world sees of marriages and families is, with few and unimportant exceptions, all that there is to see. Families and marriages
exist to be seen and recognized by the world, not to please their
component members.

Nevertheless, there must be some mechanism for formally send-
ing a heroine out of the family and into the world to find a mate.
In Austen's novels, this mechanism is the process of education. As
this process is portrayed in these novels, one sees how social forms
manage to retain so much power even though they are so difficult
to interpret and so impossible to relate to an actual order and
wholeness in society. In fact, one sees that it is the very ambiguity
of behavioral codes that serves to reinforce the power of society in
the formation of personal desire. One sees, in other words, that the
very conception of an ideal order that cannot be achieved in common life serves to maintain all the repressive aspects of that life. As
individuals are humiliated by their failure to achieve the ideals held

out to them by society, they are forced to submit to all the faults of that society. Having no way to account for the discrepancy between social forms and social ideals, they are led to interiorize this discrepancy as a fault within themselves. Those conflicts between aristocratic and middle-class values that contribute so much to the difficulty of judging behavior in these novels, then, are but a part of a more general social process that leads to the formal subjugation of individuals in general and women in particular.

In this matter of education as in so many others in Austen's fiction, Richardson provides a precedent. One has only to listen to Harriet Byron. "In every case," she says, "the teacher is the obliger. He is called *master,* you know: And where there is a *master,* a *servant* is implied."[23] Those who read Austen's fiction idealistically can follow Richard Simpson's 1870 review in giving an entirely positive interpretation to this relationship – "Miss Austen," he wrote, "seems to be saturated with the Platonic idea that the giving and receiving of knowledge, the active formation of another's character, or the more passive growth under another's guidance, is the truest and strongest foundation of love"[24] – but an attention to the social implications of this relationship, in history and in Austen's fiction, gives one a different point of view. In Austen's novels, all education is imitation and all imitation is in emulation of a mastery that one imagines others to possess. Instead of being led to rebelliousness, the individual is led to an attitude of submissiveness by the recognition that social signs are ambiguous and society itself an ideal order that is not practically manifested in one's experience of the world. The heroine who finds her experience conflicting with the social forms for experience can only imagine that it is herself who is at fault and can only hope that this fault may be corrected through an appeal to the assumed superiority of others – such as Henry Tilney or Mr. Knightley – who do not seem to feel that anything is out of order.

It is because of the mastery of this process of education, for instance, that Catherine Morland is so confused when she talks with Mr. and Mrs. Allen about the propriety of young people driving about together. In this scene as in that in which she has dinner with the Tilneys for the first time, her problem is her failure to understand that decorum is not a clearly codified system of rules applicable to any situation but rather an ideal understanding that maintains its power through the very ambiguity of its application to the practical conduct of life. She fails to realize that the rule of decorum is a rule of domination. She fails to realize, in other words, that the idea of decorum represents an imaginary mastery over behavior that is not sustained by the actual reality of behavior in society but rather through a systematic subordination of behavior to the interpretation of society. The constitutive basis of decorum is not really in questions of right or wrong behavior but rather in the rule that no desire, action, or meaning is acceptable unless it gives evidence of deference and doubt before the power of society. The individual must be taught that uncertainty is meant to inspire submissiveness rather than curiosity. The prevailing attitude is the same as the one that brought Dr. Johnson to write, "What state of life admits most happiness is uncertain; but that uncertainty ought to repress the petulance of comparison, and silence the murmurs of discontent."[25] After all, as Mandeville noted, "It is incredible how necessary an Ingredient Shame is to make us sociable."[26]

The kind of communication that results from this process of education may be exemplified by a famous exchange between Tilney and Catherine in *Northanger Abbey*:

> "With you, it is not, How is such a one likely to be influenced? What is the inducement most likely to act upon such a person's feelings, age, situation, and probable habits of life considered? – but, how should I be influenced, what would be *my* inducement in acting so and so?"
> "I do not understand you."
> "Then we are on very unequal terms, for I understand you very well."
> "Me? – yes; I cannot speak well enough to be unintelligible."
> "Bravo! – an excellent satire on modern language." (*NA*, 132–3)

Satire, indeed – but whose satire? Should it be attributed to Catherine, who speaks it? to Tilney, who recognizes it? to Austen, who wrote it? or to the society of her novels, which makes an intelligibility like Catherine's unintelligible, and which demands that intelligence be manifested through a submissive reserve?[27] As Austen writes in another famous passage – a passage so famous that few take the trouble to examine its obvious reference to her own art –

"A woman especially, if she have the misfortune of knowing any thing, should conceal it as well as she can" (*NA*, 111). Tilney's claim that he understands Catherine perfectly is especially significant in this respect, for perfect understanding can exist in Austen's novels only as an unreciprocal relationship between someone who assumes mastery over communication and someone who is ignorant of its rules. Rather than implying the transference of intelligence from one person to another, communication implies the setting up of one person as a master over another. The acknowledgment of this relationship is always more important than the supposed content of the communication.

This rule is maintained throughout Austen's novels, so much so that there is really very little of parody in this passage in *Northanger Abbey*:

> To be disgraced in the eyes of the world, to wear the appearance of infamy while her heart is all purity, her actions all innocence, and the misconduct of another the true source of her debasement, is one of those circumstances which peculiarly belong to the heroine's life, and her fortitude under it what particularly dignifies her character. (*NA*, 53)

Shame is essential to the development of the heroine because it is only through an admission of shame that she can be brought to the attitude of deference demanded by the command of society over desire. All of Austen's heroines are brought sooner or later to the point of shame at which the individual takes upon herself responsibility for the enigmatic errancy of social forms and signs.[28] Once this violation is thus accepted as a fault of personal character rather than an instability and partiality in the character of society, the education of desire can proceed along its proper path, as in that scene in *Northanger Abbey* which concludes with "a lecture on the picturesque . . . in which his instructions were so clear that she soon began to see beauty in every thing admired by him, and her attention was so earnest, that he became perfectly satisfied of her having a great deal of natural taste" (*NA*, 111). Whether it be human, scenic, or social, nature is always found in Austen's novels through such a process of submission; and therefore it should not be surprising to find that the nature of love in her novels is governed by social circumstances, or that the nature of the family in her work is an ersatz nature subject to a potentially endless series of supplantments.

This potential may be exemplified by the beginning of *Emma*, where Austen states that "it was Miss Taylor's loss which first brought grief" to Emma (*E*, 6) – not the loss of her mother, whose place the governess had taken. In her attempt to overcome this loss, Emma puts herself in Miss Taylor's place by taking under her care Harriet Smith, a bastard, only to find at the end of the novel that she should have taken care of Jane Fairfax, a legitimate orphan. The novel ends, finally, as Emma places herself under the care of Knightley, learning "to grow more worthy of him, whose intentions and judgment had been ever so superior to her own." The story thus described is not a love story in any conventional sense, but rather a lesson in "humility and circumspection" (*E*, 475) directed to a heroine who had failed to realize that education is only adventitiously concerned with the formation of "opinions and . . . manners" (*E*, 4) and is primarily concerned with the discipline of desire. Emma seeks to remove Harriet's shame and to stimulate her desire, and thus the mastery she arrogates to herself in her attempt to teach Harriet must be proved to be false and damaging. Harriet is unable to become another Pamela not because she is the bastard daughter of a tradesman – for this fact remains in question until the end of the novel – but because she is brought to approach a higher social rank through the incentive of pride rather than through the deference of humility and abject imitation.

The case is the same with the other novels, though the drama of attachments and supplantments is played out in different ways. In *Mansfield Park,* for instance, Edmund supplants Fanny's brother, William; Fanny supplants Miss Crawford; she and Edmund are married; and then her younger sister comes to take her place at the Bertrams' house. In a passage that critics generally ignore, Austen writes,

> Susan could never be spared. First as a comfort to Fanny, then as an auxiliary, and last as her substitute, she was established at Mansfield, with every appearance of equal permanency . . . and after Fanny's removal, succeeded so naturally to her influence over the hourly comfort of her aunt, as gradually to become, perhaps, the most beloved of the two. (*MP*, 472–3)

In this case the stability of Fanny's place in the novel is qualified by at least four major considerations: her attraction to Edmund was secondary to her feeling for her brother; Edmund had originally preferred Miss Crawford to her; she could easily be replaced in the Bertrams' household by her sister; and her sister could, "perhaps," exceed her place there. If one adds to these considerations the casual nature of her parents' ties to her and the affection that we are told she would have had for Henry Crawford if she had not had a previous love for Edmund, the portrait that emerges completely transfers desire from the realm of individual expression and spontaneous affinity, where it is sentimentally thought of as existing, to a realm where it is little more than the intersection at a particular place and time of a great host of vagrant attachments and supplantments. And this intersection yields no promise of continuation beyond the next change of cirumstances unless it should be preserved through a rigorous submission to social forms, even when those forms are so unclear that one can only fall back into silence, secrecy, and reserve. If one reads Austen's novels with attention to such intersections, one can see in their composition the emergence of desire from the complex, contradictory, equivocal, unsympathetic forces of society. Austen's novels may be seen as attempts, first of all, to identify this process that is so destructive of individual identity and of individual expression; and, second, to describe the ways in which an individual may hope to maintain at least a minimal control within this conflict of life. As Mrs. Grant says,

> There will be little rubs and disappointments every where, and we are all apt to expect too much; but then, if one scheme of happiness fails, human nature turns to another; if the first calculation is wrong, we make a second better; we find comfort somewhere. (*MP*, 46)

6

READING THE WORD OF NATURE

❧

I N RECENT YEARS there have been critics who have questioned C. S. Lewis's famous judgment that "the great abstract nouns of the classical English moralists are unblushingly and uncompromisingly used" in Jane Austen's novels, in which he said that everything was "hard, clear, definable; by some modern standards, even naively so." Already in 1953 Andrew H. Wright was analyzing at some length the complexities in Austen's narrative point of view, but especially in the last twenty years the major criticism of Austen has shown what seems to be a growing consensus that her language is by no means simple or unblushingly easy to grasp. Frank W. Bradbrook, for instance, notes that the question of speech in these novels "is not so simple as it might appear," because "it does not provide an absolute standard of either intelligence or integrity." J. F. Burrows argues that "Jane Austen uses words with the freedom of a novelist rather than the necessary rigidity of a lexicographer," supporting this argument by analyzing her usage of such terms as "sense," "reason," and "fancy." E. Rubenstein writes, "If the eighteenth-century moralists gave Austen their vocabulary, they do not appear to have given her the certainty that Lewis implies they themselves enjoyed." K. C. Phillips points out how such words as "sense" and "sensibility" are "overburdened with meaning" in her work. Norman Page says that Austen is concerned with "defining and refining the ethical vocabulary through which her judgments are conveyed," the implication being that the vocabulary she inherited could use such definition and purification. Jane Nardin further develops Wright's analysis when she describes how "we must never trust the narrator in Jane Austen's novels, no matter how Johnsonian her moral commentaries may sound, for the Jane Austen narrator is merely a complex of functions, rather than a reliable or even consistently portrayed persona." Stuart M. Tave says that there are few 'good' or 'bad' words in Jane Austen's lexicon, as there are relatively few things good or bad in themselves." Darrel Mansell comments upon the "relentless obliquity" of Austen's fiction, "this relentless deflection of the potential, narrated, objective fact into someone's version of it." In a chapter entitled "Verbal Disputes," Lloyd W. Brown describes how variously a word like "nature" may appear in Austen's work. In another allusion to Lewis, D. D. Devlin says that "the great confident abstract nouns which are a feature of her vocabulary . . . are perhaps less monolithic, and more shifting, than they seem." And in writing of Austen in the context of the latest developments in literary criticism, Alistair M. Duckworth goes so far as to say that it seems true "that even a 'classic' author like Jane Austen will leave . . . indeterminacies to be repaired in her works."[1] In short, whatever disagreements may arise among these and other critics of Austen in their evaluation of her work, there seems to be a growing agreement that her language does not even have the appearance of naiv-ité, much less the substance of it.

It can be somewhat surprising, then, to see how little the interpretation of her work is affected by this growing agreement upon the nature of her language. To put it simply, the complexity acknowledged in the language of her fiction is not extended to the meaning of that work. There is a great gap between the fine analysis her critics give to the details of her novels and their final interpretation of them, which almost invariably presents them as falling in line with simple, conservative, Christian moralisms and manners. As David Daiches has written, Austen "does not usually get credit for her perceptions."[2] Even if one did not expect her to receive the presumption of complexity, ambiguity, and depth of meaning routinely given to a Proust or a Joyce, the attention that critics have given to the complexity of Austen's language might lead one to expect that they at least would acknowledge as much difficulty in deciding when she is being ironic and when she is not

as other critics have acknowledged in writing of a novelist like Defoe; but this is not the case.[3] Despite all the qualifications they place
upon Lewis's observations, virtually all of these critics show no
hesitation in jumping directly from those qualifications to definitions of Austen's "real meaning" and "true character." And though
the picture of the author that they develop from these definitions
may not be as egregiously sympathetic as Austen was made to appear in Henry James's characterization of her as "our dear, everybody's dear, Jane,"[4] still the prevailing portrait is a remarkably simple one that is not unfairly summarized by W. A. Craik's description
of her as "a writer who appeals to all the reasonable and rational
qualities in her reader."[5] Even a so-called subversive critic like Marvin
Mudrick is quite sure that he knows who the real Jane Austen is,
for all his talk of her ironic detachment.[6] In other words, the large
amount of credit that Austen is given for linguistic subtlety is with-
drawn when it comes to the final judgment of her work, owing to
the prevailing critical assumption that *as a person* Jane Austen is
clear and definable and the meaning of her writing, therefore, in-
ordinately easy to establish. A kind of cloying Janeite assumption
of intimacy thus lingers on in otherwise quite sophisticated contemporary criticism.

In his essay *"Emma* and the Legend of Jane Austen," Lionel Trilling posed a question to himself based on this tendency among Austen's readers to find that her work offered so little resistance to their
interpretations and to their appropriation of Austen herself. He wrote:

> If Jane Austen is carried outside the proper confines of litera-
> ture, if she has been loved in a fashion that some tempera-
> ments must find objectionable and that a strict criticism must
> call illicit, the reason is perhaps to be found not only in the
> human weakness of her admirers, in their impulse to self-flat-
> tery, or in whatever other fault produces their deplorable tone.
> Perhaps a reason is also to be found in the work itself, in some
> unusual promise that it seems to make, in some hope that it
> holds out.[7]

Trilling concluded that Austen's work elicits this kind of reaction
because the world of her novels, or at least of *Emma,* is an idyllic
one. Whatever one's opinion of that conclusion may be, however,
I would suggest an alternate one that might do more to account for

the general survival of such an assured understanding of Austen's meaning in the face of quite elaborate analyses of the complex methods, techniques, and ambiguities in her use of language. I would suggest that Austen's novels are designed to satirize the apparent understandings between people, and that the prevailing assumption that one can clearly understand Jane Austen shows just how extensive her irony can be – so extensive that it allows readers to see all sorts of misconceptions in her characters while satirically seducing those readers into ignoring their own misconceptions. The famous correspondence between Austen and the Prince Regent's so persistently dense librarian might serve as an apt illustration of this extensive irony; but one can take a more direct approach to it by considering one word, "nature," which is so central to the eighteenth-century diction supporting her writing. For all of her irony must be presumed to develop from this word, since it is only by one's awareness of the "natural" point of view of things that it is possible to appreciate the exaggerations, contradictions, and misconceptions that deviate from such a point of view. It is through an understanding of nature that one is brought to appreciate affectation, delusion, dissimulation, and imitation; and so one would suppose that in such well-understood work as Austen's this word, at least, would have some hardness and clarity so that it could serve as a kind of rhetorical anchor. One finds, however, that this is not so.

Consider the multiplicity of meanings this word may have. At times the nature referred to in Austen's fiction is landscape, inanimate nature; at other times it is this landscape enhanced by artistic development and then further enhanced by the tastefully educated appreciation with which characters approach it. One can speak of being good-natured or ill-natured, as this word is drawn into a simple dichotomy descriptive of a character or of how a character appears at any particular time. Nature may be nothing but the expression of an individual's scale of values, as when John Dashwood finds the disposition of a church living at the greatest possible price to be "a point of such common, such natural concern!" (*SS*, 295); or it may come to express the difference between such scales. Willoughby, for instance, speaks of "those false ideas of the necessity of riches, which I was naturally inclined to feel" (*SS*, 323), whereas Elinor Dashwood considers his disposition to have been "naturally open and honest" (*SS*, 331) before it was changed by those ideas. Both portraits are in agreement: The only difference is in which side of the difference one chooses to mark with the word "naturally."

Nature may be the basis of all attributes – "Catherine, who had by nature nothing heroic about her" (*NA*, 15) – or it may be positively distinguished from certain attributes: "Feelings rather natural than heroic possessed her" (*NA*, 93). It may be a reference that supplements and authenticates another, as in the descriptions of Mrs. Price's "natural and motherly . . . joy" (*MP*, 371) and Emma Woodhouse's "desirable, natural, and probable" plan for a match between Harriet Smith and the Reverend Elton (*E*, 35). It may signify an ultimate ground of goodness, as when Anne Elliot decides that Mrs. Smith's character has to come "from Nature alone" (*P*, 154); or it may be a frailer substance, as Mrs. Smith gently tries to inform Anne.

Moreover, that which is natural may form a curious relationship between the achievement of satisfaction and the realization of loss:

> On the morning appointed for Admiral and Mrs. Croft's seeing Kellynch-hall, Anne found it most natural to take her almost daily walk to Lady Russell's, and keep out of the way till all was over; when she found it most natural to be sorry that she had missed the opportunity of seeing them. (*P*, 32)

Or, rather than forming a relationship between satisfaction and regret, nature may link knowledge and ignorance. This is the case when Edward Ferrars becomes convinced of Lucy Steele's "wanton ill-nature," only to have Elinor convince him "that nothing could have been more natural than Lucy's conduct, nor more self-evident than the motive of it" (*SS*, 366–7). This is also the case when Jane Bennet writes to her sister Elizabeth, after learning that Elizabeth was correct in saying that Miss Bingley did not really care for her:

> "But, my dear sister, though the event has proved you right, do not think me obstinate if I still assert, that, considering what her behavior was, my confidence was as natural as your suspicion." (*PP*, 148)

In both of these cases, the question of whether one calls something natural depends upon whether or not one finds it understandable, even if that understanding may be shown to be mistaken.

Nature can also be that which is customary, as it is when Fanny thinks that "every thing natural, probable, reasonable was against" Henry Crawford's proposal to her (*MP*, 305), just as it is when Sir Thomas Bertram quite contrarily speaks of Henry's desire for an interview with Fanny as "a request too natural, a claim too just to be denied" (*MP*, 321). Nature may be nothing but probability, as when Mr. Knightley says, "It is a great deal more natural than one could wish, that a young man, brought up by those who are proud, luxurious, and selfish, should be proud, luxurious, and selfish too" (*E*, 145). Or it may be that which is convenient, as when Knightley says, "The nature and the simplicity of gentlemen and ladies, with their servants and furniture, I think is best observed by meals within doors" (*E*, 355). Or, to give one last and appropriately summary example, nature may actually be a sign for the "liberty" of differing opinions. It is in this manner that the engagement of Fanny and Edmund Bertram is announced:

> I purposely abstain from dates on this occasion, that every-one may be at liberty to fix their own, aware that the cure of unconquerable passions, and the transfer of unchanging attachments, must vary much as to time in different people. – I only entreat every body to believe that exactly at the time when it was quite natural that it should be so, and not a week earlier, Edmund did cease to care about Miss Crawford, and become as anxious to marry Fanny, as Fanny herself could desire.
>
> With such a regard for her, indeed, as his had long been, a regard founded on the most endearing charms of innocence and helplessness, and completed by every recommendation of growing worth, what could be more natural than the change? (*MP*, 470)

Many other examples could be brought forth and many further distinctions could be made, providing a list of usages for Austen's fiction akin to Lovejoy's list of the philosophical usages of this word.[8] And from one point of view this multiplicity of usages certainly should not be surprising: scholars of the eighteenth century have long recognized the multiple and frequently contradictory uses of this word,[9] and eighteenth-century writers themselves sometimes noted this situation, as when Voltaire considered how in civilization the image of nature may become "so different from itself" that one cannot easily "submit to general laws the arts over which custom, which is to say inconstancy, holds such empire."[10] The only problem is that the nature of Austen's work has so often seemed to critics to be a secure inheritance from eighteenth-century moral theory and from her own Christian belief, even though the word "nature" is so demonstrably variable and insecure in its meaning, not only in her novels but also in the eighteenth-century works to which she owes much of her vocabulary. All of Austen's critics give her credit for commanding the moral and psychological diction of the eighteenth century, but she is rarely, if ever, given credit for being conscious of this vocabulary; for using it, that is to say, with an awareness of its internal contradictions. Critics have too often accepted as a rhetoric of truth the words and phrases that Austen used because they had cultural power – even as she showed the radical disharmonies, inconsistencies, and inequalities from which standards such as that of "nature" gained their power in society. And one cannot say that the divergent meanings of this word were controlled by an implicit cultural understanding and thus explain why critics find Austen so easy to understand despite this disorderly variety of meanings, because it is precisely the lack of such an implicit understanding that leads to the trials of the heroines in all of her novels. They come up against a society that appears to promise them secure grounds for understanding in language as well as in other kinds of signs, and what they find is that they cannot rely on either promises or appearances. If Austen is not credited with a great depth of meaning in her work, then, and if critics seem to be able to arrive at a remarkably secure conception of her identity despite the paucity of biographical evidence, it may be because her work seems idyllic or at least very limited, controlled, and safe; and yet it only appears to be so safe because we mistake our sense for hers.

The nature of Austen's work is remarkable because it seems to agree with everybody, whether one is a reader of her novels or a character in them. And this is the point of her satire: that understanding in general, like the understanding of nature, is neither safe, nor certain, nor real. Understanding is the agreement we imagine between ourselves and others, and all of Austen's writing dramatizes the dangers in this presumption of agreement. Like Hawthorne, Austen is concerned in her writing with the extraordinary fragility of all those aspects of life that we ordinarily think so unbreakable that we hardly notice them at all. If her writing, like Hawthorne's, does not usually seem disagreeable – if it seems to represent a conservative attachment to society and to the dominant social powers – it is because her readers ignore the lack of agreement in what passes for agreement in her work.

Austen's style is not a style of wholeness but of partiality, and partiality so relentless that semantic authority never settles in any one place, person, idea, or word. In all the aspects through which her novels can be viewed – plots, imagery, characters, conversations, and so on – her style serves to wean the reader from expectations of certitude and stability. Thus, when Elizabeth Bennet asks the question "Where does discretion end, and avarice begin?", it remains unanswered throughout her story, because it cannot be answered within the society she inhabits. This lack of response is not simply an indication of uncertainty, but of uncertainty dramatized as the condition of all discourse. When it comes to such questions, practical answers of a sort may be established through the brute facts of marriages, inheritances, benefices, and the like; but the disposition of such matters does not make an individual's moral status any more certain. If one learns how the power of such practical facts is established, one is enabled to act, and to act with a fair assurance of avoiding disaster; but that is all. The true nature of things – the nature on which all understanding must rest – is available only through limited, partial, delusive appearances.

At one point in *Pride and Prejudice,* for example, Jane is referred to as possessing "a strong sisterly partiality which made any admiration of Elizabeth appear perfectly natural" to her (*PP,* 224). What is deemed to be natural in Austen's novels is always related to such a qualifying partiality. Nothing comes to representation without suffering qualification from such a variety of sources and for such a variety of ends as to make impossible the idea of any measure other than the satirical. The most authoritative pronouncements come not from nature or sense but from assertions of power, a consideration satirized in *Mansfield Park* when the narrator abruptly discards the major topics that have occupied the novel simply because of a personal inclination that may or may not be "ironic":

> Let other pens dwell on guilt and misery. I quit such odious subjects as soon as I can, impatient to restore every body, not

greatly in fault themselves, to tolerable comfort, and to have
done with all the rest. (*MP*, 461).

Similarly, rather than dramatizing a comprehensive authority, the
positions of the narrator and of the characters at the ending of a
novel may simply serve to reiterate the lack of impartiality that had
provided the impetus for the beginning of the story. As Austen
writes of Catherine Morland,

> though Henry was now sincerely attached to her, though he
> felt and delighted in all the excellencies of her character and
> truly loved her society, I must confess that his affection orig-
> inated in nothing better than gratitude, or, in other words,
> that a persuasion of her partiality for him had been the only
> cause of giving her a serious thought. It is a new circumstance
> in romance, and dreadfully derogatory of an heroine's dig-
> nity; but if it be as new in common life, the credit of a wild
> imagination will at least be all my own. (*NA*, 243)

As in *Northanger Abbey*, where it is "authorized" by "a page full of
empty professions" from General Tilney to Mr. Morland, the endings of these novels are always mere formalities, as is indicated by
the perfunctory rhetoric with which they may be accomplished:
"Henry and Catherine were married, the bells rang, and every body
smiled" (*NA*, 243).[11]
Because of this prevailing partiality, Austen's is always a style of
second thoughts – a style of reconsideration. Where a qualification
by contraries seems to be announced, all that is received is the slightest
of modifications:

> I will only add in justice to men, that though to the larger and
> more trifling part of the sex, imbecility in females is a great
> enhancement of their personal charms, there is a portion of
> them too reasonable and too well informed themselves to de-
> sire any thing more in a woman than ignorance. (*NA*, 111)

Where a character's motives are concerned, they are never simple
and singular, and never entirely selfless:

> She soon recollected, in the first place, that she was without
> any excuse for staying at home; and, in the second, that it was
> a play she wanted very much to see. (*NA, 92*)

When the outcome of a novel might be expected to satisfy those
readers who choose to identify with the trials and morality of their
heroines, vengeance upon their enemies is not allowed:

> That his repentance of misconduct, which thus brought its
> own punishment, was sincere, need not be doubted; – nor
> that he long thought of Colonel Brandon with envy, and of
> Marianne with regret. But that he was for ever inconsolable,
> that he fled from society, or contracted an habitual gloom of
> temper, or died of a broken heart, must not be depended on
> – for he did neither. He lived to exert, and frequently to enjoy
> himself. (*SS, 379*)

There is no achievement of the ideal of justice – poetic, legal, or
otherwise – in Austen's novels. There are only lessons in language
based upon a recognition of the injustices of power, the inequality
and instability of social circumstances, and the demand for a rigorous circumspection consequent to these conditions. The endings
of these novels can be considered to be happy only if one ignores
all that has taken place before those endings. The heroines do always get married, but the significance of those marriages has been
brought into question throughout the narration of their adventures.

As with the word of nature, one can even follow the partiality of
Austen's fiction down to the level of individual words or phrases
in her writing. On this scale, one often sees words that are coupled
together as if they were naturally married to each other in a secure
order of meaning – and yet, closely considered, the apparent naturalness of this union often proves to be just as questionable as are
the marriages that conclude these novels. Once one actually analyzes such couplings – once one actually reads Austen's writing
rather than an image of Austen – the meaning of her work becomes
no less complex than the style of her writing. Frank Churchill, for
instance, is said to have been "given up to the care and wealth of
the Churchills" (*E, 16*). Are care and wealth then presumed to be
allied as are power and wealth in these novels? Anne Elliot is said

to have been able to find "no second attachment, the only thoroughly natural, happy, and sufficient cure, at her time of life" (*P*,
28). As these adjectives specify the nature of the cure under discussion, how does the introduction of a word like "sufficient," with
its air of a rather spartan satisfaction, affect the meaning of "happy"
and "natural"? When telling of Mrs. Elton's attitude toward Jane
Fairfax, the narrator of *Emma* says "she was not satisfied with expressing a natural and reasonable admiration" (*E*, 281), and again
the question is of the relationship between a natural admiration and
one that is reasonable. Is the reference to that species of reason which
moves Mr. Knightley to opine that meals within doors are "natural" to ladies and gentlemen? Or, in *Sense and Sensibility*, when Willoughby listens to Marianne and is said to be impressed by "the
force of her arguments and the brightness of her eye" (*SS*, 47),
what does this conjunction between reason and beauty indicate about
the nature of persuasion – and the real power of beauty – throughout Austen's novels?

Again, many more examples could be listed, although these should
be sufficient to indicate the characteristics of Austen's style. Words
that otherwise might seem to have a definite significance are disturbed by other words that would seem just as definite, characters
and conversations by other characters and conversations, plots by
plots, until the only basis for the judgment of meaning comes to be
the success that certain words, characters, and plots entertain over
others. And rather than being natural or sensible or true, this success always represents nothing more than the realities of social power
or some response to those realities in a particular area of life and
language. Consider, for example, the relationship between beauty
and power represented by the drama of Anne's face in *Persuasion*.

When Anne is first reunited with Captain Wentworth and his
presence revives the grief she had felt at their separation, her face is
like a landscape deserted by its tutelary deity. As Austen writes,
"*Once* she felt that he was looking at herself – observing her altered
features, perhaps, trying to trace in them the ruins of the face which
had once claimed him" (*P*, 72). Having earlier been informed that
it was as a result of their separation that Anne's "bloom had van-
ished early" (*P* 6), the reader subsequently witnesses a momentary
revival of this lost youthfulness as Austen describes Anne and
Wentworth passing by William Elliot on the steps at the beach:

They ascended and passed him; and as they passed, Anne's face caught his eye, and he looked at her with a degree of earnest admiration, which she could not be insensible of. She was looking remarkably well; her very regular, very pretty features, having the bloom and freshness of youth restored by the fine wind which had been blowing on her complexion, and by the animation of eye which it had also produced . . . Captain Wentworth looked round at her instantly in a way which showed his noticing of it. (*P*, 104)

The face that was a wilted blossom and then an indecipherable archaeological wreckage can thus become a flower once again under the combined influences of the weather and of the two men who will be rivals for Anne's affection. Finally, then, as the resumption of Anne's engagement with Wentworth approaches, Lady Russell and Sir Walter Elliot also remark upon an improvement in her appearance, as if to hint that their erstwhile opposition to her romance with Wentworth may be overcome. Thus it is that Anne's face seems to be a symbolic representation of her romantic destiny, a representation that waxes and wanes in accordance with the vagaries of her emotional situation.

But even though many critics have followed Virginia Woolf in seeing this novel as marking a change in Austen's novelistic temperament toward a softer, more romantic tone,[12] the case is not so simple. For just as the romantic plot in *Persuasion* is set in motion by that vanity which caused Sir Walter and Lady Russell to oppose Anne's initial engagement to Wentworth, and just as the action that revivifies this plot stems from Sir Walter's aristocratically vain expenditures and the consequent need for a removal of his family to Bath, so is Anne's beauty intimately allied with this form of partiality. Like the high rank and wealth achieved by Wentworth during the period of his estrangement from Anne – which a romantic vision would have one believe is incidental to the renewal of their connection, whereas a more realistic vision would note a stronger relationship – Anne's face appears as a symbol of romance only to those who ignore how such romance is designed to assert aristocratic values. As this novel shows so well through the vanity of Anne's father, beauty is as much an aristocratic value as is social rank; and the fact that Anne's romance with Wentworth should finally revive in economic and social circumstances more satisfactory to her vain family is a strong blow to her own particular vanity: the belief that she does not belong to that family. Or, to put it another way: the belief that she could ever be romantically beautiful without belonging to such a family.

Anne's beauty, then, is at least as much a desirable representation of her social condition as it is a representation of her romantic fortunes. The most powerful marriage in this novel is not that between Anne and Wentworth but rather the marriage that reconciles Anne and Wentworth to her family at the end of the novel. The truth of romance allegorized in Anne's face is that beauty is an aristocratic possession. This possession, we learn, will be lost if one has inappropriate desires, and it may be regained only if one's desire endures the discipline of aristocratic control. Anne regains her beauty because she learns to accept her family's vanity, and Wentworth desires her beauty because it represents to him all that aristocratic power which Austen shows in this novel to be as inextricably involved in the literary depiction of romance and romantic desire as it was actually involved in determining all sorts of values in the society of her time.

That Anne should have to let her face speak and act for her in this manner is by no means a peculiarity of *Persuasion,* either; for the lesson held out to all of Austen's heroines is that they must protect their speech from those misunderstandings that result from the partiality of all understanding, and that they can do this only through silence or disguises. In order to preserve their meaning, they must withhold it. Speech must be recognized as a strategy, just as honesty must be recognized as a policy. In their successful moments Austen's characters recognize the dangerous diffractions of meaning in their world; they are foolish when they have faith in communication and therefore fail to recognize that there is no secure ground for communication in "nature" or in any other word. In this respect, Austen's novels are as different as they could possibly be from Radcliffe's. Instead of showing itself in fullness and immediacy in these novels, meaning must always wait upon events as those events are worked out according to the distribution of power within society – a consideration dramatized more clearly than anywhere else in the opening of *Sense and Sensibility,* where John Dashwood's deathbed assurance to his father that he will look after Mrs. Dashwood and her daughters is attenuated to the point of nothingness through the combination of his selfish partiality and the legal inconsequentiality of that last promise. In other words, the language of Austen's novels can never be easily and completely understood because it can never be taken in isolation from the complexities of the social background in which it appears. It is this background that determines meaning, and so language in Austen's novels is always, in effect, *quoted* language: language that does not originate with her characters or with the narrator herself but that instead derives from a social and cultural context that will finally determine one's meaning. This circumstantial background is the only "nature" of Austen's work, and one cannot understand that work apart from it. To give another characterization of Austen's heroines, then, one can say that they are wise when they gain some idea of the traditions and conventions they are quoting, and foolish when, like Marianne Dashwood, they believe that they can disregard this background and communicate freely and immediately with others.

A virtually paradigmatic illustration of this environment of quotation in Austen's work may be taken, again, from the example of Anne Elliot. At one point in *Persuasion* Austen describes her on a walk in the country,

> repeating to herself some few of the thousand poetical descriptions extant of autumn, that season of peculiar and inexhaustible influence on the mind of taste and tenderness, that season which has drawn from every poet, worthy of being read, some attempt at description, or some lines of feeling.

Overhearing in the course of this walk an especially friendly conversation between Captain Wentworth and Louisa Musgrave, Anne finds her memory disturbed. Overhearing is always a dramatic form of quotation in Austen's works, as words are detached from their immediate context to be judged within another one; and this second quotation drives away those on which Anne had been musing:

> Anne could not immediately fall into a quotation again. The sweet scenes of autumn were for a while put by – unless some tender sonnet, fraught with the apt analogy of the declining year, with declining happiness, and the images of youth and hope, and spring, all gone together, blessed her memory.

Captivated by this second quotation, Anne finds that the other quotations disappear, "unless" some new reference appropriate to her disappointments in love and beauty should divinely intercede. Yet a little farther, then, and Anne comes upon a view of fields being plowed, "counteracting the sweets of poetical despondence" (*P*, 84–5).

Anne thus moves from a solitary walk in the autumn countryside to a walk in the world of a poetical *topos,* to an imaginary excursion into the minds of others, to (perhaps) the world of a sonnet appropriated from the world of literature as if it had been written especially for her, into a final view of cultivated fields "meaning to have spring again" and serving in the world of Austen's novel to foretell Anne's own second spring of beauty and love. The part of Anne's walk that seems most natural and immediate – the appearance of the fields that drive away poetry somewhat as Milton's Christ in "On the Nativity" silences the pagan oracles – is the most literary, an image of renewal as old as literature itself and deliberately used as such in this passage. The excursion of this heroine is thus an excursion of tropes, this landscape of nature the topography of a mind exhibiting the cultural background to this heroine's thoughts and emotions and textual situation. And even though, with the final renewal of her engagement to Wentworth, Anne is said to have "never been supplanted" (*P*, 241), with the implication being that there is something original and natural in their connection, the delay between her original engagement and her second engagement *is* such a supplantment. Just as previous attachments to other persons appear between lover and beloved elsewhere in Austen's works, the passage of time intervenes here to characterize the nature of love as the repetition or "quotation" of an earlier experience that is not personal and immediate but cultural and historical, and embodied in literature as in the institutions of society. It is foolish characters like Marianne Dashwood who only believe in first loves and are led to disaster on that account; whereas those who succeed, like Anne and Wentworth, succeed because they surrender the apparently clear understanding of nature to the decidedly unclear meanings of art. Implicitly or explicitly, they accept the fact that they are in a dependent position of repetition rather than one of originality.

It is true that in Austen's novels the discourse of lovers is distinguished from all other forms of discourse in that it does not experience this repetition as such. Although Elizabeth Bennet finds that

Sir William Lucas's tales become boring through repetition; although "the usual rate of conversation" is described in *Emma* as "a few clever things said, a few downright silly, but by much the larger portion neither the one nor the other – nothing worse than every day remarks, dull repetitions, old news, and heavy jokes" (*E*, 219); although all that can be said of the conversation of Catherine Morland and Miss Tilney is that there "might" be something uncommon in the manner in which they use expressions "made and used some thousands of times before, under that roof in every Bath season" (*NA*, 72), the case is different with lovers:

> For though a very few hours spent in the hard labour of incessant talking will dispatch more subjects than can really be in common between any two rational creatures, yet with lovers it is different. Between *them* no subject is finished, no communication is ever made, till it has been made at least twenty times over. (*SS*, 363–4)

Even though lovers find such originality in their repetitions, however, the novel as Austen wrote it is not a discourse of love or of lovers. This kind of narrative instead shows originality to be nothing but a convention, a repetition, or a trope. Even if it seems to be a kind of ultimate trope, transfiguring all that it touches, love is still exposed as the product of a cultural order of which the lovers must necessarily be ignorant. Their partiality toward each other is directly related to a certain blindness toward their world, but as a narrator Austen did not adopt the lover's point of view except to satirize it. Her novels show love to be at best a kind of harmless delusion that palliates the harsh effect of inescapable social conditions; at worst, a conviction of originality that so utterly blinds one to these conditions that it may lead a character like Marianne Dashwood to say, "I detest jargon of every kind, and sometimes I have kept my feelings to myself, because I could find no language to describe them in but what was worn and hackneyed out of all sense and meaning" (*SS*, 97). The danger, of course, is not in Marianne's dissatisfaction with language, which is entirely justified; the danger is in her belief that there may be a language, that transfiguring language of love, which is not made up of "worn and hackneyed" quotations. Perhaps Austen did believe, as a writer and as a person, in the existence of a love that is not on a scale of relatively dangerous delusions; at times, the reader of Austen's novels might feel that such a sense of love lies somewhere behind her words; but if it does exist, it does so only within that impenetrable reserve that Austen shows as the only home where "true" understanding can survive the misunderstandings that reign over communication in a society governed in all its aspects by various forms of partiality.

There is nothing sentimental in Austen's fiction, then, but there also is nothing of despair, which in fact is shown to be sentimental indulgence or extreme partiality toward one's self. And intellect, it should be noted, is especially protected from sentimentality, as Mary Bennet, the most intellectual character in these novels, reads and makes extracts and ends up with – quotations. Austen's writing, then, is directed against readers like Catherine Morland and John Knightley's children, who think that the stories told to them ought always to be told in the same way, and also against readers like Marianne Dashwood, who believe that they possess all the originality in the world and therefore interrupt stories because they feel confident that they can foretell the endings. Austen's writing diverts us between naive passivity and intrusive self-assertion, telling us stories that are familiar and yet new because they examine the relationship between what we find familiar and what we think is new. If Austen's work possesses originality, it is in its insistence upon the absence of originality.

Austen's novels are lessons in the need for doubt, but they are lessons that demonstrate the inescapable pressure for credulity. They are lessons in language, but lessons given with Elizabeth Bennet's recognition that "we all love to instruct, though we can teach only what is not worth knowing" (*PP,* 343). They are stories told with Anne Elliot's recognition that quotations are unfair to women because "men have had every advantage" over them in telling "their own story" (*P,* 234), and yet they are stories written with the recognition that all heroines, like Catherine Morland, "must read to supply their memories with those quotations which are so serviceable and so soothing in the vicissitudes of their eventful lives" (*NA,* 15). (And it is relevant to note that Anne's argument itself is a quotation, whether deliberate or accidental, from one of Steele's early papers in *The Spectator.*[13]) After all, Austen knew very well the deceptions that may be played among books; as she wrote to her sister Cassandra, alluding to Cowper's poem on Alexander Selkirk, "I am alone in the Library, Mistress of all I survey – at least I may say so & repeat the whole poem if I like it, without offence to anybody" (*L* 2: 335). Her novels always show that the nature surveyed by men and women is not a matter of the external world or of the heart or of God's will, but a matter of language – and they show, further, that one can command the nature of language only when one is alone in a library. As soon as one steps outside or allows another person to come inside, this power vanishes. The reality of history and of social circumstances sets in, and then one can only try to survive through secrecy and through silence. One lives through partiality and survives by partial satisfactions, for "where other powers of entertainment are wanting, the true philosopher will derive benefit from such as are given" (*PP,* 236). Of course, it is difficult to summarize the meaning this recognition draws from Austen's novels; but perhaps it may be represented by the mixture of wit, pathetic desolation, and rigorous strength conveyed by another comment to Cassandra: "I do not think it worth while to wait for enjoyment until there is some real opportunity for it" (*L* 1: 56). The nature of Austen's writing is never more intriguing than in the difficulty of deciding where irony begins and where it ends in such a statement.

PART III

SIR WALTER SCOTT

∾

Walter Scott has no business to write novels, especially good ones. It is not fair . . . I do not like him, and do not mean to like "Waverley" if I can help it, but fear I must.

— JANE AUSTEN, *Letters*

7

BLIND ROADS

~

The strong contrast produced by the opposition of
ancient manners to those which are gradually sub-
duing them affords the lights and shadows necessary
to give effect to a fictitious narrative; and while such
a period entitles the author to introduce incidents of
a marvellous and improbable character, as arising out
of the turbulent independence and ferocity, belonging to old habits of violence, still influencing the
manners of a people who had been so lately in a barbarous state; yet, on the other hand, the characters
and sentiments of many of the actors may, with the
utmost probability, be described with great variety
of shading and delineation, which belongs to the
newer and more improved period, of which the world
has but lately received the light.
    – SIR WALTER SCOTT, *The Fortunes of Nigel*

IN THE FOREGOING PASSAGE as in all of Scott's novels, the reader is promised a certain line of distinction between
some version of ancient and of modern times. As it appears in
the various novels, this borderline between the old and the new
comes to be set in many different periods of historical transition,
but it always serves the same narrative function. It might be called
the engine of Scott's fiction, this line that allows him to distinguish
that which is doomed to recede into history from that which bears
the stamp of the future, for it organizes the basic conflicts of his
fiction while at that same time serving to predict the resolution of
those conflicts. As Scott presents the situation, the modern forces
must win, despite whatever virtues may belong to the past and
despite whatever flaws the future may bring – and yet the situation
is not as simple as he tries to make it appear. For although clear
distinctions between ancient and modern times are absolutely necessary to Scott's picture of history as a progressive development

toward more refined societies, a close reading of his work does not uphold these distinctions. In fact, even as Scott's narratives promise readers that they will see strongly marked borderlines so that they can appreciate the changes through which the world has passed, his narratives so obscure those borderlines as to make them all but illegible. The most profound conflict, then, is not being waged between any individual or social or political forces but between this drawing and obscuring of borderlines; and this conflict in the mode of his narration needs to be evaluated before one can approach any full understanding of the dramatic conflicts portrayed in that work. Ultimately, this narrative conflict can be seen as the result of a division in Scott's sympathies as a narrator between aristocratic and middle-class values. An awareness of this division and of the conflicts resulting from it can lead the reader to a more complex appreciation for Scott's importance in the development of the historical novel.

At first glance, the differences within Scott's novels do indeed seem to contrast as greatly as light and shadow. The pattern appears so clear and so uniform, in fact, that all the factors that are ancient might be tallied on one side of a line and all that are modern on another. On the side of the past in various novels are such elements as violence, superstition, disorder, pagans, Saxons, Catholics, Scotland, the Highlands, and the Stuarts, and on the side of the present are law, reason, peace, Christians, Normans, Protestants, England, the Lowlands, and the Hanoverians. Naturally, this list could be extended through additions and through further subdivisions of the categories already given. The difference between the Independent and the Presbyterian Protestant, for instance, would fall along this line, as would that between the traditional genre of romance and the modern romance or novel. As it distinguishes between anachronistic and progressive elements in these novels, this borderline passes through every area of judgment within them. On the one side is all that has passed or is passing, bearing the general character of powerful simplicity and romantic excess; on the other, all that is progressive, bearing the character of refinement and inhibition. Scott's novels are typically set in a time of disorder just before the emergence of a new order, and they are typically elegiac, mourning what is about to be lost while announcing what is to come. They are set, in other words, on a borderline between different historical, political, social, and psychological states – or so the author maintains, and an overview of the novels gives one no reason to quarrel with him. The usual approach in Scott criticism, in fact, is to see him as a mediator of such differences, whether that mediation is thought to eventuate in "Engels's 'triumph of realism,' "[1] in "the complex balanced attitude toward the historical turning point" bespoken by Donald Davie,[2] or in D. D. Devlin's judgment that Scott "follows a complex middle way between an Enlightenment view of history, with human nature as the one great and totally fixed point, and an historicist approach to the past."[3] One even finds the same approach in a volume of after-dinner speeches given in memory of Scott: Almost every one emphasizes his sane, sensible, rational, reconciling imagination.[4]

Regarded more closely, however, this borderline central to the development of civilization comes to resemble that "species of path, visible when looked at from a distance, but not to be seen when you are upon it . . . called on the Border by the significant name of a 'blind road' " (*M,* 211n).[5] Although it is clear to the historical romancer who regards his subject from afar, this boundary becomes increasingly imperceptible as one moves with a writer like Scott into the thick of the action. One cannot try to follow it without falling into a severe confusion, for not only do elements supposed to belong definitively to one side of the line instead appear quite disconcertingly on the other, sometimes openly and sometimes in disguise, but the elements as such are even liable to be mistaken. Boys appear as girls, or girls as boys; noblemen appear as commoners and a common barber as the counselor of a king; loyalists and rebels exchange places as a result of subterfuge, time-serving hypocrisy, ideological persuasion, or social change; superstition and reason are inextricably intertwined; law is used as an instrument of violence, or violence to establish law; and so on. In sum, even as they are introduced as belonging to a period in which the reader will see the disorders of the past surrendering to the order of more modern times, all the elements of these novels are given such a capricious life that no convincing vision of modern order is finally possible. One is led to expect certain distinctions by a narrator who wishes to picture change as a systematic and progressive process, and one instead is conducted by that narrator to a blind road along which all distinctions are blurred into a vast shadow of loss.

It is true that not every distinction is challenged. In his editorial

comments, Scott assumes that he is writing for an audience of Protestants who belong to the middle and upper classes and who believe
in the virtues of commerce and conservative politics as in an unal-
terable dispensation, and the corresponding assumption that the
nineteenth century is a conclusive and just age of law is never thought
to warrant discussion. This assumption, however, is not really very
significant to the novels he produced. It accounts only for a few
moral homilies sprinkled throughout their narration, some few
contentious asides from that narration, and perhaps the choice of
an occasional metaphor, as in his presentation of the relationship
between the writer and his audience as a contractual one. Although
certainly of interest, these aspects of his novels are of little importance relative to the more central and almost continually posed
problem of order. The fictional situations developed around this
problem do not support the confident values of the modern anti-
quarian, advocate, and aspirant to the aristocracy that these editorial comments, excerpted from Scott's texts, might otherwise lead
one to suppose as conclusively his own. As it is dramatized over
and over again in these novels in an almost obsessive manner, this
problem of order instead comes to possess a cumulative force that
belongs more to obscurity, unhappiness, and guilt than to the comfort of morality.

To begin, then, as the general question of order is raised in the
introductions to the Waverley novels and in the commentary upon
events given within the narration of those novels, Scott's position is
that a fundamental human identity is preserved within every historical change. This identity is said to become increasingly perfected in the progressive course of time until it reaches his own age,
beyond which no different future seems to be imagined. David
Daiches goes astray when he argues that Scott was so completely
different from Enlightenment historians as to realize that "human
nature could and did change,"[6] for Scott's writing always appeals
to a basic constancy beyond a superficial mutability. As "Laurence
Templeton" writes in his dedicatory epistle to *Ivanhoe,*

> What I have applied to language, is still more justly applicable
> to sentiments and manners. The passions, the sources from
> which these must spring in all their modifications, are gener-
> ally the same in all ranks and conditions, all countries and
> ages; and it follows as a matter of course that the opinions,

habits of thinking, and actions, however influenced by the peculiar state of society, must still, upon the whole, bear a strong resemblance to each other. (*I, xxv*)

This entirely ordinary expression of humanist belief often makes its appearance in these novels in one form or another, and it would seem to constitute a secure ground for Scott's study of social differences and historical change. In some versions, however, this vision of permanence may not be quite so reassuring. Instead, it becomes as unreliable as all those other shifty characters and qualities that travel with such impunity across the borderlines of his fiction.

Compare the preceding quotation from *Ivanhoe,* for example, to one of Henry Morton's meditations in *Old Mortality:*

> Let the tide of the world wax or wane as it will . . . enough will be found to fill the places which chance renders vacant; and, in the usual occupations and amusements of life, human beings will succeed each other, as leaves upon the same tree, with the same individual difference and the same general resemblance. (*OM,* 375)

The Olympian detachment of this pronouncement sorts strangely with the progressive idea of history in Scott's novels, and it is not so very different from that despairing vision by which characters in Thomas Hardy's works are given to see the anonymous members of the human race partaking of an unimportant succession of repetitious events. Despite its unremarkable imagery, there is an eerie quality to this passage. It is as if Morton were attending, although at a controlled distance, to the violent misanthropy of the protagonist in *The Black Dwarf.* This character gives a somewhat more dramatic version of human identity, reaching through allusion to comparisons with *Troilus and Cressida* and *Hamlet:*

> "Why should not the whole human herd butt, gore, and gorge upon each other till all are extirpated but one huge and overfed Behemoth, and he, when he had throttled and gnawed the bones of all his fellows – he, when his prey failed him, to be roaring whole days for lack of food, and, finally, to die inch by inch of famine; it were a consummation worthy of the race!" (*BD,* 27–8)

Although these passages are spoken by individual characters and so need not be regarded as contradicting the general point of view that organizes these novels, they indicate a problem of order that goes well beyond the boundaries of individual characters. It is the borderline that distinguishes individual characters as such, in fact, that is put into question. For these passages raise the possibility that one might look upon humanity from the bird's-eye view of these historical novels and, in so viewing humanity as a whole, lose all sense of individual differences. All changes, all variations, all discriminations would be absorbed within an impersonal corporate identity that would be seen to be at least dehumanizing, if not actually fearsome. Far from being a vision that reconciles the various elements in these novels, Scott's vision would collapse into disorder precisely because it sees so many similarities among the various elements that it can no longer distinguish among them. And this possibility is not only voiced by individual characters but also appears in images furnished by the narrator of these novels. In a description of a battle in *The Fair Maid of Perth,* for example, such an impression of impersonality behind all the varied surfaces of this particular situation in life completely eliminates from view all individuals. As the scene is described, it is

> a tumultuous chaos, over which the huge swords rose and sunk, some still glittering, others streaming with blood, appearing, from the wild rapidity with which they were swayed, rather to be put in motion by some complicated machinery than to be wielded by human hands. (*FMP*, 415)

A terrible loss of individuality is depicted here through just the sort of scene in which Scott's protagonists usually are called upon to prove their individual courage and virtue. Therefore, the dramatic crisis of the battle is in effect a crisis of the narration, since this image of the battle runs so contrary to the formulaic borderlines that organize the picture of history in Scott's fiction. How can one recover the meaning of such battles as testing grounds for the individual heroes of the novels once a picture so destructive of individuality is allowed into view? The question is not a casual one, for such images are by no means unusual in these novels. A comparably threatening moment, for instance, is when Julia Mannering discovers that once plots are set in motion by human hands, they may escape the control of those hands. Here, again, one receives an image of human beings subjected to an impersonal fate under which they virtually disappear as individuals:

> "I feel the terrors of a child who has in heedless sport put in motion some powerful piece of machinery; and, while he beholds wheels revolving, chains clashing, cylinders rolling around him, is equally astonished at the tremendous powers which his weak agency has called into action, and terrified for the consequences which he is compelled to await, without the possibility of averting them." (*GM*, 203)

And a similar effect is created when Julian Peveril is imprisoned in connection with the seventeenth-century Popish Plot and hears a mysterious voice that says,

> "There is no condition in life, no degree of talent, no form of principle, which affords protection against an accusation which levels conditions, confounds characters, renders men's virtues their sins, and rates them as dangerous in proportion as they have influence, though obtained in the noblest manner, and used for the best purposes." (*PP*, 419)

The point is that the vision of history that Scott explicitly proposes as the controlling vision in these novels is directly challenged in every situation of these novels – and there are many of them – in which their protagonists experience themselves as being helpless before essentially impersonal forces responsible to no order of reason, progress, or truth. In such situations, all elements are leveled and confused with each other. Consequently, his characters are almost continually beset by uncertainty as they try to distinguish between the ancient and the modern, the outmoded and the refined, disorder and order, lies and enlightenment.

This uncertainty is most powerfully manifested in the tendency of the judgment of Scott's characters to be so swayed by the muddle of transient circumstances as to hopelessly confuse the line between public order and individual feelings. They cannot take that grand bird's-eye view of events claimed by the narrator, and the result is that one may mistake a political conflict for an opportunity to be exploited on behalf of one's private feelings, as in *Waverley;* a personal tragedy as proof of a universal malignancy, as in *The Black Dwarf;* a literary example as a guide to life, again as in *Waverley,* or *The Bride of Lammermoor,* or almost all of these novels; a social difference as a difference in character, values, appearance, or political affiliation, again as in almost all of the novels; and so on through all the plots that Scott constructs out of the confusion that may spread from the drawing of borderlines. The uncertainty of the borderline between the ancient and the modern in Scott's work is reflected in this uncertainty felt by his characters in every area of their experience.

When Quentin Durward, for example, learns that a man who had originally appeared to him in a humble guise is actually Louis XI, he reacts in the same way as he will when he later learns that a woman who attracted him is actually a countess. The past is altered and perception transformed so as to sweep this knowledge of rank through every category of sensibility:

> Those eyes which, according to Quentin's former impression, only twinkled with the love of gain, had, now that they were known to be the property of an able and powerful monarch, a piercing and majestic glance; and those wrinkles on the brow, which he had supposed were formed during a long series of petty schemes of commerce, seemed now the furrows which sagacity had worn while toiling in meditation upon the fate of nations. (*QD,* 88)

His perceptual judgments are at the mercy of his prejudiced opinions, as in a similar fashion Guy Mannering observes that many gypsies "set out by being imposters and end by becoming enthusiasts, or hold a kind of darkling conduct between both lives, unconscious almost when they are cheating themselves and when imposing on others" (*GM,* 334–5). Just as Quentin finds society so glamorous that he is unable to maintain a separation between appearances and their social disposition, so does Guy observe the difficulty of maintaining a course of action without coming to be so fascinated by it as to lose one's judgment – a difficulty, incidentally, from which Guy himself is not exempt. In short, so vulnerable is identity in Scott's novels that it does not even give individuals clearly outlined images of themselves, much less of others. There is always this tendency in the novels for elements that are apparently defined with the utmost clarity to drift beyond borderlines toward a general condition of disorder and confusion.

One sees the judgment of Scott's characters threatened in a related way when Darsie Latimer is imprisoned under the pretext of madness and considers the possibility that he may actually go mad, as others have, merely through "the action of exterior and contagious sympathies" (*R*, 192–3). Though he is not treated severely, he recognizes that the very fact of any association between himself and madness, however undeserved, is dangerous and liable to make itself true. Identity is so vulnerable here that simple contiguity may overcome all power of reason. So Richard Middlemas, unjustly confined in an unwholesome hospital, "longed, though he struggled against the impulse, to vie in curses with the reprobate, and in screams with the maniac" (*SD*, 68). And when the narrator describes one of the more dramatic scenes in which Quentin Durward participates, noting that "whoever had seen Quentin Durward that fatal night, not knowing the meaning of his conduct, had accounted him a raging madman; whoever had appreciated his motives had ranked him a hero of romance" (*QD*, 235), the implication here as elsewhere in Scott's work is that noble sense and insane nonsense are closely associated and often may be confused with each other. As one sees this confusion so extensively developed throughout these novels, it begins to seem more significant than the rational, orderly, reconciling conclusions that critics usually take as their guides in reading them. Like Radcliffe's and Austen's, Scott's novels show a certain disharmony between the superficial ideology of the narrative and the structure of that narrative; but although these disharmonies can be seen to be related to a continuing problem in the establishment of social values, the specific form that this disharmony takes in Scott's work is to be distinguished from its appearance in Austen's novels just as the specific problems of her works are to be distinguished from those that occupy Radcliffe's imagination.

Scott's characters continually are facing situations in which they cannot even come close to adopting the detached and objective point of view that enables Scott, as a historical novelist, to see order in history. The question that arises, then, concerns the significance of a point of view that has value only in retrospect. If the borderlines that organize Scott's view of history and that serve to chart the progressive course of that history mean nothing to individuals in the midst of historical circumstances, can they mean anything at all? Just what does it mean if one cannot find in the drama of the novels the order Scott claims to see controlling them? This is not the naive question that one could ask of all writers in regard to their creations – how can they know more than their characters? – for Scott's narrative itself often seems to incline toward favoring the disordered point of view of the characters rather than the orderly point of view that otherwise is proposed as the author's own. One notes, for example – and here lies a similarity to Austen – that the marriages, reconciliations, and inheritances that occur in the conventional endings of most of Scott's novels[7] generally are given succinctly, abruptly, and self-consciously, as if begrudged. And even though no writer speaks of a desire to adapt his or her writing to the tastes of the public more than Scott does, the very frequency with which he admits this disarming desire might lead one to regard it as being symptomatic of some kind of dissatisfaction.

To be sure, in some respects this dissatisfaction may appear to be completely reasonable. For instance, Scott's novels are dedicated to the time of youth and yet are written in the belief that the time of youth can be recognized only through memory, since youth does not fully appreciate its own blessings. It is only to be expected, therefore, that the mourning in these novels for what disappears through change should always be greater than the celebration for what has arrived. And yet this conclusion raises disturbing questions. Even though Scott assumes, for example, that his readers "are, have been, or will be lovers" (*AG*, 338), he describes love as an emotion founded upon loss:

> The period at which love is formed for the first time, and felt most strongly, is seldom that at which there is much prospect of its being brought to a happy issue. The state of artificial society opposes many complicated obstructions to early marriages; and the chance is very great that such obstacles prove insurmountable. In fine, there are very few men who do not look back in secret to some period of their youth at which a sincere and early affection was repulsed, or betrayed, or became abortive from opposing circumstances. It is these little passages of secret history which leave a tinge of romance in every bosom, scarce permitting us, even in the most busy or

most advanced period of life, to listen with total indifference
to a tale of true love. (*PP, 125*)

As it is described in this passage and dramatized throughout Scott's
novels, the interest of romance flows from a wound in experience
so deep that a cure is not even desirable. In a curious way, in fact,
the wound actually seems to be positively desired, because of the
effect it finally will bring to the lover. Thus, the interest of Scott's
novels is dedicated to "that delightful season when youth and high
spirits awaken all those flattering promises which are so ill kept to
manhood" (*SRW,* 18), but one finds compensation for those bro-
ken promises in "the spirit of romantic melancholy which perhaps
is ill exchanged even for feelings of joyful rapture" (*PP,* 220). Or,
to put it another way, the love of which these novels tell may form
"the most delightful hours of human existence" but also and just
as frequently leads "to those which are darkened by disappoint-
ment, fickleness, and all the pains of blighted hope and unrequited
attachment" (*QD,* 271). Given this understanding, it is really
something of an understatement to note, as has Robert C. Gordon,
that there is a "basic energising dissatisfaction that lies behind the
Waverley Novels."[8] It is necessary to add, at least, that this dissatisfaction not only energizes the novels – for instance, giving an
impression of vivid reality to precisely those scenes of violence and
irrationality that are supposed to be so foreign to the modern order
of life – but also leads to narrative complications within the novels
so severe that they might themselves be called violent. The borderlines of Scott's historical fiction are transformed into blind roads by
this secret history of an attachment to the lost past.

This is the case, for instance, with Scott's repeated adversions to
the comprehensibility that may be demanded of fiction, though not
of life. As he writes in *The Fair Maid of Perth:*

> The incidents of a narrative of this kind must be adapted to
> each other, as the wards of a key must tally accurately with
> those of the lock to which it belongs. The reader, however
> gentle, will not hold himself obliged to rest satisfied with the
> mere fact that such and such occurrences took place, which
> is, generally speaking, all that in ordinary life he can know of
> what is passing around him; but he is desirous, while reading

for amusement, of knowing the interior movements occasioning the course of events. This is a legitimate and reasonable curiosity; for every man hath a right to open and examine the mechanism of his own watch, put together for his proper use, although he is not permitted to pry into the interior of the timepiece which, for general information, is displayed on the town-steeple. (*FMP*, 285)

Fictional order is here allowed to be an amusement, a concession to the reader, and little more than a mechanical formality. It is not spurned, but it is trivialized, as if the narrator could throw this admission as a veil over that unsuccessful struggle to maintain order which is waged throughout his work. In effect, in this passage Scott simultaneously attempts to proffer and to withdraw significance from his work by drawing a line between those illusions of art that are not to be taken seriously and the realities of experience that alone are to be judged important. And yet the problem of determining this very line forms a theme of great dramatic interest throughout Scott's works, as has already been noted, so that the distinction that here is said to be exterior to the author and his audience is within the same narrative made intrinsic to their clear communication with each other. The result is that this passage, closely analyzed, appears so full of internal contradictions as to be incomprehensible; and one finds similar contradictions in all of Scott's comments of this type. They are significant contradictions, though, not just faults of writing or logic, for they point to that great tension in Scott's work between his commitment to the present and his yearning for the past.

More frequent even than this type of comment, though, are Scott's repeated warnings against presumptions upon futurity, and these warnings are similarly bound to the uncertainty of borderlines. Since Scott's novels imply that the end of history has virtually been achieved in the early years of the nineteenth century – since there does not seem to be any suspicion that an age could arrive that would make his own age appear barbaric, according to his usual engine of duality – these admonitions against divination are especially significant. They serve to defend the position of complacency he tries to appear to occupy, although this defense does not prove to be any more effective than any of the others that he tries to make against the problems of disorder.

An instance of this kind of warning occurs in the Introduction to *Guy Mannering*, where Scott speaks of

> those singular coincidences which occasionally appear, differing so widely from ordinary calculation, yet without which irregularities human life would not present to mortals, looking into futurity, the abyss of impenetrable darkness which it is the pleasure of the Creator it should offer to them. Were everything to happen in the ordinary train of events, the future would be subject to the rules of arithmetic, like the chances of gaming. But extraordinary events and wonderful runs of luck defy the calculation of mankind and throw impenetrable darkness over future contingencies. (*GM*, xiii)

The moral of this passage goes at least as far back as the pronouncement of the chorus at the end of *Oedipus Rex,* so it is not for its originality that it is significant. Somewhat more remarkable is the fact that this notice should serve as much to promise variety in life as to bridle pride, but even this elaboration upon the traditional piety was not unusual in a century in which John Stuart Mill could fret that there might be no new musical melodies to be composed. What *is* particularly interesting about this comment is that the event to which it refers is the fulfillment of an astrological prophecy. A calculation of the future that proves to be accurate is thus used as evidence against the possibility of calculating the future: a rather singular mode of argument, and yet one typical of the way the lines drawn in Scott's fiction work contrary to their supposed identities and ends.

No less tortuous a destination, for instance, is reached by Scott's most common explanation for the settings of disorder and impending change that almost always are the basis of his plots. He glosses a particular scene in *Ivanhoe* in the same way as he generally explains his habit of dwelling upon the disordered past:

> A moment of peril is often also a moment of open-hearted kindness and affection. We are thrown off our guard by the general agitation of our feelings, and betray the intensity of those which, at more tranquil periods, our prudence at least conceals, if it cannot altogether suppress them. (*I,* 267)

The specific qualities of kindness and affection are here spoken of in the same way that the truth of human nature is addressed in similar passages in other novels. They are considered to be positive qualities, and yet it is implied that they require force – even the force of evil – if they are to be fully expressed. Men and women must be taken by surprise if their true identities are to be revealed, and the only surprise sufficient to bring them forward is that afforded by violence. The true order of human identity, in other words, is so rigorously dependent upon the disorder in which it is allowed to appear that it is practically impossible to think of it as something other than a term in a formal narrative equation; it is equally difficult to consider the value assigned it as anything other than an inflection with which it is arbitrarily marked. For if what is called truth must be persuaded to be free, and if the means of persuasion are invariably those of falsehood, treachery, and physical force, then the identity of truth as something radically at variance with these means becomes rather difficult to maintain. The question is not simply that of guilt by association, although the syntax of metonymy should not be overlooked in evaluating dramas such as Scott's; the question here, as in the related case of Radcliffe's novels, is where one can draw the line between the discovery of truth and those conditions necessary to this discovery. Here, again, is a narrative crux in which the definition of elements in Scott's novels is thoroughly confused with a background of violence and loss.

It is this situation that is thrown into the relief of caricature in *St. Ronan's Well,* Scott's only novel set in his own time, as a retired military man is described as assuming the double role of fomenting and quelling conflict. The narrator comments:

> We have heard of men of undoubted benevolence of character and disposition, whose principal delight was to see a miserable criminal, degraded alike by his previous crimes and the sentence which he had incurred, conclude a vicious and wretched life by an ignominious and painful death. It was some such inconsistency of character which induced honest Captain MacTurk, who had really been a meritorious officer, and was a good-natured, honourable, and well-intentioned man, to place his chief delight in setting his friends by the ears, and then acting as umpire in the dangerous rencontres which, according to his code of honour, were absolutely nec-

essary to restore peace and cordiality. We leave the explanation of such anomalies to the labours of craniologists, for they seem to defy all the researches of the ethic philosopher. (*SRW,* 129)

Like the redoubtable Peregrine Scrogie Touchwood, a character appearing in the same novel as one who "with the best intentions in the world, chose to have everything in his own way; and, like most petty politicians, was disposed to throw intrigue and mystery over matters which had much better be prosecuted boldly and openly" (*SRW,* 401), Captain MacTurk might be said to caricature Scott in his role as a narrator. For the narrator is always a double agent in these novels, at once evoking and dissipating illusion, ignorance, mystery, crime, and evil. The domestic circle that is usually the final destination of his characters may be the unexceptionable locus of "real history" (*Wa,* 371), but the narrator admits that a situation so comfortable "is, of course, utterly uninteresting," since interest depends upon "uncertainty and misfortune" (*GM,* 130). The wild romance of the past that Scott displays as a realm of experience inferior to the destiny slowly built through the ages and conclusively achieved by his audience nevertheless is the native realm of heroic passion and as such is the object of nostalgia – the only kind of passion available to civilized moderns. The result is that the beliefs the narrator chides and dismisses, on the one hand, are those to which he lends dramatic support, on the other. There is a continual vacillation between a commitment to modernity and all that it entails and an attraction to the past and all that belongs to it. There seems to be an air of guilt about this attraction, but then nostalgia is generally a guilty passion, as desire is deflected from the dangers of fulfillment in the present world by an attachment to the lost past. Actually, then, it would not be going too far to say that Scott's writing is no less prurient in its vivid descriptions of historical disorder than it is in its more patently sexual manipulation of Catherine Glover, the Fair Maid of Perth, after she has fainted on her lover's doorstep:

> As she withdrew not her hand from her lover's hold or from his grasp, we must in charity believe that the return to consciousness was not so complete as to make her aware that he abused the advantage, by pressing it alternately to his lips and

his bosom. At the same time we are compelled to own that
the blood was colouring in her cheek, and that her breathing
was deep and regular, for a minute or two during this relapse.
(*FMP,* 226)

Just as a woman is thus compelled by the narrator to agree to her
own abuse, so does that narrator try to lock his readers within the
delusions of immature eras of history even as he speaks of regret-
ting the imprisonment of his characters within those times. He makes
the disorder of the past so appealing that it overwhelms the ordered
vision of the present with which he claims to be viewing it. This
duplicity is the narrator's representational policy; it is the method
of all the Waverley novels; it is, for better or for worse, the entertainment offered by these novels. The distance at which Scott seems
to stand from the past in his role as a narrator does not secure his
narratives from the blindness – and violence – of history as it is
lived by his characters.

"Distance, in truth," Scott writes in *Waverley,*

> produces in idea the same effect as in real perspective. Objects
> are softened, and rounded, and rendered doubly graceful; the
> harsher and more ordinary points of character are mellowed
> down, and those by which it is remembered are the more
> striking outlines that mark sublimity, grace, and beauty. (*Wa,*
> 187)

This kind of observation upon the gentling effect of time is a commonplace of both eighteenth- and nineteenth-century literature and
is closely associated with the characterization of writing as a tran-
quilizer that extends from Aristotle to Addison's description of literary terror as "a dead Monster"[9] and to the reflections that Scott
himself makes through the person of Darsie Latimer in *Redgauntlet:*

> A thousand vague fears, wild expectations, and indigested
> schemes, hurry through one's thoughts in seasons of doubt
> and of danger. But by arresting them as they flit across the
> mind, by throwing them on paper, and even by that mechan-
> ical art compelling ourselves to consider them with scrupu-
> lous and minute attention, we may perhaps escape becoming
> the dupes of our own excited imagination.

Perspective, memory, and writing all serve to tame sensations and events; they are all civilizing tools that withdraw one from the dangers of immediacy as they withdraw one from action; they are supposed to put an end to disorder; and yet Scott can maintain an interest in the history to which he applies these tools only by seeking to excite in the reader an appetite for the very dangers they are designed to eliminate. From such a blatant contradiction great confusion must inevitably result, even if that confusion often goes unnoticed because the readers of Scott's work side wholeheartedly with the viewpoint of the moderns or the excitement of the past – or some balance of the two – while failing to see how Scott demonstrates that these two positions are completely unreconcilable. Scott does show history moving forward, but he shows that it does so – like his narratives – only by means of violence, disruption, and irreparable loss.

This conflict within Scott's narratives is not, however, one peculiar to him as an individual. It is not a matter of psychological ambivalence, at least not in the common acceptance of that term, and it is not accurately described by the supposed conflict between Scott the Rationalist and Scott the Romantic that has been argued so extensively from his day to our own. It is rather the appearance in the design of Scott's narratives of a conflict between aristocratic and bourgeois inclinations that leads to the uncertainty of all the borderlines in his fiction. It is this tension between two great social orders of value – a tension certainly very prominent in Scott's time, as England moved forward into its era of Reform – that explains why the very elements that make his writing interesting also tend to lead it to moments of actual incoherence.[10]

One must see, for instance, that no matter how dreary the humor may be in the pseudonymous trappings Scott gave to his works before formally acknowledging their authorship in 1827, it is not incidental to those narratives that the "Chronicles of the Canongate" should picture the writer as an aristocrat who exhausted his patrimony in his careless youth and who has since seen the estate that used to be his taken over by a businessman, vulgarized, and lost again; or that Peter Pattieson, the narrator of *The Bride of Lammermoor,* should attribute his disinclination to public recognition to a desire not "to make sport for the Philistine lords and ladies" who have their place as he has his (*BL,* 2); or, to give a final example from among many more, that the "Marquis de Hautlieu" should be invoked with admiration in the Introduction to the first edition of *Quentin Durward*. Even in such "light" moments, Scott's imagination is immediately drawn into dark considerations of rank and its derogation. His claim that the astigmatism of "those who argue for party's sake" is overcome in his writing, which "will please neither Whig nor Tory" (*Wo,* 129), is really beside the point; for it is not the differences of party but those of blood that capture the imagination of his novels, though he would pretend otherwise. The rift in his mode of narration that leads to so many confusions within the novels stems from the divisions in his commitment to the emerging middle-class world of Victorian England and to the basically aristocratic world of the recent past. In his historical novels, in other words, one sees Scott's view of the history of his own time.

The aristocratic values toward which Scott's writings lean are primarily those of humanistic intellectuality, unthought bravery, and personal loyalty. The first quality is seen, for instance, when Quentin Durward makes a vow and the narrator comments that "its purpose being sincere, we can scarce suppose it unacceptable to the only true Deity, who regards the motives and not the forms of prayer" (*QD,* 199). The assurance thus given has little to do with modern approaches to ecumenicism. Rather, just as classical mythology and legend were reverently plundered by Renaissance humanists who believed that they could be made to agree with, support, or prefigure Christian truth, and just as this attitude toward the past was rationalized by the philosophers of the eighteenth century into an eclectic tolerance of different religions, so is unenlightened devotion here absorbed within the true spirit of religion. And following this attitude, all of the earlier conditions of which Scott tells, whether they be those of seventeenth-century Scotland or of fourth-century Constantinople or of any other time or place, are treated in the same way. Although the different ages are presumed to possess different manners and degrees of enlightenment, the problems, beliefs, and emotions ascribed to them are always parallel to those of all other times. As Avrom Fleishman has written, Scott's novels are moved by "polarities not only of the time but of all periods of transition."[11] History is taken up whole within the syncretic grasp of Scott's borderline between less- and more-advanced nations, and all consciousness of historical differences is strictly limited by the belief that all ages are fundamentally the same both in the passions by which they are moved and in the demands made upon those passions. The approval of unthinking bravery arises in conjunction with this humanistic attitude because there is no sense in Scott's novels that one could ever honorably differ from the notions of honor current at any particular time, however vicious or misguided they may be. The same kinds of rules always apply, even if those rules differ in the particulars; there may be different codes of honor, but honor must be obeyed without hesitation. A Flemish weaver, therefore, may save through legal trickery a noble castle that otherwise would be lost *(The Betrothed);* but he is pictured as a vulgar commoner because he employs such means in place of armed force. Similarly, Catherine Glover is made to learn that "men rarely advance in civilization or refinement beyond the ideas of their own age" so that she will appreciate the "exuberant courage" of her suitor, the blacksmith, over the more sensitive but also more hesitant attitude of the young Highland chieftain who also loved her (*FMP,* 434). (The situation thus described is a rare one in Scott's novels, since a commoner triumphs over a nobleman; but the smith eventually is offered a knighthood, and thus the affirmation of aristocratic rank that concludes almost all of Scott's novels is restored.) And following the same rule, loyalty is valued in all times, no matter who or what one may be loyal to. In these novels the violation of one's word is always held to be a more heinous crime than the execution of that pledge, however immoral it may be. Thieves' honor, it seems, is aristocrats' honor; and thus even thieves are accorded some respect on this basis, as in *The Fortunes of Nigel.* It is this aristocratic side to Scott's writing that Mario Praz missed when he described the bourgeois aspect of Scott's work, and he missed it because he ignored the structural constants and confusions in this work in favor of an emphasis upon Scott's descriptions of customs, habits, and intimate scenes.[12]

On the other hand, the bourgeois values toward which these writings lean are those of professionalism, industry, and law. Although these values are not logically opposed to the comparable aristocratic values – the demand for law, for instance, would not seem necessarily to contradict the demand for loyalty – they do prove to be opposed in their practice. Rather than taming violence, the written word of law is shown to deaden the living voice of honor even as the *Phaedrus* warned that writing would damage the truth of dialectic. The need for stability, regularity, and repetitious labor associated with industry conflicts with the spontaneity and variety demanded by the aristocratic life of adventure and bravery. The discipline and economics of middle-class professionalism similarly fail to agree with the aristocratic taste for disinterested and generalized humanistic talents.

Less space need be expended in describing middle-class values because, Praz and Lukács to the contrary, Scott places so little emphasis upon them in comparison to the attention he lavishes upon the more "foreign" or "ancient" values of the aristocracy. As has been noted, the middle class is more an assumption than a dramatic reality in his work, which is preoccupied with the aristocratic values of the past; and yet this assumption of modern values displayed so unremarkably must be an object of distaste to those who follow the anachronistic interest of these novels – if that interest itself is not to be distasteful. The result is not a final choice of one side or the other but rather a continual vacillation of the narrative – and, presumably, of its ideal reader – between the two kinds of values. The result, in other words, is a confusion between enlightenment and the darkness of ignorance: a blind road.[13]

The duplicitous style of Scott's writing, then, is more significantly representative of a social than of an individual confusion, and yet it is not a commonly defined social reality that is represented. It is not, for example, strictly comparable to the conflict between Loyalists and Jacobites in Scott's portrayals of these types, for upholders of aristocratic values can be found on both sides of their struggle, just as Waverley's allegiance is torn between the two sides. The conflict is better typified by that between Waverley and Flora MacIvor, the Highland lass whom he cannot reach because her devotion to one side of the conflict is single-minded. They must part, just as the lines of Scott's narrative must part into irreconcilable versions of order, each of which is destructive of the other. To be sure, the passage of history in these novels is always a passage toward modern middle-class values; the death of romance is always announced;[14] and yet the aristocratic figures of romance always reappear, no matter how distant or close the age to which Scott refers, as if in aggression against the very audience that he claims to be humbly soliciting.

There are, then, four major ways in which Scott's novels fail to maintain their own borderlines. These boundaries are weakened by elements that travel freely across them; by the transformation of human identity into a nightmarish impersonality; by contradictions between narrative statements and dramatic situations; and, most generally, by this conflict within the very process of drawing borderlines, which is never successfully terminated and which ultimately is attributable to the contradictions between aristocratic and bourgeois values. The reader should not be surprised, then, at other disharmonies in Scott's writing, as when that same approval extended in his novels to a great number of poets both minor and major (not excluding himself) is also extended to "Rochefoucault, who has torn the veil from so many foul gangrenes of the human heart" (*HM*, 117), through imitation as well as through more open flattery: "There is, perhaps, no time at which we are disposed to think so highly of a friend as when we find him standing higher than we expected in the esteem of others" (*HM*, 438). Nor should it be surprising that the criticism consistently given to gambling in these novels should, at least once, be extended to the business habits that otherwise are presented as being diametrically opposed to those of gambling: "Trade has all the fascination of gambling without its moral guilt" (*RR*, 4). The young woman whose life, like those of so many other heroines in these novels, is said to be divided between "frankness and mystery" (*RR*, 153) might well be understood to be part of this larger pattern of duplicity, as might the mock advertisement for the "editor's" services as a language teacher that follows *The Heart of Midlothian*'s pious conclusion. And Scott's admission that he used characters in the original introductions to his novels as "the means of communicating his own sentiments to the public" (*Ab*, xii) will not seem so very reassuring, since the dualities that seem to organize these novels are so duplicitous and so unsettling to the reader's understanding of Scott's sentiments. There is, finally, only one borderline that remains secure throughout Scott's writing: the line between the aristocratic hero, passionate and doomed, and those common readers who have given over strong emotions to the entertainment of books so that they may live reasonably, triumphing over their erstwhile superiors through nostalgia, the middle-class passion: the superior form of condescension.

8

SUPERSTITION AND THE
ENCHANTED READER

∾

I am, I own, no great believer in the moral utility to
be derived from fictitious compositions; yet, if in any
case a word spoken in season may be of advantage
to a young person, it must surely be when it calls
upon him to attend to the voice of principle and self-
denial, instead of that of precipitate passion.
   – SIR WALTER SCOTT, *The Fortunes of Nigel*

SUPERSTITION IS A MAJOR ELEMENT in almost
all of the Waverley novels and would merit attention if only
for that reason.[1] Its significance, however, goes beyond the
fact that it is a characteristic topic in Scott's fiction as well as in
other works loosely grouped under the title of Romanticism, such
as "the Rime of the Ancient Mariner." For the attitude Scott takes
toward superstition is a contradictory one, at once rational and superstitiously irrational in its own right; and this contradiction is
repeated in the attitudes he takes toward the past, women, class
differences, and the reader. By analyzing the appearance of superstition in Scott's work, in fact, one may come to a new reading of
that work that not only helps to restate its importance in literary
history but that also helps to show how the contradictions within
it are essential to its masterly style.

Superstition would be an entirely uncomplicated topic in Scott's
novels if the rational notice taken of it were allowed to pass un-
challenged. The following reference to an incident at the Tower of
Ravenswood is representative of such comment:

> The peasant who shows the ruins of the tower, which still
> crown the beetling cliff and behold the war of the waves,
> though no more tenanted save by the sea-mew and cormo-
> rant, even yet affirms that on this fatal night the Master of

Ravenswood, by the bitter exclamations of his despair, evoked some wild fiend, under whose malignant influence the future tissue of incidents was woven. Alas! what fiend can suggest more desperate counsels than those adopted under the guidance of our own violent and unresisted passions? (*BL*, 22)

Throughout Scott's fiction, passages like this one draw a didactic line between the interest one may legitimately take in dramatic or marvelous events and the disgust one must feel at the surrender of self-control. For this is what the supernatural is in Scott's novels: a realm primarily distinguished from that of ordinary events by the fact that it strips individuals of power over themselves. It transforms individuals from responsible masters of themselves into irresponsible servants of forces foreign to their understanding. Though generally associated with sublime scenery, characters of heroic dimensions, and intensely dramatic situations, the realm to which man is tempted by superstition is one of submissiveness. Whether the particular superstition be directed to religious, political, familial, or individual concerns, belief in it always involves a surrender of rational control that makes one, in Scott's moral judgment, childish.

A method Enlightenment skeptics used to discredit traditional authority – the psychologizing of the supernatural – is therefore used in such passages as a tool to enforce moral orthodoxy. These passages are, as it were, moments of chastisement. They inform the reader that the individual is indeed responsible for his actions and responsible in all situations, no matter how fantastic, extreme, or literary. In this case, Ravenswood's father has just been buried and his estate expropriated; but Ravenswood still has no more excuse than does the unfortunate Janet Dalrymple, whose mother's supposed witchcraft "consisted only in the ascendency of a powerful mind over a weak and melancholy one," as "it is needless to point out to the intelligent reader" (*BL*, xvii).

Superstition is also checked in these novels through attributions of its origin to the lower classes, to Faustian seekers of wisdom, and to the immaturity of the past in general; but these sources are still made to fall under the rule of psychology, which is assumed to reign over the moral affairs of the nineteenth century just as firmly and conclusively as law reigns over its social affairs and a rather latitudinarian Protestantism over its spiritual concerns. Superstition will be allowed to be interesting to Scott and to his readers because it is so often associated with dramatic, legendary, or historical events, the propensity of unenlightened mankind having been to prefer fantastic explanations to those that are rational; but the fact that it is so common does not mitigate its error. History – even history overtly manipulated to suit the requirements of romance – must be detached from the ideas of prescience and occult influence.

It is true that these ideas are not always directly opposed to rationality in Scott's novels, for they may darkly figure the judgments of reason, as in Coleridge's "Destiny of Nations." This is the case, for instance, when Lord Mentieth says that Allan M'Aulay "persuades himself that the predictions which are in reality the result of judgment and reflection are supernatural impressions on his mind, just as fanatics conceive the workings of their own imagination to be divine inspiration" (*LM,* 195). This is also the case when Scott interprets the Puritan search for divine inspiration, psychologizing it even as he claims to refrain from "entering into an abstruse point of theology":

> One thing is plain; namely, that the person who lays open his doubts and distresses in prayer, with feeling and sincerity, must necessarily, in the act of doing so, purify his mind from the dross of worldly passions and interests, and bring it into that state when the resolutions adopted are likely to be selected rather from a sense of duty than from any inferior motive. (*HM,* 146)

Despite this relationship to reason, however, these superstitions are definitely opposed to the development of the individual as a mature and responsible agent in society. All extremes, including those of reason, are rejected in these novels, because they tend to become independent of those balanced judgments which are the only kind Scott allows to be true. Even superstition, then, while generally intolerable, may be granted a limited virtue by way of balance:

> It seems that human nature, when its original habits are cultivated and attended to, possesses on similar occasions, something of that prescient foreboding which announces the approaching tempest to the inferior ranks of creation. The cultivation of our intellectual powers goes perhaps too far when

it teaches us entirely to suppress and disregard those natural
feelings which were originally designed as sentinels by which
nature warned us of impending danger. (*RR*, 286)

Psychology is so conclusive that in this passage it can even afford
to grant a measure of reality to the opponent it generally forces into
complete nonexistence. It can be so generous because it can explain
away all the power that superstitions wield over men – and yet this
very explanation becomes the source of further superstition.

For every comment in these novels that portrays the supernatural
as a projection of psychological processes upon the physical world,
a simple confusion of the exterior and the interior, there is an event
that dramatically confirms superstitious beliefs and so contradicts
such narrative deliberations. It is in this contradiction that the use
of the supernatural in Scott's novels differs from the use Radcliffe
made of it. Thus, a Highland seer who predicts the death of an
English colonel in battle and a chieftain who claims to have seen a
vision that tells of his own imminent captivity are both borne out
by events (*Waverley*); a horoscope drawn up as a playful exercise
proves to be in accord with a wild gypsy's prophecies, and these
prophecies come true to the last detail (*Guy Mannering*); a young
man follows a prophecy of Thomas the Rhymer by dying in quick-
sand after the woman he loves stabs her husband on their wedding
night, goes crazy, and dies (*The Bride of Lammermoor*); the corpse of
a man issues blood in the presence of his murderer just as it is expected to in the superstitious ceremony of the bier right, and in the
same novel the legend that a boy who was suckled by a doe would
grow up to be a coward and lead his Highland clan to destruction
is perfectly fulfilled (*The Fair Maid of Perth*); a girl persuaded to stay
in a chamber that is said to be haunted by a family spirit sees that
ghost and finds her life fitting its predictions (*The Betrothed*); horse-
shoe-shaped stigmata and a tendency to be involved in losing causes
are handed down, as prophesied, to the descendants of a man who
had accidentally killed his own son (*Redgauntlet*); the exiled Queen
Margaret tosses a black feather and a red rose to the wind that re-
turns the rose to her attendant, thus foretelling the future return of
the House of Lancaster over that of York (*Anne of Geierstein*); and
so on. No matter how often Scott allows comments within his
narratives that explain supernatural affairs as some sort of psychological misapprehension or the result of deliberate trickery (as in

some episodes of *Woodstock, The Antiquary, Rob Roy,* and *The Pirate*), he just as often directs the plots of his novels so as to fit them to superstitious predictions.

If one does not ignore it – as most critics do – or dismiss it as a sign that Scott "was cheerfully inconsistent in his position as omniscient author,"[2] the contradiction is so blatant as to seem cynical. Positions advanced thematically are undercut dramatically; the discovery of psychology is announced even as the evidence of superstition is shown to be beyond its power; the assurance given with one hand is taken away with the other. And yet this device only seems cynical because it is, finally, just as artless as it is methodical.

Scott subjects his psychological explanations to the exploitation of his plots because the interest of his fiction demands such double-dealing. Institutionalized law, the domestic life, responsible professional activity, a tolerant but pious religiosity, middle-class values in general: All these aspects of that life of reason which is taken to be definitive of the nineteenth century are most certainly considered to be superior to the features that defined earlier times. No man in his right mind would wish to exchange the mature present for the childish past, commercial progress for feudal tradition, enlightenment for ignorant delusion; and yet the violence, the romantic intrigue, the chivalrous relations, the rude but intense religious beliefs, and the aristocratic values that characterized the life of superstition are interesting. In seeing ignorant delusion as a source of poetical imagination, Scott follows the tradition represented by Richard Hurd's *Letters on Chivalry and Romance,* Thomas Weston's *History of English Poetry,* Vico's *New Science,* Rousseau's *Essay on the Origin of Language,* and the writings of Herder. As Scott notes, "Superstition, when not arrayed in her full horrors, but laying a gentle hand only on her suppliant's head, had charms which we fail not to regret, even in those stages of society from which her influence is well-nigh banished by the light of reason and general education" (*P,* 219). Superstition is so interesting, in fact, and in this character so vital to the appeal of literature, that it is not necessary that the marvelous conditions of its appearance be persuasively evoked through some sort of powerfully affective description or rhetoric. It is only necessary that the marvelous be *named,* and named by this device which restores to a narrative in a purely formal way what had been taken from it through reason.

It is this interest that is artless, beyond the explanations of Scott's reason. According to these novels, an interest in superstition can only imply a state of immaturity in which human agency is surrendered to the powers of fate and, by association, the rational progress of the middle classes submitted to the arbitrary power of aristocracy. But although Scott's reason can make this diagnosis, it cannot provide either the etiology or the cure for this fascination. For this immaturity is not of the past but of the present; it is what is thought to give literature its enchanting, captivating, bewildering influence; and it is a topic treated in all of Scott's novels, especially in the characters of their heroes. Although the adventures of these heroes are almost always directed to a definite end, which involves a change in their status from that of untested youths to that of mature and married men, these adventures do not so much resemble *rites de passage* as they do a repetitive, unprogressive, apparently interminable meditation upon the intertwined natures of mastery and submission.

Scott's male protagonists are much more fully individualized than is sometimes admitted, but they do come in two basic varieties. One kind, represented by characters such as Ivanhoe, Quentin Durward, and Hereward in *Count Robert of Paris,* is the stalwart but unimaginative youth with the weakness of the good soldier: a passionate and naive temper. Though they do prove themselves as men through their loyalty, devotion, and combat, these protagonists are as children in matters of authority and superstition, and this side of their nature never changes. The significance of their credulousness becomes clear when one considers the second kind of protagonist, represented by characters such as Waverley and *Redgauntlet's* Darsie Latimer, who are just as brave when conditions call upon them to be so but who are less impetuous, more intelligent, and therefore more sensitive to the childishness they enjoy in common with the other kind of hero. Whereas captivity, frustration, and bewilderment generally appear to the first kind of hero as nothing but obstacles of greater or lesser difficulty, they are more likely to appear to the second kind as symbols that bespeak immaturity. Nigel Olifaunt, for instance, notices that he has been "a thing never acting but perpetually acted upon" (*FN,* 263), and Darsie Latimer complains that those who are holding him in confinement treat him "as they would do a spoiled child" (*R,* 188). These latter characters, in other words, are at least partially aware of a truth that the first kind of hero never even guesses: that all the contests in Scott's novels are contests against the mastery of enchantment. It is this aspect of Scott's novels that Alexander Welsh has described as involving "the perverse pleasure of being acted upon."[3] Good and evil, rich and poor, Christian and pagan, Whig and Tory, old and new: Whatever the divisions of a conflict or trial may be, they always involve this division of consciousness between sober control and an anachronistic, tortuous, perversely fascinating state of submissiveness. The narrative style that Scott claims as that of "a humble English postchaise, drawn upon four wheels, and keeping his Majesty's highway" (*Wa*, 30) only maintains that character at the price of a guilty and even morbid sense of oppression.

Because he is one of the most petulant and ineffective and awkward of Scott's protagonists. Roland Graeme represents the situation common to them all in the most vivid terms. As he protests to his mother, who has just revealed herself as the witch to whom he was led by a girl whom he has not yet discovered to be a boy,

> "I have been treated amongst you – even by yourself, my revered parent, as well as by others – as one who lacked the common attributes of free-will and human reason, or was at least deemed unfit to exercise them. A land of enchantment have I been led into, and spells have been cast around me – every one has met me in disguise – every one has spoken to me in parables. I have been like one who walks in a weary and bewildering dream; and now you blame me that I have not the sense, and judgment, and steadiness of a waking, and a disenchanted, and a reasonable man, who knows what he is doing, and wherefore he does it." (*Ab*, 296–7)

"Enchantment" is a word Scott often uses to name the effect of literature upon men as well as the effect that may be produced by superstition, women, and the glamor of the aristocracy; and the enchantment that leads his protagonists into confusion and distress is entirely parallel to that which he expects to exert through his narratives. The reader of Scott's romances faces the same problems of deciphering their treacheries, dangers, and spells that the characters within those romances face. Not only is there the duplicitous matter of superstitious plots to be considered, but also equivocations in description – "the apparition, whether it was real or whether it was the creation of a heated and agitated imagination" (*BL*, 218)

– and analyses that are not only equivocal but that also confuse the very distinction between the internal and the external presupposed by Scott's psychology: "All that could be collected from her conversation seemed to imply that she was under the influence either of a spell or of a vow – there was no saying which, since she talked as one who acted under a powerful and external agency" (*Ab,* 17). The fact that so many of Scott's dramatic mysteries are easily penetrated by the reader – the identity of Richard the Lion-Hearted in *Ivanhoe,* for example, or the difference between Catherine Seyton and her twin brother in *The Abbot* – is no more destructive of their enchantment than is the mechanical way in which Scott turns his plots to contradict his reason. The enchantment is not in the style with which the ends of the narrative are dissimulated or its secrets hidden any more than the interest of the scenes of bewilderment within the novels lies in the actual mechanics by which they are developed and escaped. Scott is not a creator of puzzles but rather a commentator upon the puzzling nature of desire. When he personifies superstition, he writes of "that state of excited terror which she fears and yet loves" (*An,* 233); and one can see how Poe could be interested in his work. In the case of Scott's readers as in that of his heroes, it is the admission of enchantment that is significant, not the literary formalities – disguises, switches in identity, sublime vistas, misdirected messages – that are used to name this fascination.

For the reader, making this admission entails nothing more than showing a willingness to read to the end of one adventure and then, perhaps, to start another and then another of these novels. The significance of this willingness, however, is another question. For to make such an admission of enchantment, whether one is a hero or simply a reader, is to admit a desire for subjection – for that very condition of childishness which Roland Graeme so laments. Like the heroes in Spenser and in medieval romances, the hero of Scott's novels must always face further enchantments, at least until he settles down as *paterfamilias* in the last chapter; and the reader who continues to read must know that only further surrender to the narrative is possible. The enchanted reader must feel the similarity between the narrative and those tales of murder read by Nigel Olifaunt, which, "strange and shocking as they were to human feeling, possessed yet the interest of sorcery or of fascination, which rivets the attention by its awakening horrors" (*FN,* 287). Scott treats the enchantments of literature exactly as he does those of superstition, criticizing their unreality within the very novels that resuscitate and give even greater life to that unreality. He does, however, give sufficient warning of his double-dealing through the many examples he presents of those who are led by a fondness for romances into the discovery that the enchantment of literature is not a phenomenon over which the reader has control, since the very existence of this enchantment signals the loss of distance, reason, veracity, and the power of responsibility.

The case of Lucy Ashton is typical in this regard, although untypically female and thus leading to death rather than to wedded bliss (just as Amy Robsart's similar indulgence in romantic fantasies leads to her similarly unfortunate end in *Kenilworth*). Having been accustomed to "identify herself with the situation of those legendary heroines with whose adventures, for want of better reading, her memory had become stocked," Lucy finds that "the fairy wand, with which in her solitude she had delighted to raise visions of enchantment, became now the rod of a magician . . . serving only to invoke specters at which the exorcist trembled" (*BL,* 276). She is thus like Waverley, who finds his taste for romance turning to disgust in the course of his adventures, except that she is a young woman and therefore must suffer the punishment reserved for women who admit a willingness to surrender themselves.

Some male characters, such as Darsie Latimer and Quentin Durward, take romances as the patterns for their lives and are entirely successful in their imitations – and Waverley at least survives, becomes wealthy, and is married – but Lucy's unhappy story is still relevant to their fate, and relevant even in its peculiarly female conditions. For as it is described by Scott, the childish nature of superstitious and literary enchantment is also a female nature, both in the figure of the oppressor and in the figure of the oppressed – the victim of enchantment, who is drawn to yield to his situation of distress with all the shame, guilt, morbidity, and secret pleasure with which women have traditionally been thought to yield to rape. And it is according to this same pattern that middle-class values are drawn to yield to aristocratic values in Scott's work.

One of the most remarkable examples of this pattern in which Scott's rational psychology yields to perverse forms of persuasion occurs in *Redgauntlet*. Having been kidnapped by a man whom he does not yet know to be his uncle, Darsie Latimer is forced to ride with this captor and is forced to disguise himself in female clothing, including a mask that appears to be velvet but is actually a steel helmet locked around his head. Thus attired, he is permitted during the journey to converse with a girl he had heretofore admired only from afar; but he finds himself confused:

> It was in vain that, in order to avail himself of a situation so favourable for indulging his romantic disposition, he endeavoured to coax back, if I may so express myself, that delightful dream of tender and ardent passion; he felt only such a confusion of ideas at the difference between the being whom he had imagined and her with whom he was now in contact, that it seemed to him like the effect of witchcraft. What most surprised him was, that this sudden flame should have died away so rapidly, notwithstanding that the maiden's personal beauty was even greater than he had expected, her demeanour, unless it should be deemed over kind towards himself, as graceful and becoming as he could have fancied it, even in his gayest dreams. (*R*, 336–7)

Scott goes on to suggest that the reason for Darsie's lack of interest may be that "the lover's pleasure, like that of the hunter, is in the chase" and then further digresses from this rather un-Victorian argument into a more respectable plea that marriages based on reason should not be slighted in favor of those based on passion. These comments, however, turn out to be a smokescreen for the revelation that this girl is Darsie's sister. The witchcraft Darsie experiences is that of incest; it would be scandalous for Scott to allow his desire to continue at such close range; and yet this sexual taboo does not explain why Darsie should be forced to experience the change mandated for his feelings while he is locked into the appearance of a woman. One must either ignore this incident, discuss it as a *bizarrerie*, or, if one wants to understand it, analyze it as a highly condensed version of the drama of sexual differences played out in all of the Waverley novels. Seen at a distance, as all attractive women must be seen in Scott's code of chivalry, a girl may arouse one's passion; but one can approach her more closely only by involuntarily becoming a woman oneself and by accepting the other woman as a sister. In other words, this scene shows in an extraordinary and yet entirely typical way Scott's attitude toward marriage as opposed to romantic passion and toward the present in general as opposed to the distance of the past. According to these novels, the civilizing process demands the enchanted imprisonment, infantilization, and feminization of men. This does not mean, however, that Scott sees more room for passion in the past than there is in the present; for all the ordeals his protagonists undergo are civilizing ordeals. No matter what era of history these ordeals may appear in, they are lessons in inhibition. Since the difference delineated in all these novels between the immediacy of the present and the distance of the past is continually swept forward through history by the progress of time, it is simply a device to enchant the reader into a willingness to endure – and even to desire – frustration.

According to the usual critical discussion of Scott, romantic passion and civilized reason are the two great conflicting forces in his work. One of these forces is usually described as finally dominating the other, although some critics do argue that a compromise of some sort is reached between the two.[4] The argument was already articulated in his own day, with one view holding Scott to be a man infatuated with the past while the other held him to be a rationalist, albeit one who found his reason a rather pale thing in comparison to the vivid excitements of history. These are still the terms in which critical discussion is commonly carried out, and yet they are misleading. These two terms are elements in a single formulation dramatized throughout Scott's work: the argument that one needs to learn prudence by accepting humiliation at the hands of others. "Reason" and "romance" really are peripheral to the power of this argument, which dominates all the adventures in Scott's novels and determines not only the structure of their plots but also the way in which the relationships of past to present, women to men, aristocrats to commoners, and author to readers are imagined within that structure. Scott's novels do indeed let us hear "the voice of principle and self-denial," but this voice cannot be found within oneself unless one submits to the voice represented by superstition. The rational mastery that seems so secure in Scott's psychology can be won only through enchantment. Self-denial can be achieved only through a submission to others that must be a humiliating and childlike experience because it cannot be reasonable.

This argument not only explains the aforementioned scene in *Redgauntlet* but also a number of otherwise inexplicable and generally unexamined dramas, such as the one involving Ursel in *Count Robert of Paris*. Having been a competitor for the Byzantine throne held by Alexius Comnenius in this novel, Ursel has disappeared and is thought by some to be dead. Near the end of the novel, however, a different fate is revealed. It seems that Ursel, having been seized by Comnenius, was subjected to a phony operation designed to make him believe that he had been blinded. Since he was subsequently imprisoned in a dark dungeon, he did think that he was blind. He became so accustomed to the darkness, in fact, that when he is released at the end of the novel and allowed to overlook the city, he shrieks because the spires of its buildings seem to leap into his eyes. Showing an odd mixture of irritability and submissiveness, he then fulfills the condition under which the Emperor released him. He uses his popularity with the people to support that very man who had imprisoned and tortured him, and then he retires to a monastery. And as strange as it may appear even in the work of a writer who could end one novel (*The Surgeon's Daughter*) with the villain stomped to death by an elephant, the pattern of this peculiar drama – humiliation and the extortion of one's consent for that humiliation – is that of Scott's writing in general.

Another example of this pattern, perhaps an even more remarkable one, occurs in *Ivanhoe*. Already humiliated because he is lying injured and captive inside a castle that is being attacked by those seeking to release its prisoners, Ivanhoe is forced further to endure the triple indignity of allowing others to fight in his defense, of relying upon Rebecca to learn the progress of the battle that she observes through a window, and of listening to the preachments against violence and the vanity of honor that Rebecca adds to those reports. Thus tortured, thus set at such a great distance from the action of the story as almost to be in the position of a reader who vicariously submits to its thrills – an invalid reader, say, who hallucinates his health and glorious power[5] – Ivanhoe lashes out at Rebecca as one who is made hopelessly ignorant by her religion and sex:

> "Rebecca," he replied, "Thou knowest not how impossible it is for one trained to actions of chivalry to remain passive as a priest, or a woman, when they are acting deeds of honor around him. The law of battle is the food upon which we live

— the dust of the *melee* is the breath of our nostrils! We live not — we wish not to live — longer than while we are victorious and renowned. Such, maiden, are the laws of chivalry to which we are sworn, and to which we offer all that we hold dear." (*I, 275*)

Ivanhoe's statement is notably at odds with Scott's descriptions of the civilizing functions played by chivalry at its best, and it is in accord with the sanguinary brutality he identified with the worst aspects of this code of manners. This fact is of interest not only because it allows the notation that the best and worst aspects of chivalry are not separated in these novels by the borderline of individual character, but also because it shows Ivanhoe's appeal to the demands of chivalry to be superstitiously abject and irrational. Even more interesting, then, is that warfare should be defined through its difference from women (as well as through its difference from priests, who are practically identical to women in this context). The notion of female passivity as a contrast to and occasional threat against male activity is common enough throughout these novels, as in the history of literature generally, where it is sanctioned by misogynistic interpretations of dramas such as those involving Adam and Eve, Samson and Delilah, or Caesar and Cleopatra. Its articulation here is remarkable, however, because it occurs with the utmost formality and vehemence at just that point when the hero is unmanned and bound in the swaddling clouts of sickness, oppression, dependence, and — as he considers the faith of his nurse — superstition. Furthermore, he owes his life to the care this woman gave him when he was injured, and he owes the renown he gained in a tournament before his injury to the armor she procured for him. Given this background, his animadversion against womanliness can only be an outburst against himself, especially since he can only deny his present condition of passivity by pleading his devotion to another source of female oppression: chivalry itself, with its central allegiance to the commands of women.

"In all civilised society," writes Scott in *The Fortunes of Nigel,* "the females of distinguished rank and beauty give the tone to manners and, through them, to morals" (*FN,* 155). A similar passage occurs in *Peveril of the Peak,* where he writes about "that noble tone of feeling towards the sex which, considered as a spur to 'raise the clear spirit,' is superior to every other impulse save those of religion and patriotism" (*PP*, 38). And, indeed, the prevailing attitude throughout the Waverley novels is that it is only in the most barbarous societies that women are not so placed as to be reverenced by and thus given command over men. The peculiarity in Scott's use of this doctrine, which became the standard middle-class attitude in the Victorian period, is that his women are completely bewildering in their commands. When Anne of Geierstein appears and disappears from Arthur Philipson's presence, giving him unexplained orders and forcing him to endure the humiliation of having his life saved by her several times, she is not only similar to Rebecca in *Ivanhoe* but is also entirely typical of Scott's women in general. Their rule appears in his novels to be arbitrary and unpredictable, and it is in just this fashion that the attitude toward women enjoined by chivalry is described:

> But it was peculiar to the time of chivalry, that in his wildest rapture the knight imagined of no attempt to follow or to trace the object of such romantic attachment; that he thought of her as of a deity, who, having deigned to show herself for an instant to her devoted worshipper, had again returned to the darkness of her sanctuary, or as an influential planet, which, having darted in some auspicious minute one favourable ray, wrapped itself again in its veil of mist. The motions of the lady of his love were to him those of a superior being, who was to move without watch or control, rejoice him by her appearance or drive him to despair by her cruelty. (*I*, 50–1)

The situation thus described prevails even in those novels set in more modern times, though it is more directly dramatized in some than in others. One novel, albeit a brief one, is devoted in its entirety to the story of a fanatical mother who destroys her son by the tricks she uses to make him live up to her anachronistic notions of honor (*The Highland Widow*); and, for all their differences, such figures as Flora MacIvor in *Waverley*, Meg Merrilies in *Guy Mannering*, Madge Wildfire and her mother in *The Heart of Midlothian*, Norna in *The Pirate*, Queen Elizabeth in *Kenilworth*, Ulrica Wolfganger in *Ivanhoe*, Lady Ashton in *The Bride of Lammermoor*, the Countess of Derby in *Peveril of the Peak*, the titular heroine of *Anne of Geierstein*, Magdalen Graeme in *The Abbot*, and Adela Montreville in *The Surgeon's Daughter* are alike in the oppressive and humiliating force they exert upon the men around them.

The contradictory attitude Scott's writing assumes toward superstition is directly related to this double character it assigns to women, proclaiming them both objects of veneration and sources of oppression. As they act through this double character to reduce men to impotent passivity even as they demand that men be heroically active, women govern the adventures of Scott's male protagonists. It is easy to understand, then, why superstitious beliefs should be described in these novels not only as psychological misapprehensions but also as primitive forms of that social control later to be perfected through law. Like the female characters in these novels, whether they be maidens who civilize the chivalrous knight or fanatics who force their sons blindly to follow their dictates, superstitions place limits on behavior that must be allowed to have some significance, no matter how irrational or brutal they may be. Like Gibbon before him, Scott saw that the superstition of the common people could be used by the higher powers of the state as a means of control.[6] For this is the fear, after all, that lurks behind Scott's voice of principle and self-denial: that antisocial impulses within the individual might be so powerful that rational law by itself is insufficient to tame them. By eliminating the greater force of repression that comes from the externalization of law in superstitious attitudes toward nature, women, and hierarchical social structure, rational law might actually be leading itself to extinction. The fear, in other words, is that only irrationality may be strong enough to fight against irrationality. Thus arises not only the interest in enchantment in these novels, but, finally, the power of necessity given to that enchantment.

In some cases, to be sure, the significance of superstition as a form of social control is quite prosaic, nothing more than the discovery that actions based on superstitious belief could sometimes be inadvertently responsible to truths. As Scott writes of witches,

> The worst of the pretenders to these sciences was, that they were generally persons who, feeling themselves odious to humanity, were careless of what they did to deserve the public hatred. Real crimes were often committed under pretence of magical imposture; and it somewhat relieves the disgust with which we read, in the criminal records, the conviction of these

wretches, to be aware that many of them merited, as poisoners, suborners, and diabolical agents in secret domestic crimes, the severe fate to which they were condemned for the imaginary guilt of witchcraft. (*BL,* 278)

In other cases, however, superstition plays a somewhat more complex role, as in Scott's description of the *Vehmegericht,* the secret and superstitiously dreaded organization in the fifteenth-century Germany of *Anne of Geierstein:*

> Such an institution could only prevail at a time when ordinary means of justice were excluded by the hand of power, and when, in order to bring the guilty to punishment, it required all the influence and authority of such a confederacy. In no other country than one exposed to every species of feudal tyranny, and deprived of every mode of obtaining justice and redress, could such a system have taken root and flourished. (*AG,* 254)

Although Scott so carefully circumscribes the situation in which this secret society is said to have arisen, it is important to note that the institution given his qualified but definite commendation is shown in the novel to act in a capricious, vicious manner that is only checked by the observance among its members of a very limited sense of honor. Scott will approve even such an institution rather than allow the possibility that superstition could exist as something completely foreign to the governing purposes of modern psychology and law. It can be seen, then, how this connection between superstition and social control lends some rationality even to belief so definitively irrational and thus not only confuses still further the condemnation Scott otherwise passes upon it but also shows something of the arbitrary demands of authority that actually prevail in the conduct of reason. Given this connection, the disturbed judgment in the following portrait of the condemned man at a modern execution might almost be predicted:

> He no longer stalks between the attendant clergymen, dressed in his grave-clothes, through a considerable part of the city, looking like a moving and walking corpse, while yet an inhabitant of this world; but, as the ultimate purpose of punish-

ment has in view the prevention of crimes, it may at least be doubted whether, in abridging the melancholy ceremony, we have not in part diminished that appalling effect upon the spectators which is the useful end of all such inflictions, and in consideration of which, unless in very particular cases, capital cases can be altogether justified. (*HM,* 18)

While superstition must always be checked and the unreasonable enjoyment of its romance chastised, it can never be completely rejected and one's regard for it can never be completely analytic, because no matter what else it may be, it is always powerful – of compelling interest. Like the enchantment of literature, it is so powerful that it may be impossible to control it except by exploiting it. In fact, Scott's image of superstition is in effect sustained by the very chastisement directed against it, for the punishment thus prepared for those readers who fall victim to superstition is like the punishment that so oppresses and yet so stimulates his heroes.

The situation could not be otherwise, given the values that direct Scott's writing. For whatever this writing may yield to a psychoanalytic reading, its description of desire as a quest by men for a humiliating transformation into a childish, feminine, powerless condition depends upon the larger quest for aristocratic recognition portrayed in every aspect of his work. In a society governed by aristocratic ends – as Scott's still was, despite the rise of the middle class[7] – all desire is finally turned to those ends by the powerful tropism of value exerted as much through literature as through any other institution and practice; and Scott's novels are hardly the only works of art in which these teasingly aloof and mysterious ends are assigned to women as the character that makes them so attractive and *for the same reason* so punishingly forbidding and so worthy of punishment. Although the particular form that this pattern takes in Scott's case may certainly be of interest, it must first and finally be understood as a social and ideological pattern rather than the style of an individual psyche. Though apparently contradictory, Scott's attitudes toward superstition, the past, women, and class differences are not ambivalent, at least not in the common sense of that word whereby one is said to desire two different and opposed objects. These attitudes belong to a single and entirely consistent formulation of that desire, which aims at the recognition given by masters to those beneath them.

After George Lukács has described the greatness of Scott's novels as consisting in their depiction of popular life, quoting George Sand to the effect that Scott "is the poet of the peasant, soldier, outlaw, and artisan,"[8] and after Mario Praz has begun a chapter on Scott in a well-known work by writing, "the novels of Sir Walter Scott made a notable contribution to the process by which Romanticism turned bourgeois,"[9] it may seem odd to emphasize the aristocratic nature of Scott's work. To assert that aristocratic values direct his work might seem almost as perverse as the contradictions in Scott's portrayal of superstition, especially if one considers Scott's enormous contribution to popularizing and legitimizing the novel, this genre so closely associated with the rise of the middle class and the end of literacy as a prerogative of the upper classes. Praz, however, could sustain his point of view only by assuming that "the best of Scott" is to be sought "in his descriptions of Scottish habits and customs . . . or in small scenes of intimate interiors"[10] – in other words, by assuming what he asserts and by ignoring the structural relationships and organization in Scott's writing that contradict his viewpoint. And even though his essay remains one of the most valuable ever written on Scott, Lukács is forced to argue for an almost magical objectivity in Scott's writing, a " 'triumph of realism' over his personal, political and social views."[11] In fact, I would argue that Lukács goes wrong in his essay not because his Marxism distorts the emphasis of his reading but – perversely enough – because he finally reads as one who is dominated by aristocratic values. That is to say, he is enchanted by Scott's writing just as all Scott's readers are supposed to be enchanted. When he summarizes Scott's achievement at the beginning of his essay – "Scott ranks among those great writers whose depth is manifest mainly in their work, a depth which they often do not understand themselves, because it has sprung from a truly realistic mastery of their material in conflict with their personal views and prejudices"[12] – one could not ask for a more traditional description of the aristocratic master, and it is to this figure that Lukács submits in his reading. To understand this situation and what it means for the contradictions discussed previously, it is necessary to consider just what mastery means in Scott's writing and in its literary context.

Whether the specific reference be to social, aesthetic, or personal power, whether the organization with which Scott is concerned be that of a girl's face or of a landscape or of a nation or of a mind, the form of mastery to which his writing appeals is one that grants control only where there is no apparent history to that control. Aristocratic favor may be earned through various forms of service, flattery, or attendance, but mastery itself can be said to exist only where it is given as if through an inheritance from nature rather than through labor, education, or any other primarily cultural means. A control thus defined must of necessity always remain strange and elusive, even to those in whom it is invested and by whom it is exerted over others, since it is not denominated by any signs more determinate than the misty group of organic and theological metaphors traditionally associated with such words as "presence," "beauty," "nobility," "grace," "virtue," "honor," and "taste." The paradox of mastery, in other words, is that it cannot be mastered. This concept of control that reigns over aristocratic values and over those societies governed either directly or indirectly by such values can be approached only through submission and humiliation. It is not elusive as a Platonic idea, say, is inviolate in its immaterial perfection, the pattern for those flawed representations with which men must be contented on earth. The fact that no one sign is adequate to it – not even that of aristocratic birth – does not reveal a world apart from its perfection but rather the radical uncertainty of the concept itself. This uncertainty is precisely what constitutes its power. As in the novels of Jane Austen, mastery is a knowledge that one imagines to be absent from oneself and possessed by others – unless one realizes that mastery is nothing but this imaginary discrepancy between oneself and others.

Mastery is established, then, through the impression of a control that exists both within and beyond the surface of its appearance. Since one cannot master mastery – since one can only call upon it as a phenomenon, even a phenomenon in one's own person, by submitting to this control that must always be unwarranted because it is finally anchored only in the rhetoric with which it is described, a rhetoric that can possess a society but for that very reason can be possessed by no individual – even those who possess it must submit to its exteriority. They must experience the very control that they wield as something alien to themselves, something Frankensteinian, overpowering them from without even as they draw it from within themselves to use over others. Mastery is not associated with or incidental to this paradox: It *is* this paradox.

As the references to the work of Austen and Mary Shelley might indicate, Scott's novels are by no means peculiar in their emphasis upon compulsion and its relationship to mastery. This emphasis, in fact, is essential to the Romantic sublime, the concept of perception in which one is overpowered, mastered, by a presence that is definitely articulate, beyond the power of conventional perspectives and signs. Consider, for example, "The Rime of the Ancient Mariner," that touchstone of Romanticism so fraught with superstitious overtones.

"The Ancient Mariner" is a virtual catalogue of compulsions. A ship is compelled to immobility and later forced to drive northward; its crew is compelled to muteness, to the witnessing of disgusting scenes, to death, and later to a seeming revivification in which they are forced to work the ship; the mariner is compelled to wear the albatross, to live beyond the death of his shipmates, to bless the water snakes, to look away from the corpses of his shipmates to the boat that rescues him, and to perform his penance by compulsively repeating his story; and the Wedding Guest is, of course, compelled to hear it. One of the very few acts in this poem that is not said to be committed under a mastery foreign to the agent is the shooting of the albatross with the mariner's crossbow, and the motivation of this act is elided. What we have, then, is a didactic dissociation of knowledge from power. The Wedding Guest's lesson – and, by implication, the reader's – is his alienation from the social ceremonies and celebration. It is the lesson, in other words, of the Faustian legend so dear to the Romantics, including Scott: that the true marriage is between knowledge and sadness and that this marriage enjoins one to quietism. Like "This Lime-Tree Bower My Prison," in which the experience of compulsion is made to yield the lesson that "sometimes / 'Tis well to be bereft of promis'd good, / That we may lift the soul, and contemplate / With lively joy the joys we cannot share," this poem is designed to display action as the crucifixion of the real and submission as the path to the true mastery of the imagination. The situation is the same in "Dejection: An Ode," as the power of the imagination so affects the author that "fruits, and foliage, not my own, seemed mine."[13] Rejecting the actual disposition of property and power, the imagination is designed to accept oppression and through this acceptance to extend its own mastery.

It is understandable, then, that the secret of Scott's novels should so frequently turn on the discovery of the protagonist's nobility, just as it is fitting that the concluding lines of "The Ancient Mariner" should be quoted to characterize the state of the hero near the end of *Waverley*. Whether this discovery of rank in the novels' conclusions is made for the first time (as in *The Abbot* and *Redgauntlet*) or whether the endings of the novels serve to reaffirm a status cast into doubt by the protagonist's poverty or obscurity (as in *Quentin Durward*), the significance is the same: Mastery has been indicated. For despite the fact that nobility alone is an insufficient sign for mastery, so that Scott's narratives are a record of the anxiety consequent to this insufficiency, it is nonetheless true that nobility is the closest thing to a conventional index for mastery that could be found in his time. Thus it is that the primitivist did not argue the value of the savage's *difference:* He argued his nobility. And thus, although it may not be a guarantee of mastery, not one of Scott's male protagonists can be allowed to conclude his adventures without some form of aristocratic rank, just like heroes in the Spenserian and fairy tale traditions. Even Harry Smith, the artisan hero of *The Fair Maid of Perth,* is offered a knighthood at the end of the book; and though he refuses it, he does not do so "proudly," as Lukács says, because "burgher he is and free burgher he will die,"[14] but rather "humbly," as he himself says, and "dejectedly," as Scott says (*FMP,* 423). Moreover, he refuses it because he does not want war to take him away from his beloved. He sacrifices his chance for this rank on behalf of a woman – and there is no better way than this of showing one's "true" nobility, in contrast to the corrupt noblemen, such as the Duke of Rothsay, who appear in this book.[15]

Furthermore, given the patriarchal force assumed within mastery – for this concept that so dominates aristocratic values is not an abstract one but rather one built upon historical life and drawn from that life into the themes and traditions of philosophy, science, and art – it is also understandable that the solicitation of its grace should be feminizing as well as humiliating. Although this patriarchal force is so frequently expressed through women in these novels, this fact only serves to show how important the relationship is between the women whose favor was entreated by Troubador poets and their Renaissance descendants and those women in Romantic and Victorian poetry and prose who are no less idealized, though they may be less carnal. In both cases, the women are finally stand-ins for the figure of the patriarchal master. The love relationship is guided by the manner in which men submit to each other in their social, economic, and political relationships.

To be sure, Scott is torn: Else there should not be such interest. As he himself never tires of repeating, one reason he so frequently sets his novels in times of danger and disorder is because it is in such times that men can rise by merit who might otherwise be held back by birth. Not one hero introduced by this gesture toward middle-class values, however, can be suffered to go entirely without the imprimatur of rank. Scott admires ability – after all, it is the modern style of character – but in these works dedicated to the past he can allow the just reward of skill to rise above the vulgarity of mere money. Hence the contempt expressed in *The Fortunes of Nigel* and other novels for mercenary soldiers: Scott, the most professional of writers and of men, nevertheless assumes the values of the amateur, because amateurism is the style of the aristocracy, and fighting for honor rather than pay is its ancient right. Scott does not finally value the disorder of the past for the room it gives to merit but rather because the ordeals involved in this kind of situation, just as they can allow women to be met in a politely prurient dishabille, can also convey in an almost prurient manner the experience of aristocratic desire. Mark Twain may have been unfair in blaming the American Civil War on "the Sir Walter disease," but he was perfectly correct in saying that Scott's novels teach "reverence for rank and caste, and pride and pleasure in them."[16] In his novels Scott is both literally and figuratively writing against himself, pursuing a life that he claims is dead while fleeing what he announces as the present and future of England. The reason for this apparently contradictory movement, of course, is that the modernity he proclaims and the history he mourns are not radically divided but are rather so much involved with each other that it is finally the aristocratic past – superstitious, fearful, punitive, and yet rewarding – that reveals its mastery in the present.

Also understandable, then, is the reason Scott should admit *The Monastery* to be a failure. For *The Monastery* is the only novel in which he goes beyond his narrative equivocations and contradictions concerning the subject of superstition to the point of actually portraying a spirit, the White Maiden of Avenal, who interferes in the action of the story several crucial times. This spirit is that figure of mastery evoked throughout all of Scott's writing: "But it would seem there is something thrilling and abhorrent to flesh and blood in the consciousness that we stand in presence of a being in form like to ourselves, but so different in faculties and nature that we can neither understand its purposes nor calculate its means of pursuing them" (*M,* 96). D. H. Lawrence, another great novelist of the search for aristocratic recognition, could hardly have said it better; but Scott sees this novel as a failure for the very reason that so many critics, reading as if enchanted by aristocratic values but unwilling or unable to admit this attitude, have seen much of Lawrence's work as a failure: because it too explicitly describes a concept, a figure of mastery, disseminated less directly in his other writing. Scott writes of "the introduction of the supernatural and marvellous, the resort of distressed authors since the days of Horace, but whose privileges as a sanctuary have been disputed in the present age, and wellnigh exploded" (*M,* xii). In other words, he confesses to a violation of modern taste: the taste for a *discreet* submission to aristocratic values that he captures so well in his other writing. The reader will no longer be enchanted, it seems, if he can see the master to whom he is surrendering. It is easy to conceive that a novelist who felt this way might desire, rationally and superstitiously, to remain anonymous.

9

VIOLENCE AND LAW

~

In youth . . . there is a sort of freemasonry, which,
without much conversation, teaches young persons
to estimate each other's character, and places them
at ease on the shortest acquaintance. It is only when
taught deceit by the commerce of the world that we
learn to shroud our character from observation, and
to disguise our real sentiments from those with whom
we are placed in communion.

  – SIR WALTER SCOTT, *The Monastery*

IN ALL OF SIR WALTER SCOTT'S NOVELS the difference between the modern world and the world of the past
is defined by the difference between the rule of law and the
rule of violence. At every period of history described in these works[1]
the progressive elements of civilization are distinguished from the
anachronistic on the basis of their commitment to the increasing
sublimation of violent conflict within formal regulations, especially
the written regulations of law. In the modern world "the attorney
is . . . a man of more importance than the lord of the manor" (*I*,
xxii), and the modern attitude toward society is that represented by
Mr. Pleydell in *Guy Mannering* as he explains why the faults that
may be found in the legal system should not be unduly distressing:

> "In civilised society law is the chimney through which all that
> smoke discharges itself that used to circulate through the whole
> house, and put every one's eyes out; no wonder, therefore,
> that the vent itself should sometimes get a little sooty." (*GM,*
> 271)

This pacific and tolerant attitude would seem to be the controlling one in the novels, since it finds so much support in Scott's
narrative meditations upon the course of history and the enlightenment that history has brought to mankind. Within these same nov-

els, however, there is another attitude, which finds that the serenity and peace brought by law actually may be the source of greater insecurity and a worse violence than ever existed before this advancement in civilization. As Karl Kroeber has noted, there is in the Waverley novels not only a wealth of legal proceedings and references but also "an implicit questioning of the whole concept of civilized law."[2] Moreover, this questioning not only suggests that law may lead to violence rather than enlightenment but further suggests that the violence law was invented to curb may not have been entirely undesirable. According to this questioning attitude, violence may come to appear as the best and truest law among men; and as this attitude appears in Scott's novels in the form of that nostalgia for youth and for the youthful ages of the world so common among the Romantics, an examination of it may help to deepen appreciation for Scott's achievement and serve to suggest a productive approach to some of the characteristic problems and concerns of Romanticism.

Regarded broadly, then, the problem of law in the Waverley novels is the problem of distinguishing civilization from decadence. For law does not come without a price, according to these novels, and this price is the loss of the open and immediate relation between men that is presumed to have existed before the organization of society – times when there were no social forms that men could wear as masks to their individuality. Civil laws in particular and behavioral codes in general are the necessary first steps to any sort of sociality, but according to these novels this codification of behavior entails an obscuration of the human spirit. As soon as one enters an organized society and so leaves behind that "merry warld" of which Rob Roy nostalgically speaks, when "every man held his ain gear wi' his ain grip, and when the country-side wasna fashed wi' warrants and poindings and apprizings, and a' that cheatry craft" (*RR*, 233), one also leaves behind the unmediated presence of men to each other. The result is that laws give birth to lies. The more that relations among men are governed by social conventions, the greater the possibility that a sophisticated adaptation to such conventions may disguise the real nature and true meaning of men. For example, one sees this situation in the contrast Scott sketches between the "cross-grained fidelity" of the domestics of the old world and "the smooth and accommodating duplicity of the modern menial" (*OM*, 42). The problem of law is that the sublimation of violence is accompanied by a sublimation of the human spirit and that the latter process tends to subvert the former. Consequently, the reign of law – like the reign of decorum in the novels of Radcliffe and Austen – may be thought to increase the confusion and injustice among men instead of ordering the commonweal more fairly and efficiently. The progressive enlightenment of law may end in an unnatural darkness.

Even Mr. Pleydell sees the problem. As he says, "Law's like laudanum: it's much more easy to use it as a quack does than to learn to apply it like a physician" (*GM*, 415). He is speaking of civil law, of course, but the same rule holds for all types of behavioral codes in Scott's fiction, including the religious doctrines at the heart of so many of the conflicts he describes. One need only consider the number and intensity of these conflicts to see that his characters always find it easier to abuse sacred scripture than to use it in the right spirit – so much easier, in fact, that its proper use is never specified in these novels except by the vaguest of references to contemporary Protestant belief. The Bible, it seems, is also like laudanum. As Rebecca says to Brian de Bois-Gilbert in *Ivanhoe,* "If thou readest the Scripture . . . and the lives of the saints, only to justify thine own license and profligacy, thy crime is like that of him who extracts poison from the most healthful and necessary herbs" (*I,* 216). Since variant readings of the scriptures do occur, it seems clear that some corruption must exist in their readers if not in the texts themselves; and yet that corruption is not as easily identified as one might suppose. Even though Rebecca seems to speak as a physician and not as a quack, for instance, and even though she finishes her life in serving humanity and thinking of heaven, she herself must be considered as one who has been "erroneously taught to interpret the promises of Scripture to the chosen people of Heaven" (*I,* 214). She may have a special skill in the use of herbs and medicines so that she can cure Ivanhoe of his wounds, just as the infidel Saladin may possess a healing stone that will aid a Crusader (*The Talisman*); but this association of therapeutic powers with individuals who otherwise stand beyond the modern law of these novels does not serve the purposes of reconciliation. It serves rather to make the distinction between the proper use of law and its abuses even more difficult to identify, since people cannot be sorted into the simple categories of physicians and quacks but instead must be judged according to specific acts and situations that do not become conclusive precedents for any other acts and situations.

So violence has the virtue of openness and law the demerit of obscurity, and the problems of interpretation caused by this obscurity may finally lead to more violence; thus a great confusion arises in the moral *chiaroscuro* of Scott's work. Laws of all kinds must be judged according to the spirit with which they are used, but it is precisely this spirit that laws obscure. The result is that the attempt to govern a society by controlling violence may actually be an incitement to greater violence. And though there may be at least some historical basis for this problematic image of law – Lawrence Stone has described how the code of dueling developed in the sixteenth and seventeenth centuries led to an explosion in litigation and finally spurred violence over trivia that otherwise might have been of no significance[3] – still Scott's use of this image is not really based on historical analysis. The image of law in his novels comes to be violently torn by contradictory attitudes that now see it as progressive, now as degenerate, because of a positive *desire* for violence that enters into Scott's writing. The passage of violence into law and thence into new causes of violence is recorded again and again in all of the Waverley novels, and through this passage one can trace a desire to imagine a world of the past where there were no problems in interpreting the world or the relation of one man to another within that world.

Take, for example, the way law passes into violence in *Count Robert of Paris*. In this novel, a character named Hereward and Count Robert fulfill a challenge and fight almost to death even after they have become friends and supporters of each other, because the code of chivalrous honor is felt to supersede these personal considerations. Similarly, although some of the many rivals who appear in Scott's novels are given personal reasons to be in conflict with each other that might have led them into violence under any conditions, quite often the conflict between them is shown as having nothing to do with an individual enmity. One thinks of such rivals or antagonists as Waverley and Colonel Talbot, Rudolph Donnerhugel and Arthur Philipson in *Anne of Geierstein,* Hector M'Intyre and Lovel in *The Antiquary,* Athelstane and Ivanhoe, Henry Morton and Lord Evandale in *Old Mortality,* Henry Seyton and Roland Graeme in *The Abbot,* and even Sir Kenneth and Saladin in *The*

Talisman. Even if it be at the moment of death, as in *Anne of Geier-stein* and *The Abbot,* they eventually are reconciled to each other in such a way as to discount the motives that had brought them into conflict. Not only are the supposed causes of their enmity shown to be entirely exterior to them as individuals, but no matter how important those reasons may be to society at large, they are made to look trivial when compared to the immediate relation of the one man to the other. Religious, political, economic, and military problems all pale in comparison to this relation. The characters of the rivals do not change, but the pressures for precedence bred by social forms are allowed to drop away from them so that they can confront each other freely and openly, as if in that outlaw's paradise that is imagined to have existed in the world's youth. According to the historical structure of these novels, in other words, these men have come full circle as they have moved from being restrained by law to fighting on account of laws and then to meeting each other with the transparency imagined to have existed before there were any laws to restrain the fighting among men.

These men, then, have revolved upon the paradox that generates the nostalgic appeal of Scott's writing and that can be summarized in a formula at once very simple and extremely complex: Etiquette makes enemies and violence creates intimacy. Or, to formulate it somewhat more discursively: The codes of behavior required by society make it so difficult for men to have a sure understanding of each other that a pressure develops for a violence that would pene-trate social forms, and this pressure becomes so great that violence in and of itself may appear to have a positive value. Thus it is that Scott can write of the conflict between the Crusaders and the Sara-cens and claim that war, "in itself perhaps the greatest of evils,"

> yet gave occasion for display of good faith, generosity, clem-ency, and even kindly affections, which less frequently occur in more tranquil periods, where the passions of men, experi-encing wrongs or entertaining quarrels which cannot be brought to instant decision, are apt to smoulder for a length of time in the bosoms of those who are so unhappy as to be their prey. (*T,* 9)

The air of reluctant discovery about this passage is disingenuous, for all of Scott's writing pushes the reader toward this idea that the truth of one man's relation to another is to be established only through violence.[4]

It might be objected that Scott's rivals usually are brought into conflict not only as the result of large-scale social interests but also because of jealousy over women, in accordance with Rob Roy's remark that "women and gear are at the bottom of a' the mischief in this warld" (*RR,* 351). The idea that women are an important cause of such rivalry, however, is belied by the greater intensity in Scott's depiction of the relations between men as opposed to those between men and women. Women are simply the means by which men place themselves in relationship to each other, as Scott suggests when he says that "the regard of women is generally much influenced by the estimation which an individual maintains in the opinion of men" (*B,* 142). It is not women but the wary circumspection necessitated by the complexity of social codes that causes these men to be alienated from each other. Like Sir Aymer and Sir John at the beginning of *Castle Dangerous,* they come to be rivals because the formalities of such codes make them "jealous of every punctilio" (*CD,* 231). In other words, according to the drama that structures these novels it is only because these men cannot establish the strength of their "ain grip" when they first meet that they must find religious or romantic or economic or other reasons to separate them: It is thus that men fight who otherwise would be friends. Only when the secondary violence resulting from law takes on the extreme character of the primitive violence pictured as having antedated the rule of law can Scott's men return to their real selves.

Given this understanding, one sees why the dramatization of legal proceedings in these novels so often should reveal them to be irrational or unjust in their origins and capricious in their resolution. In *Redgauntlet,* for instance, the case with which Alan Fairford must make his first appearance at the bar is the suit of a madman, Peter Peebles. The case yields nothing to that of Dickens's Jarndyce and Jarndyce in point of awful complexity; like the affair in *Bleak House,* it seems to exist for no reason but that of generating writings so stupefying in quantity that their only significance is in the sheer mass of the paper they occupy. Peter's madness, moreover, seems to consist in nothing more nor less than his extreme passion for the law and the elaborate technicalities of its language, as he is maniacal but not incompetent in pursuing his obscure claim. The case is still further complicated by the discovery, in the course of the novel, that the crazy but seemingly harmless Peter had once been a landlord who drove one of his tenants to the poorhouse; her daughter to prostitution, crime, and transportation; and the girl's lover, as a consequence, to an irregular and despairing course of existence on the sea. To be sure, the case is presented as an extraordinary one, and Fairford takes it only in obedience to his father's hope that it will distract him from the adventures of his friend, Darsie Latimer. This legal process, however, in addition to being explicitly linked with the labyrinthine illegalities of some smugglers in the novel, is also comparable to situations in other novels. *Redgauntlet* is set in the eighteenth century, but the situation described in it conforms to the early seventeenth-century dramas of *Peveril of the Peak* and *The Fortunes of Nigel* and to the fifteenth-century drama of *Anne of Geierstein*.

Julian Peveril and his father are implicated in the tortuous accusations of the Popish Plot. Their trial, luckily, falls at a time when belief in the plot is beginning to weaken, so that the judge presiding at their trial is careful of their rights; but the reader is given to understand that this respect for the law is no less undependable than the disregard for legal rights that the judge has exhibited in other cases. It is not a return of justice but simply a swing of the pendulum of political influence; and so the situation is similar to that in *The Fortunes of Nigel,* in which the hero seeks to petition the king for the payment of money owed his family so that he may retain his father's estate. In the first place, he manages to get the petition to the king only through the chance intervention of two strangers; and second, after a great many complications, he manages to get the money to redeem the lands only through the last minute efforts of Richie Moniplies, his servant, and Reginald Lowestoffe, a lawyer of doubtful repute who is able to help Nigel in his distress because he associates with the criminals of London. It is only by the help of these criminals, in fact, that Nigel manages to stay alive and healthy until the end of the story. So all the means vital to the securing of his legal rights are extra-legal,[5] based on chance, coincidence, personal favor, or crime. There also is little difference, then, between the situation of law in these two novels and its appearance in *Anne of Geierstein,* a novel in which the only regular institution of law is an illegal institution, the *Vehmegericht,* which meets secretly to condemn malefactors who otherwise would go free – or such is the principle. In reality, the justice meted out by this organization, which Scott credits as a kind of ad hoc judicial system, is entirely violent and has only the flimsiest of safeguards against false accusations. These safeguards do, as it happens, save the life of Mr. Philipson, the disguised Earl of Oxford; but it is only by chance that he is able to take advantage of them. In fact, the manner in which Philipson is taken before the secret tribunal – lowered in his bed at night down through the floor of his room and into a shadowy subterranean vault in which all the assembled members of the organization are disguised in hooded robes – seems almost a symbolic description of the nightmarish depths of law not only in this book but throughout Scott's novels.

The situation remains the same, for instance, in *The Heart of Midlothian,* even though the superficial conditions seem to differ. A girl unwilling to suborn her testimony even to save the life of her sister, who is condemned by a recently instituted legal technicality, sets out on a walk to see the queen in London. Eventually, after the inevitable adventures, she succeeds in obtaining the queen's mercy. Justice would seem to be served, but it is necessary to consider two qualifications to this conclusion. One is the fact that Jeanie Deans's royal interview is certainly extraordinary and is presented as such, so that it can have no representative authority in the description of justice. (This consideration is emphasized if one compares this novel with the situation in *Kenilworth,* in which Amy Robsart fails to obtain the help she needs from Queen Elizabeth.) The other is the fact that this *oral* interview is explicitly opposed to the *written* word that characterizes the regular administration of the law. For this is what these novels show to be most essentially debased in the law: the spoken word. Not just the spoken word, of course, but the spoken word in the immediate presence of one person to another. Therefore, although we see that the past is exemplified for Scott by a good code of honor according to which noblemen captured in battle could give their *parole* to their enemies and so be allowed to roam freely, we can also see the degeneration of such a primitive and thus unusually honest code in the reliance of modern law upon the arcane language of contracts and warrants. Or, as Jeanie Deans says,

> We must try all means . . . but writing winna do it: a letter canna look, and pray, and beg, and beseech, as the human voice can do to the human heart. A letter's like the music that

the ladies have for their spinets: naething but black scores, compared to the same tune played or sung. It's word of mouth maun do it, or naething. (*HM*, 280)[6]

As this speech by Jeanie would indicate, it is because of the value Scott places upon personal contact that the image of law in his novels is so torn by contradictions through which violence nostalgically appears as a surer justice and law as a deceptive form or cause of violence. For example, it is because the rule of law in his novels is confused by a desire for personal ties antedating legal connections that Scott could describe *Waverley* in the General Preface to the novels as a story of "brave opponents, who did nothing in hate, but all in honour" (*Wa*, xx), even though this description is so much more idealistic than the narrative itself. As Francis R. Hart has written, "for the Author of Waverley, right must be realized in terms of personal loyalties, not in terms of abstract justice."[7] As previously noted, Scott believes in the intimacy of the rude past and fears that etiquette creates enemies instead of controlling violence. This, then, is what he describes in his novels as the decadence liable to destroy all the value of civilization: the attenuation of personal bonds between men in favor of "trumpery etiquette." As he describes them, artificial codes of behavior not only weaken communication between men by creating the possibility of lies but also entirely displace the proper subjects of communication, adding "seriousness and an appearance of importance to objects which, from their trivial nature, could admit no such distinction" (*CRP*, 5). And it is such a state of trumpery that Scott's novels show as the end toward which all laws tend, while they also show that when such a decadent condition becomes especially threatening, it is only a superlative violence – a violence that recaptures the primitive youth of the world – that can restore value to its proper place.

Such is the historical lesson implicit in the Waverley novels. For the violence described in these novels is not only open, but it is personal, vital, and invigorating. The violence in Scott's novels might be called a Gothic violence, and it gives birth to the same impression of intimacy that may be seen in the general commingling of sexuality with violence in the Gothic tradition (as well as in less genteel modes of pornography). According to this image, genuine communication must be forced into being. As Scott says, we need to be "thrown off our guard by the general agitation of our feelings" during a time of "peril" if we are to show those true feelings "which, at more tranquil periods, our prudence at least conceals, if it cannot altogether suppress them" (*I, 267*). The peculiarity of Gothic violence is that its lurid terrors are meant to articulate and to provoke the highest sensibility: One must have taste to appreciate such violence. Etiquette makes enemies and violence creates intimacy: This is the overriding conviction that upsets the transition from violence to law in Scott's novels.

This understanding does much to explain that general pattern of romance in Scott's novels by which women are won only after the hero has endured situations of physical conflict, whether or not they are directly connected to his love; but the psychology represented in this pattern must be investigated further if its social provenance is to be understood. For this psychology is by no means peculiar to Scott or to Gothic writers; it is rather the product of the most tenacious of historical traditions, which holds the spoken word and the unmediated appearance of one individual to another to be the authentic forms of human relationship. As it leads to a demand for personal bonds in place of legal codes, this belief is specifically aristocratic and is based on an ideal of hierarchical and reciprocal duties transmitted more by blood than by writing; and this belief informs all of the Waverley novels. The paradise of the outlaw in these novels is the paradise of the aristocrat. In effect, Scott the lawyer is undone by Scott the laird.

That this is so may be seen, for instance, in the value Scott's writing gives to personal appearance – a value entirely parallel to the one Jeanie Deans finds in a personal interview with the queen. "The truth is," Scott writes in what he calls "a digression,"

> that a regard for personal appearance is a species of self-love from which the wisest are not exempt, and to which the mind clings so instinctively, that not only the soldier advancing to almost inevitable death, but even the doomed criminal who goes to certain execution, shows an anxiety to array his person to the best advantage. (*K, 327*)

One need not inquire as to the empirical truth of this rather remarkable passage – that is beside the point. What is significant is that Scott must regard the doomed criminal as having a vanity identical to the doomed soldier's. He cannot allow a violence to exist that condemns the individual to a condition of impersonality, even though his writing frequently raises this possibility through the repetitiousness of its formulas and its emphasis upon large-scale scenes that dwarf the individual. The "even" in the foregoing passage is disingenuous, for it is *especially* in moments of actual or threatened violence that the opacities of civilized codes are stripped away to leave what aristocratic attitudes hold to be the fundamental human relationship: the individual appealing for the recognition of others as a bondsman appeals to a master. This vanity is, of course, not "self-love" at all. It is a desire for the self to have value in the eyes of others, and this desire is modeled upon the general system of aristocratic attitudes in which individuals in each rank of society must be accepted by those above and below them if they are to accept themselves. The fact that Scott often describes how "the distinctions of rank are readily set aside among those who are made to be sharers of common danger" (*LM,* 157) does not invalidate this judgment at all, for the way in which the violent situations of his novels are arranged makes it clear that the distinctions of rank are swept away only so that true aristocrats can distinguish themselves from that false nobility which may arise under the peaceful rule of law. It is not by accident, after all, that Scott should picture the transition from openness to smooth deception in civilized manners by complaining of "the modern menial." And given the self-reinforcing system of demands for personal recognition that he describes in the previous passage, it is not at all "strange," as Arnold Biederman remarks in *Anne of Geierstein,* "that the veneration for rank should be rooted even in the minds of those who have no claim to share it!" (*AG,* 53). Nor is it strange that this veneration should consistently be found among the virtuous commoners in Scott's novels. George Heriot in *The Fortunes of Nigel* is entirely typical of such characters when he addresses the hero of that novel by saying, "But remember, my good young lord, that I do not, like some men of my degree, wish to take opportunity to step beyond it and associate with my superiors in rank, and therefore do not fear to mortify my presumption by suffering me to keep my distance" (*FN,* 81). And it is also no accident that when the Lady of Avenal in *The Abbot* believes she sees gentle blood in a boy of unknown origins – "it were shame to think otherwise of a form so noble and features so fair; the very wildness in which he occasionally indulged, his contempt of danger and impatience of restraint, had in them something noble" (*A*, 20) – this confidence in the importance of appearances and their relation to the aristocratic character is formally confirmed by the plot of the novel. In these novels as in traditional aristocratic ideology, the true aristocrat compels recognition;[8] and the disturbing appeal with which violence upsets the rule of law in Scott's writing may be said to be the narrative expression of this aristocratic compulsion.

One also sees the aristocratic attitude behind Scott's descriptions of law and violence in his adoption of the traditional idea of aristocratic grace. For instance, as Scott describes two men saluting the Lord of Kenilworth and Amy Robsart, his wife of undistinguished rank, "the earl returned their salutation with the negligent courtesy of one long used to such homage; while the countess repaid it with a punctilious solicitude which showed it was not quite so familiar to her" (*K*, 71). In other words, codes of behavior need be emphasized only among men and women of inferior birth. After all, for the true aristocrat etiquette is so familiar a second nature that it is merely a transparent veneer, not a disguise or imposition from without. Thus, the only true etiquette appears not to be etiquette but rather the nature to which a man was born. In fact, the only situation in which the appearance of etiquette is really allowed any meaning in these novels is when it confronts the vulgar – that is, when it serves to overawe and subdue – or when it serves women:

> In the higher classes a damsel, however giddy, is still under the dominion of etiquette, and subject to the surveillance of mammas and chaperons; but the country girl, who snatches her moment of gaiety during the intervals of labour, is under no such guardianship or restraint, and her amusement becomes so much the more hazardous. (*HM*, 100)

Unless they are hopelessly mad, women cannot meet on the grounds of violence and so must need the laws of civilization, whereas a man who always needs those laws might as well be a woman, as far as these novels are concerned.

Executions, interestingly enough, are scenes to which Scott likes to return for the purpose of making statements about human nature, such as the one discussed previously. As he writes in another passage:

The feeling that he is the object of general dislike and der-
eliction seems to be one of the most unendurably painful to
which a human being can be subjected. The most atrocious
criminals, whose nerves have not shrunk from perpetrating
the most horrid cruelty, endure more from the consciousness
that no man will sympathise with their sufferings than from
apprehension of the personal agony of their impending punishment; and are known often to attempt to palliate their en-
ormities, and sometimes altogether to deny what is established by the clearest proof, rather than to leave life under the
general ban of humanity. (*FN*, 372)

Again, one need not ask how many men actually suffer more from
dislike than from death. If the question were posed in a slightly
different way, it seems highly improbable that even the most sociable criminal would choose the latter to escape the former. The only
reason Scott can moralize with such unlikely assurance upon the
vanity of condemned men is because he is not really writing of
criminals. Instead, this passage actually refers to that noble code in
which death is preferred to dishonor. This is the primitive code that
regulates the actions of all of Scott's protagonists, whatever qualms
they may have about employing violence in the place of judicious
deliberation; and therefore everyone in these novels is condemned
to support it. Scott is simply exploiting the criminal character to
uphold the aristocratic, just as he exploits the unhappy intrigues of
the Earl of Leicester to keep down the lower classes:

> But, could the bosom of him thus admired and envied have
> been laid open before the inhabitants of that crowded hall,
> with all its dark thoughts of guilty ambition, blighted affec-
> tion, deep vengeance, and conscious sense of meditated cru-
> elty crossing each other like spectres in the circle of some foul
> enchantress, which of them, from the most ambitious noble
> in the courtly circle down to the most wretched menial who
> lived by shifting of trenchers, would have desired to change
> characters with the favourite of Elizabeth and the Lord of
> Kenilworth! (*K*, 409)

As in the earlier passage, Scott's ostensible subject is misleading.
He is not really writing about the troubles of Leicester, as one can

see from the fact that he has drawn the same moral earlier in the novel merely by describing the present-day condition of the castle of Kenilworth:

> We cannot but add, that of this lordly palace, where princes feasted and heroes fought . . . all is now desolate. The bed of the lake is but a rushy swamp; and the massive ruins of the castle only serve to show what their splendour once was, and to impress on the musing visitor the transitory value of human possessions, and the happiness of those who enjoy a humble lot in virtuous contentment. (*K*, 292–3)

Rather than writing about the Lord of Kenilworth or his castle, Scott is using these topics as occasions to write about the burdens that justify aristocratic rule. As the noble attitude toward honor guides the passage about the condemned criminal, so are these passages guided by the traditional support given to the man of noble blood on the basis of his superior responsibilities. He is in an elevated position, but he – and his castle – suffer more than the ordinary man. The attitude is the same as that displayed in the lament of the king in *Henry IV, Part 2:* "Uneasy lies the head that wears a crown" (III. ii. 31).

To be sure, the suffering Scott describes is entirely unrelated to social responsibilities, but this is the way aristocratic suffering characteristically is described in Romantic as in Gothic literature. Whether he appears in the figure of a hypersensitive poet, a criminal as much sinned against as sinning, a knight bound by a vow or a woman, or a Faustian scientist, the aristocratic figure is shown to suffer more profoundly than others; and thus these others are warned to maintain their own state instead of envying his. A general assertion of superiority is disguised in the assertion of a more vulnerable sensibility. Even if aristocracy is not explicitly referred to, the poet et al. are described as "natural aristocrats"; and thus aristocratic attitudes often may be at the very center of works, such as Wordsworth's or Shelley's, that otherwise seem to have democratic sympathies. Like the refined thoughts of philosophy and the more exquisite kinds of pleasurable feelings described under the name of taste, exquisite suffering is made a prerogative of the upper classes, implicitly or explicitly; and thus resentment toward the members of these classes is symbolically deflected at the same time as the suffering of the lower classes is effectively denied. As Samuel Johnson noted in his review of Soame Jenyns's *Free Enquiry into the Nature and the Origin of Evil*, the traditional argument that their ignorance is the bliss of the poor may actually serve to disguise "the lust of dominion."[9] The fact that few members of the lower classes would have been able to read the work of Scott or other writers who adopted this patronizing attitude and thus could not benefit from their pedagogy is beside the point, for the most basic attitudes that writers hold toward society are not necessarily exercised deliberately. These attitudes are inherited, as it were, from the life and the discourse in which they are bred; and thus one often may find social significance in passages and reflections that the writer would consider to be entirely "natural" or at least very different in significance. Still, Scott's conscious attitudes toward society do receive explicit formulation at some points in his writings; and a consideration of some of these passages may help to explain the problem of law and its interpretation in his work.

As might be expected, one of the influences that Scott calls upon on behalf of law and against violence is a strong monarchy. It is not for nothing that he dwells upon weak or irresponsible rulers in several novels: Prince Charles in *Redgauntlet* and *Woodstock*, King George II in *The Heart of Midlothian*, James I in *The Fortunes of Nigel*, King René of Provence in *Anne of Geierstein*, Robert III in *The Fair Maid of Perth*, and Emperor Alexius Comnenius in *Count Robert of Paris*. And yet this very emphasis upon sovereignty exhibits a distrust of the law and an appeal to violence, since it is the personal presence of the ruler and the possibility of royal intervention into judicial proceedings, as in *The Heart of Midlothian*, that is accorded approval. Scott's attention is directed not to the constitutional or legal authority of monarchs but rather to their personal authority and power over the regulation of civil affairs. The discussion of the distrust existing between the houses of Ravenswood and Ashton in *The Bride of Lammermoor* is typical:

> The character of the times aggravated these suspicions. 'In those days there was no king in Israel.' Since the departure of James VI to assume the richer and more powerful crown of England, there had existed in Scotland contending parties, formed among the aristocracy, by whom, as their intrigues at the court of St. James's chanced to prevail, the delegated powers

of sovereignty were alternately swayed. The evils attending upon this system of government resemble those which afflict the tenants of an Irish estate, the property of an absentee. There was no supreme power, claiming and possessing a general interest with the community at large, to whom the oppressed might appeal from subordinate tyranny, either for justice or for mercy. (*BL,* 16)

It is the personal character of the king rather than his judicial role that is appealed to, with the help of allusions to the Bible and Maria Edgeworth.[10] Scott's good monarch is simply a feudal lord on a larger scale. It is true that when such a personally acting monarch actually appears, Scott may show that he acts too personally, without sufficient consideration for legal process, as in the case of Richard the Lion-Hearted in *Ivanhoe;* but still it is an active and a strong king that is wanted, not a lawyer. For Scott the monarch is, in effect, the spirit of the laws – the inspiring presence that is supposed to settle all disputes over the interpretation of the laws – and yet these novels do not display any great confidence in finding such a man of spirit. Scott's view of kings and queens and great lords and ladies is always an ironic one. They are not entirely belittled, but they are seen to suffer from quite ordinary fears, vanities, and prejudices. It is difficult to bring these portraits to agree with the idea of a monarchy "claiming and possessing a general interest with the community at large"; and, indeed, even judging by Scott's own rules, this spirit seems just as fantastic as any of the legendary ghosts he describes elsewhere in his work. This discrepancy between the actualities and the ideals described in his novels goes a good way toward explaining why there should be more appeals to a nostalgic violence than to a real royal authority within them. It is not the presence or even the memory of an actual monarch that makes Scott feel the need for a strong ruler, but rather the absence of such an ideal monarch in the history he surveys. His novels are driven toward violence precisely because their aristocratic ideals are so compellingly high.

In addition to appealing to the need for a strong ruler, Scott also tries to support the rule of law by describing a certain theory of the nature of social change. With social theory as with monarchical, though, the very attempt to support the rule of law proves to undermine it:

But nature has her laws, which seem to apply to the social as well as the vegetable system. It appears to be a general rule that what is to last long should be slowly matured and gradually improved, while every sudden effort, however gigantic, to bring about the speedy execution of a plan calculated to endure for ages is doomed to exhibit symptoms of premature decay from its very commencement. (*CRP*, 2)

But in revolutions, stern and high principles are often obliged to give way to the current of existing circumstances; and in many a case, where wars have been waged for points of metaphysical right, they have been at last gladly terminated upon the mere hope of obtaining general tranquility, as, after many a long siege, a garrison is often glad to submit on mere security for life and limb. (*Wo*, 70)

Scott's narrative style itself is never violent, and that patience exhibited in his style is transferred to these meditations. The conservative strength of social inertia over violent change is described in a style of conservative strength. It seems only natural, according to the images of the vegetable system and the current, that gradual change should triumph over sudden disruptions. And yet the experiences described throughout all of Scott's narratives always involve disruption, rebellion, violence, and – above all else – stern and high principles. Where then do these novels take place, if not in nature? And where is nature to be found if it is not in the realm of experience described in these novels? The problem here is similar to the one that arises in relation to Scott's use of superstition. To agree with these sentiments, the reader must see the experiences described in the novels as unnatural; to identify with these experiences, the reader must find these sentiments meaningless. For if the laws of nature and narrative, like civil and religious laws, are to repress violence and to institute an orderly regulation to events, how can an interest in the violent and disordered events that occupy these novels be understood as anything other than a release of that repression? And how can law and narrative editorializing be understood as anything but trumpery etiquette? Thus do the formal structures and sentiments of Scott's novels conflict with the intimate appeal of their drama. As a modern lawyer, Scott stands at a distance from the past and holds his readers at the same distance; as an upholder of aristocratic attitudes, he plunges with his readers into the passionate transparency of the old days.

It is true that Scott does not employ the concept of nature in a completely systematic way in his writing, and thus it might be objected that the previous passages do not imply that violence is unnatural simply because they assert the naturalness of gradual change. But the argument is not that his writings are systematically contradictory; the argument is that the contradictions within them are social rather than logical. It is from their very lack of systematic order that problems of interpretation arise – that Scott's writings, too, become like laudanum. One needs to conceive of two Scotts, the lawyer and the laird, who sometimes write passages individually and sometimes together, with predictably ambiguous results. This is not to say, however, that the novels that result from this most uneasy collaboration are flawed on this account. On the contrary, it is because of the tensions at work in their associations of violence with truth and laws with lies that these novels gain a great deal of their interest.

One area of these novels that is especially interesting in this regard – and certainly important to the aesthetics of Romanticism – is that of landscape design. One finds that the tension between the lawyer and the laird appears with as much complexity in the appearance of Scott's landscapes as it does in the telling appearance of his characters or in the divided allegiances of his protagonists. In fact, all of these aspects of his work may come together in a single description in which they are all but indivisible from each other, as in the passage in *The Abbot* that describes Roland Graeme's first meeting with the regent, the Earl of Murray:

> It did not diminish from, but rather added to, the interest of a situation so unexpected that Roland himself did not perfectly understand wherein he stood committed by the state secrets in which he had unwittingly become participator. On the contrary, he felt like one who looks on a romantic landscape, of which he sees the features for the first time, and then obscured with mist and driving tempest. The imperfect glimpse which the eye catches of rocks, trees, and other objects around him adds double dignity to these shrouded mountains and darkened abysses, of which the height, depth, and extent are left to imagination. (*Ab,* 185)

Until this point in the novel, Roland Graeme has been complaining that he is always acted upon rather than acting. Here, however, he is gladly overpowered. The only way this situation differs from the others that had oppressed him is in the connection of his incomprehension with the appearance of royalty. It is this difference that leads his hitherto bewildered and upset imagination into a sublime landscape, and this consideration may help to suggest a major meaning of the sublime not only in Scott's writings but also in those of other Romantics. It is apparent in this passage that it is the mastery exerted upon the senses by the sublime that a lord holds over his subjects; and it may be said that this is the role generally played by the sublime, whether the lordship is connected with metaphysical divinity or merely with aristocratic presence. The imagination excited by the sublime is a deferential imagination. The suspense in which one is held by its appearance describes the command ceded to the master in general and, in these novels, to Scott as a narrator. Later, of course, Roland will become disillusioned; the Earl of Murray will not seem so overpoweringly natural once he meets the imprisoned Queen Mary; but the consequent wavering of his allegiances will not efface this initial impression. Instead, this wavering will indicate the impossibility of fulfilling the imagination. The impression of aristocratic mastery in these novels opens a space in the imagination that history cannot completely occupy – the idea of aristocratic mastery outruns the actualities of the world – and from the resulting sense of emptiness there arises the pain of nostalgia, the uncertainty in Scott's commitment to law, and the drive toward violence.

A somewhat different version of the sublime may help to make the point even clearer:

> The morning, which had arisen calm and bright, gave a pleasant effect even to the waste moorland view which was seen from the castle on looking to the landward; and the glorious ocean, crisped with a thousand rippling waves of silver, extended on the other side, in awful yet complacent majesty, to the verge of the horizon. With such scenes of calm sublimity the human heart sympathises even in its most disturbed moods, and deeds of honour and virtue are inspired by their majestic influence. (*BL,* 75)

Not only does the repetition of "majesty" and "majestic" along with "glorious" and "awful" show how sublime mastery is wrought on the model of royal power, but the imaginative inspiration the Romantics so often took from landscape is here a chivalrous inspiration. It is by prompting one to heroism that the sublime exerts its therapeutic influence upon "the human heart . . . even in its most disturbed moods." The experience of the sublime, in other words, is an experience as profoundly moral and political as it is aesthetic, even though Scott can find no politics or laws adequate to the imagery of his landscapes. The appearance of modern societies and even of actual kings cannot live up to the imagination excited by such descriptions, and thus one is drawn to conclude that the codifications of modernity are mendacious and that one must seek for truth among more primitive peoples and more violent times. This is why Scott's gypsies and borderers and outlaws, as they are described in these novels, suggest the condition of animated landscape. They seem figures not entirely distinct from their uncultivated surroundings, because they are so close to the paradise of unrestrained force that is recalled by the sublime natural vista. For example, a scene that Scott repeats in several novels is that of a passionate woman suddenly appearing in an elevated position, outlined against the sky: a woman who has become unwomanly and yet who is as compellingly transcendent in her violent appearance as Scott's rivals are when they meet on the grounds of violence. It is thus that Meg Merrilies "unexpectedly presented herself":

> She was standing upon one of those high precipitous banks . . . so that she was placed considerably higher than Ellangowan, even though he was on horseback; and her tall figure, relieved against the clear blue sky, seemed almost of supernatural stature . . . On this occasion she had a large piece of red cotton cloth rolled about her head in the form of a turban, from beneath which her dark eyes flashed with uncommon lustre. Her long and tangled black hair fell in elf-locks from the folds of this singular head-gear. Her attitude was that of a sibyl in frenzy. (*GM*, 49)

Scenes of such power are frequently met with in these novels; but even when Scott's landscape is more intimately picturesque and therefore without the appeal of that lordly mastery which upsets the rule of law, it still can stimulate the imagination in ways unaccountable to modern society. Scott concludes such a description in *St. Ronan's Well* by telling of

> a sort of scenery peculiar to those countries which abound, like Scotland, in hills and in streams, and where the traveller is ever and anon discovering, in some intricate and unexpected recess, a simple and silvan beauty, which pleases him the more as it seems to be peculiarly his own property as the first discoverer. (*SRW*, 2)

First, this passage helps to show how impossible it is to regard landscape as something completely other than property: a point necessary to remember in an age when landscape was literally a product designed for the aristocracy, whether on paper or on canvas or on an estate. Second, the connection between discovery and the sense of possession may provide a hint toward investigating the extent to which the idea of originality among the Romantics represents a desire to lay claim to some property exclusively as one's own. Even if that property should be entirely poetic, the fact that the originality with which it is exalted should find a precedent in the system of private property may have considerable significance. Moreover, the element of surprise that creates the sense of discovery and possession in this scene suggests that with landscape as with other men one must be caught off-guard if one's true feelings are to come to the surface, and thus one again sees the epistemic importance of violence as a way to truth. Finally, as the pleasure in the imaginative possession described in this passage reflects the pleasure of actual possession, there is desire involved in this discovery. This desire might well move one to emulate those lords whose estates – like Abbotsford – could encompass such scenes; or, alternatively, it might inspire one to admire those old days when one could appropriate landscape to match one's imagination simply by the force of one's ain grip.

In addition to speaking of civilization and decadence, then, another way of describing the problem of law in these novels is to say that it is the distance between imaginary and actual possession that diminishes intimacy and provokes violence. But this is not just any conflict between the imaginary and the real. As has been shown, the imagination in these novels is a lordly imagination; the reality is the development of law as an institution that tries to use written procedures to expel imagination from its deliberations – and, as Scott sees it, fails in this effort. Just as that later Romantic, Lord Jim, is haunted by a spirit he cannot lay to rest – the spirit of that lordly mastery he lost on the Patna – so are the Waverley novels haunted by an imaginary spirit that cannot be exorcised by any laws. Even though these novels always show that this spirit never really existed, or at least never existed without severe imperfections, the masterly appeal of the imagination is sufficient thoroughly to confuse the reasonable, temporizing, social appeal of laws. Even though an attention to the actualities of history may show this spirit to be a lie compounded of aristocratic ideology and bourgeois nostalgia, it is a lie powerful enough to make the truth of the modern world seem poisonous.

10

CONCLUSION

∾

DESPITE THEIR DIFFERENCES in form, style, and theme, the works of Radcliffe, Austen, and Scott have important elements in common. They are concerned with the proper definition of nature, especially in regard to natural landscape, and with the tasteful judgment of nature and art. Moreover, in their works the nature of social forms takes on dramatic importance in the definition of civilization as well as in the more limited definition of decorum. In relation to this treatment of social forms, the authors explore the problem of disciplining desire, especially as they focus on the place of women in a patriarchal society. The battle of reason versus irrationality and the role of unconsciousness in the psychology of desire also appear as issues of great significance. Closely associated with these issues are the intertwined problems of defining mastery and regulating violence. In addition, one can see in the work of all three writers a marked difference between the narrative form they seek to assert and the contrary sense of things created by the dramatic events and descriptions within the novels.

Thus summarized, the similarities in the works of these writers may appear trivial. However, I hope to have shown that these and other relations among the works become highly significant when one analyzes the constructions of social order implicated in all their elements of representation. I hope to have indicated that all the elements of these novels, from the finest stylistic details to the largest topics and themes, *are* constructions of social order greatly shaped by conflicts between middle-class and aristocratic values. It is this problem that makes the similarities so compelling.

From this perspective, taste plays a comparable role in the novels of Radcliffe, Austen, and Scott, despite the other attributes and sympathies in which these authors obviously differ. For all three, the proper definition of aesthetic taste is inseparable from the denomination of proper moral, social, political, and religious attitudes. Radcliffe, Austen, and Scott certainly are not in complete agreement about these attitudes, but they are as one in assuming that the definition of true art is a question of social order that must be formulated in terms of what they take to be imperative social needs. These needs, then, are articulated in terms of the perception of nature. This perception is never merely a matter of custom or subjective inclination in their works. Rather, nature is seen as a text – and test – of the social issues played out in the events and descriptions of the novels.

The complexities involved in the adoption of this standard of taste are suggested in my first chapter. Of greater moment here is the way this standard in the works of these three authors is further complicated, and contradicted, by the appearance of a different order of social and aesthetic values associated with the emerging power of the middle classes. Since the "logic" of taste is secured by an assumption of its social exclusivity, this standard runs into difficulties when it appears in works that assert the possibility of a more democratic or sentimental appreciation of art. The consequences can be seen in the way nature is equivocally represented in these novels and confusedly perceived by their characters, as well as in the other aesthetic dissonances within their composition that I have explored.

It should be emphasized, however, that the point is not that one order of value can be seen to be supplanting another. The point is that there is no such process, as far as the works of these three writers are concerned. It is not perceivable as such in their novels and could not have been perceived in any teleological way at the time. In this period these orders of value could only appear obscure, or "natural," in their origins; and their contradictory relationship was not yet fully articulated as such, at least in a self-conscious form. It is for this reason that it appears unconsciously, as it were, in the (il)logic of the relation between landscape and the privileged observer in Radcliffe's novels, or in the way taste appears in Austen's novels as both a natural development and an acquirement imposed by male authority, or in the way superstition and violence are both outlawed and embraced by the civilization of Scott's work. By the second half of the nineteenth century, middle-class values would appear dominant in the full-blown domestic sentimentality and more formally codified realism of the novels of that time; but even in this period the traditional standard of taste would continue to exert some suasion, whereas in the era with which this book deals there clearly is no way to predict the shape of social and literary history to come. Hence the debilities that must come from the analysis of literary history in terms of formal categories, such as Romanticism, which obscure the way "Romantics" like Scott or Wordsworth may be seen to have written within differing and conflicting schemes of value that can rise into a unified aesthetics only if one idealizes art and ignores the ways in which it appears as a kind of ad hoc construction of social order.

Given the marked differences in the visions of social order to which Radcliffe, Austen, and Scott explicitly dedicate their works – from the Providential scheme laid out by Radcliffe to Scott's pronounced middle-class conservatism – one would expect major differences in their depiction of the relations between individuals and social forms. As I have tried to show, however, their often similar formulations of this problem may be accounted for by the consideration that the ideologies explicitly or editorially announced by writers are the whole picture of their attitudes only if one fits their works to an idealized image of the author instead of reading them as works composed amidst schemes of value whose conflicts can never be wholly apparent to the writer.

Read in this way, Radcliffe's novels appear at least as similar to Austen's as they are different, especially in their portrayal of social forms or decorum. In both cases, the rule of decorum demands that women be peculiarly unconscious of themselves. In both cases, that is, a rigid propriety is demanded in the absence of any effective code to actual behavior, with the result that women are driven to express themselves through some variety of unconsciousness: physical helplessness, passivity, silence, self-betrayal, or willing acquiescence in their own repression. Consequently, suffering in the work of both authors may come to appear as much a positive value as an unfortunate necessity, a value that frequently serves as the measure of one's sensibility, taste, and virtue. The problem of social forms for Radcliffe and Austen is the problem of a society in which the ideal of behavior appears imperative – especially to women – and yet impossible to fulfill, because in actuality the codes with which their characters must contend are a mixture of conflicting imperatives drawn from middle-class as well as aristocratic values. Thus, the equivocal signs to which Austen's women must offer themselves can be seen to be related to the mysterious figures, sounds, flickering lights, and unstable landscapes that terrorize Radcliffe's heroines.

In Scott's works, too, a major subject is the discrepancy between the demands of social forms and the realities of social experience, although to a rather different effect. In these works, the regulating codes of civilization in all their forms appear as a feminine and feminizing force that is accepted as a progressive historical development and yet dramatized as a demeaning, vitiating influence against which men must rebel. In other words, Scott represents the laws of social order as an elevation of the feminine and so helps to develop the chivalric assumptions that were to become standard in middle-class culture during the nineteenth century. He thus provides an ideology for the experiences of shame and submission that the female characters in Radcliffe's and Austen's novels must undergo without benefit of theory, making it appear that the relative powerlessness of women in society signifies their transcendent grace – and terror. Social forms in Scott's novels are no less ideally compelling and practically confusing than in the novels of Radcliffe and Austen, but this situation is given a twist that provides a new perspective on the way that virtue is both a liberating and a terrorizing aspect of the identity of Radcliffe's and Austen's heroines. Whereas the patriarchal compulsion of the ideal appears comparatively without mediation in the work of the latter writers, or rather is mediated simply by the name of "society" as this is taken to be natural, in Scott's novels one finds it mediated by the middle-class sentiments that seem to reject the arbitrary violence of aristocratic tradition – and one also finds a rebellion against this mediation that indicates how thoroughly patriarchal rule remains itself even when authority seems to be ceded to the feminine. Its apparent transformation, like the apparent transformation of the standard of taste going on in this period, may be its revivification under a different name and with different and yet fundamentally similar social rules. Like taste, desire figures in the work of all three writers as an inclination taken to be categorically natural and yet categorized as being definitively unnatural if it does not represent the prevailing social order. Since this order cannot be coherently figured forth from the conflicting values evident in their works, the result is that desire must defile between the categories of nature and society – must establish the difference between these categories as well as their ultimate unity – by enduring the discipline of suffering. In other words, desire is another element in these novels in which the problems of their "logic" are concentrated, and suffering is the discipline that is meant to make these inconsistencies, paradoxes, and conflicts appear as if they follow a coherent and harmonious set of rules.

It might be objected that suffering as a means to the establishment of truth is a theme and narrative logic as old as literature itself, but the point here is that suffering in the works of these three writers specifically articulates the competing constructions of society with which they are preoccupied. As it appears in these works, suffering is more than a social or literary convention. Like the landscape of nature, it is a text of the values at play in these works as well as the test of their resolution. Thus it is that suffering in Radcliffe's novels is used paradoxically to prove the aristocratic fineness of one's universal sympathies; that suffering in Austen's novels represents the experience of a social confusion that must nonetheless be interpreted as a problem of individual responsibility; and that, in Scott's novels, it marks the points at which the lawyer and the laird turn upon each other. In all three cases, suffering allegorizes the orientations these authors assume toward the conflicting values apparent in their work so that they may formally piece them together and "make sense of them." In playing this role, this suffering that disciplines desire also passes through the defile of reason and unreason, of consciousness and unconsciousness, and of other important pairs of controlling categories in these works. The ideal sense of these categories can be established only by such a rhetorical movement, since this sense can be only an ideological construction.

Suffering, then, is one important means toward the achievement of the mastery that is the ideal of taste. Mastery, this fundamentally aristocratic model for judgment, is common to all three novelists. (There is no notion, for instance, of the conventional, consensual, or relativistic notions of judgment familiar in modern literature.) In addition to the patriarchal definition always given to this concept, significant in this respect is its persistence as a standard in the face of manifest contradictions. It may be that in Radcliffe's novels the talismanic significance of landscape can exist only as a textual and not as an existential reality, that the language of Austen's novels shows a proliferation of competing interpretations where one ideal meaning is supposed to hold sway, and that Scott's novels show the spirit of mastery to be a lie compounded of bourgeois nostalgia and aristocratic ideology; but the standard still holds. In effect, these writers cannot think their way through it any more than they can think their way through the standard of taste itself. It is a limit of civilization for their imaginations.

Therefore, given the persistence of this standard despite the various ways in which it is called into question in the works of these writers, it is not surprising that violence should play such a similar role in the novels of Radcliffe and Scott. Since the ideal of mastery demands that it cannot be fully possessed even by those who are taken to be in possession of it, it appears in these novels that one can be sure only of the truth that issues immediately from violence. Violence appears to pierce the necessary but vitiating reality of social forms to touch the elusive spirit of this concept of mastery. In Radcliffe's novels this drive toward violence serves to tie the virtue of her characters to the nature of their world and the providence of God, whereas in Scott's the emphasis is more on the search for a human fellowship beyond the obscure borderlines of family, party, nation, and so on; but in both cases the quality being sought is marked as an essentially aristocratic one that may appear endangered even by those middle-class qualities to which these authors give their formal approval.

Austen's case is somewhat different, since sublime or Gothic violence does not enter into her work except as a subject of satire. Nevertheless, as divinity becomes decorum in her novels, and as it appears that her "common sense" revision of the rules of Richardson's novels results in the harsher rule that no virtue exists without violation, one sees that her transference of violence from the realm of dramatic event to that of psychological drama has, if anything, increased its force. Her tone is lighter than Richardson's and Radcliffe's, and the stakes of her battles appear much more closely circumscribed and "civilized"; but the curious result of this different form of representation is that virtue cannot emerge from its trials unscathed. Moreover, the closest one comes to Radcliffe's liberating landscape is on the dance floor, with its thoroughly qualified pleasures. In Austen's case, in other words, the violence spurred by the ideal of mastery appears in that process of internalizing society with which she replaces the metaphysical conception of character found in Radcliffe's work. In effect, her psychology is a social statics akin to the realm of dramatic event in the works of Radcliffe and Scott. In this psychological realm, as in the realm of dramatic event, the emergence of truth approximates a complete form only as an experience of repression, amnesia, partiality, and other forms of mental violence.

Perhaps the most telling way in which the novels of these three authors are comparable, though, involves the inconsistencies that appear if one compares their formal resolutions (and the narrative elements prefiguring them) to certain descriptions and dramatic events within the novels. Although it may be true that such inconsistencies are bound to appear in any novel as long as one does not read it with idealist assumptions about its necessary unity and coherence, the point here is that these inconsistencies take a form characteristic of this era in social history. Furthermore, they can be seen to be related to all the similarities summarized earlier, as these inconsistencies give one the shape of that conflict among values which also shapes these other elements of representation.

Thus, in the novels of Radcliffe, Austen, and Scott one finds a marked difference between their endings, which affirm the triumph of an order oriented to aristocratic values, and the narratives leading up to those endings, which frequently propose a different and conflicting scheme of things. In Radcliffe's novels this contradiction appears most dramatically in the gap between their repetitive events and their proclamations of a transcendent closure, as these proclamations imply a progress toward truth that is not in accord with the structure of repetition; but it also appears in the way democratic sentiments approved in the course of the narratives are disclaimed by their formal conclusions. Austen's novels, more detailed in their delineation of manners and social circumstances, show in these terms a mixture of aristocratic values (for instance, in the importance given to economic concerns in marriage) and values more closely associated with the middle class (as in her concern with professional comportment and moral seriousness). In general, although the value of traditional social rank as such is severely qualified in these novels, it is not discounted even when it appears to hold an arbitrary power; and some of the tensions consequent to this mixed situation can be seen in the way the conclusions of her novels seem to prove the existence of an order that, nonetheless, is not implicit in the events that precede these conclusions. And the contradictions in play are even clearer in the case of Scott's works, as the deliberately expressed sentiments of their narrators are all on the side of the Protestant, professional, commercial values of Scott's time, whereas the aristocratic status accorded to their protagonists and the dramatic interest of their plots are on the side of the values of the past.

In all three cases, then, the disharmonies of form in these novels may serve to reveal, first, how much all their elements are shaped by these conflicting values and, second, how these different orders of value do not appear in a pure form but rather in what psychoanalysts might call a "compromise formation." My argument has been that this formation, this text of social change, ought not to be rationalized into a coherent unity if one is concerned to understand literary creation for the active, material, human process that it is. There are many other ways that one could approach these texts aside from this question of class and aesthetic values, but my argument has been that any approach is seriously flawed if it does not take into consideration the heterogeneity of the discourse given to artists by their culture, the complex "logic" of ideologies (which are not free of contradiction and conflict even when they appear relatively stable, as in the case of taste in the eighteenth century), and the way the smallest as well as the most prominent elements of representation in a literary text are constructions of social order related to the values at play in the society in which these texts were produced.

Of course, I do not claim to have proved these contentions. Even if historical and textual arguments such as those involved in this study were susceptible of "proof," my aim has been, as I indicated in my introductory chapter, a limited one. Nonetheless, it has been my intent, through my study of three such different authors, to argue for a conception of literature as a creation that is social before it is individual: social not simply in the sense that it partakes of conventions or traditions, but rather in the sense that its use of and contribution to its culture is bounded by the discourses available to

the author, with all their "laws," "logic," "truths," and "nature."
The differences in the works of these three writers are also significant, as I hope I have also emphasized in the sections individually devoted to them. For instance, there is the comparative absence of an introspective form of psychological representation in Radcliffe's novels as well as the absence of abundant physical detail. Although both of these forms of description would be vital to the representation of reality in the Victorian novel, too often they have been taken to show a refinement of representational technique rather than a change that is important, to be sure, but without any truth value or aesthetic superiority in itself. Austen represented a psychological interiority that would become part of the standard of realism for later writers, such as Dickens, Eliot, and Hardy; but she did not for this reason have access to a truth of human character to which Radcliffe was blind. Rather, she participated in the formulation of a discourse of character comparable to the eighteenth-century discourse of taste. This was a scheme of representation that was well adapted to a society in which the figure of the individual and the issue of the individual's private judgment and affective domestic relations became of vital concern, a scheme helpful in answering the problem of a social order increasingly fluid in terms of class position, property, and environment and thus looking for a center of control that would supplement such aspects of church, state, and social tradition as were apparently becoming outmoded.

Thus, the difference in psychological representation in the works of Radcliffe and Austen can help one to judge the orientation of their work in terms of the large-scale changes in society between the eighteenth and nineteenth centuries, and the similar psychological issues that nonetheless appear in their work may serve to indicate the danger of distinguishing "better" from "worse" forms of representation according to the degree to which they favor our own values, assumptions, and habits of perception. Austen's works are no more an accurate portrayal of her society than are Radcliffe's, except for those who think they can identify a simple ideology in her novels and who then identify themselves with that system of representation. It therefore has seemed to me that a more valuable approach is one that critically examines the social significance of aesthetic form – the politics of rhetoric, as it were – without assuming that the work of any writer is any more coherent in its ideology than the society in which it was composed.

Conclusion

Perhaps the most significant difference between Radcliffe's novels and Scott's has to do with the way culture and society become the subjects of a self-conscious representation in Scott's works. That is to say, Radcliffe's blithe disregard for historical differences bespeaks a habit of mind that might almost be called pre-historical (hence the almost mythical impression of a world given by her melodrama), whereas Scott's novels are dedicated to the constitution of a historical discourse within fiction. Even though the historical consciousness thus represented proves to function remarkably like Radcliffe's landscape of nature – as a kind of Providence that can be seen coherently only from afar – the attention to change and the assumption of progress in the works of Scott (as well as in those of Austen) indicate a major shift in values, of which their narratives attempt to make sense. (Hence the significance of the attention to manners and physical details in the novels of Austen, Scott, and the Victorian novelists that followed them, which bespeaks a perception of society as being in history and thus requiring a notation and accumulation of detail if it is to rise out of the flux of change and appear to us in a coherent way. The material solidity characteristic of the Victorian novel is a sign of the perceived transience of society.) And even in this respect, Radcliffe is not entirely different from Austen and Scott. The absence of supernatural agency in her novels (all their mysteries are rationalized by the end of the narratives) indicates a secular boundary to metaphysical belief and thus implies the sort of faith in the human mind that was to become the subject of nineteenth-century psychological discourse.

I have intended the title of this study, *The Civilized Imagination,* to be a kind of oxymoron – as indeed it must appear to those who take the eighteenth-century concept of civilization and the Romantic concept of the imagination to be as radically opposed to each other as some Romantics, at times, portrayed them to be. What I have tried to explore is the way aesthetic values are of necessity subject to such paradox – or to contradiction, irresolution, logical gaps, and other forms of conflict – because of their nature as constructions of social order within societies that fall short of the ideal.

Notes

I. INTRODUCTION

1 David Hume, "Of the Standard of Taste," *Essays and Treatises on Several Subjects,* 2 vols. (London: Cadell, 1784), 1: 245, 248. See also Bernard Bosanquet, *A History of Aesthetics* (London: Allen and Unwin, 1892), p. 174.

2 Edmund Burke, "Introduction on Taste," *A Philosophical Enquiry into the Origin of Our Ideas of the Sublime and the Beautiful,* ed. with an introduction and notes by James T. Boulton (London: Routledge and Kegan Paul, 1958), p. 13.

3 R. G. Saisselin, *Taste in Eighteenth Century France* (Syracuse: Syracuse University Press, 1965), pp. 64–5.

4 There are writers – such as Francis Hutcheson and Thomas Reid – who elevate natural over educated perceptions to some degree, but the question then becomes what kind of "nature" they are referring to and whether, in fact, it is not related to aristocratic privilege. See Section V of this Introduction.

5 Alexander Gerard, *An Essay on Taste* (Edinburgh, 1764; rep. New York: Garland Publishing, 1970), p. 131.

6 Henry Home [Lord Kames], *Elements of Criticism,* ed. Abraham Hills, 3 vols. (New York: Huntington and Savage, 1845), 1: 471.

7 Hugh Blair, *Lectures on Rhetoric and Belles Lettres, The Rhetoric of Blair, Campbell, and Whately,* ed. James L. Golden and Edward P. J. Corbett (New York: Holt, Rinehart, and Winston, 1968), pp. 35–6.

8 René Wellek, *A History of Modern Criticism: 1750–1950,* 4 vols. (New Haven: Yale University Press, 1955), 1: 24.

9   L'Abbé du Bos, *Réflexions critiques sur la poësie et sur la peinture*, 3 vols. (Paris: Pissot, 1755), 2: 351. (Translations not otherwise noted are mine.)

10 Thomas Reid, "Taste and the Fine Arts," *Thomas Reid's Lectures on the Fine Arts*, transcribed from the original manuscript, introduction and notes by Peter Kivy, International Archives of the History of Ideas Series Minor 7 (The Hague: Martinus Nijhoff, 1973), p. 47.

11 Bernard Mandeville, *The Fable of the Bees: Or, Private Vices, Publick Benefits*, commentary by F. B. Kaye, 2 vols. (Oxford: Oxford University Press, 1924), 1: 199.

12 Home, *Elements*, 1: 469.

13 Samuel Richardson, *Pamela: Or, Virtue Rewarded*, Shakespeare Head Edition, 4 vols. (Oxford: Blackwell, 1929), 3: 324.

14 Jonathan Richardson, "The Science of a Connoisseur," *The Works of Jonathan Richardson* (London, 1792), p. 191.

15 Jean le Rond d'Alembert, "Reflexions sur l'usage et sur l'abus de la philosophie dans les matières de goût," *Oeuvres complètes de d'Alembert*, 5 vols. (Paris: Belin, 1822), 4: 333.

16 Denis Diderot, "Essai sur la peinture," *Oeuvres*, ed. with notes by André Billy (Paris: Editions Gallimard, 1951), p. 1169.

17 Charles Batteux, *Les beaux arts réduits à un principe, Principes de la littérature* (Paris, 1775; rep. Geneva: Slatkine Reprints, 1967), p. 88.

18 On this point and others related to this essay, see Harry Payne, "Elite *versus* Popular Mentality in the Eighteenth Century," *Studies in Eighteenth Century Culture* 8 (1979).

19 François Voltaire, *Dictionnaire philosophique, Oeuvres complètes de Voltaire*, 52 vols. (Paris: Garnier Frères, 1879), 19: 282.

20 John Donaldson, "Reflections on the Harmony of Sensibility and Reason," *The Elements of Beauty* (Edinburgh, 1780; rep. New York: Garland Publishing, 1970), pp. 84–5.

21 Voltaire, *Dictionnaire philosophique*, 279.

22 Charles Montesquieu, "Essai sur le goût," *Oeuvres complètes de Montesquieu*, 3 vols. (Paris: Editions Nagel, 1950), 1: 629.

23 Hume, "Of the Delicacy of Taste and Passion," *Essays and Treatises*, 1: 4.

24 Gerard, *An Essay on Taste*, p. 115.

25 Home, *Elements*, 1: 61.

26 Sir Joshua Reynolds, *Discourses Delivered to the Students of the Royal Academy*, introduction and notes by Roger Fry (London: Seeley, 1905), p. 194.

27 Francis Hutcheson, *An Inquiry into the Original of Our Ideas of Beauty and Virtue, Collected Works of Francis Hutcheson*, 7 vols. (London, 1725; rep. Hildesheim: Georg Olms Verlagsbuchhandlung, 1971), 1: 11.

28 Immanuel Kant, *Kritik der Urteilskraft,* Der Philosophischen Bibliothek, Bd. 39a (Hamburg: F. Meiner, 1959), p. 41.
29 *The Spectator,* ed. with an introduction and notes by Donald F. Bond, 5 vols. (Oxford: Oxford University Press, 1965), 3: 538.
30 Ibid., 1: 4.
31 Richard Payne Knight, *An Analytical Inquiry into the Principles of Taste* (London: Hansard, 1808), p. 191.
32 Humphrey Repton, *The Art of Landscape Gardening,* ed. John Nolen (Boston: Houghton Mifflin, 1907), p. 67.
33 Kant, *Kritik der Urteilskraft,* p. 47.
34 Mandeville, *The Fable of the Bees,* 1: 123.
35 Samuel Johnson, *The Idler, The Yale Edition of the Works of Samuel Johnson* (New Haven: Yale University Press, 1958–), 2: 116.
36 Aristotle, "De Memoria et Reminiscentia," tr. Richard Sorals, *Aristotle on Memory* (Providence: Brown University Press, 1972), p. 57.
37 Jean-Jacques Rousseau, *Emile, Oeuvres complètes,* 4 vols. (Paris: Editions Gallimard, 1919), 4: 407–8.
38 Plato, *The Republic,* tr. Paul Shorey, *The Collected Dialogues of Plato,* ed. with an introduction and prefatory notes by Edith Hamilton and Huntington Cairns, Bollingen Series 71 (Princeton: Princeton University Press, 1963), p. 640.
39 *The Spectator,* 4: 69.
40 Seran de la Tour, *L'Art de sentir et de juger en matière de goût,* 2 vols. (Paris, 1762; rep. Geneva: Slatkine Reprints, 1970), 2:57.
41 Thomas Mann, *Confessions of Felix Krull, Confidence Man* [*The Early Years*], tr. Denver Lindley, Vintage Books Edition (New York: Random House, 1969), p. 71.
42 Anthony, Earl of Shaftesbury, *Characteristics of Men, Manners, Opinions, Times,* etc., ed. with an introduction and notes by John M. Robertson, 2 vols. (Gloucester, Mass.: Peter Smith, 1963), 2: 255.
43 See Katharine Everett Gilbert and Helmut Kuhn, *A History of Esthetics,* rev. ed. (Bloomington: Indiana University Press, 1953), pp. 233–6.
44 Walter Jackson Bate, *From Classic to Romantic: Premises of Taste in Eighteenth-Century England* (New York: Harper and Row, 1961).
45 Reynolds, *Discourses,* pp. 206, 209.
46 In this regard, see Kant's essay, "What Is Enlightenment?" in *Critique of Practical Reason and Other Writings in Moral Philosophy,* tr. and ed. with an introduction by Lewis White Beck (Chicago: University of Chicago Press, 1949). Kant defines enlightened freedom as the liberty to publish – but not necessarily teach or practice – one's thought.
47 Lester G. Crocker, *Two Diderot Studies: Ethics and Esthetics,* The Johns Hopkins Studies in Romance Literatures and Language, Extra. vol. 27 (Baltimore: Johns Hopkins Press, 1952, p. 98).

48 See J. H. Plumb's remark that "as in our days the spread of culture amongst the masses was regarded as a decline in standards" by such writers as "Hume, Johnson, Burke, Goldsmith, Reynolds." "The Public, Literature and the Arts in the Eighteenth Century," in *The Triumph of Culture: 18th Century Perspectives*, ed. Paul Fritz and David Williams (Toronto: Hakkert, 1972) p. 47.

49 Cf. Raymond Naves, *Le Goût de Voltaire* (Paris: Garnier Frères, 1948), esp. pp. 3-4, 56-60 and 100-4.

50 Home, *Elements*, 1:468.

51 Rousseau, *Emile*, 4: 264n.

52 J. de Crousaz, *Traité du beau* (Amsterdam, 1715; rep. Geneva: Slatkine Reprints, 1970), pp. 64-5.

53 Richardson, *Pamela*, 4: 11.

54 Reynolds, *Discourses*, p. 211

55 Jane Austen, *Northanger Abbey, The Works of Jane Austen*, ed. R. W. Chapman, 5 vols. (Oxford: Oxford University Press, 1933-54), 5: 28.

56 See Thomas J. Schlereth, *The Cosmopolitan Ideal in Enlightenment Thought: Its Form and Function in the Ideas of Franklin, Hume, and Voltaire, 1694-1790* (Notre Dame: University of Notre Dame Press, 1977), esp. Ch. 1, "The Sociology of an International Intellectual Class."

57 Voltaire, "Essai sur la poésie épique," *Oeuvres*, 8: 312.

58 Nicolas Trublet, "Du goût," *Essais sur divers sujets de littérature et de morale* (Paris, 1754-60; rep. Geneva: Slatkine Reprints, 1968), p. 277.

59 Archibald Alison, *Essays on the Nature and Principles of Taste*, with corrections and improvements by Abraham Mills (New York: Carvill, 1830), p. 71.

60 Cartaud de la Villate, *Essai historique et philosophique sur le goût* (Paris, 1736; rep. Geneva: Slatkine Reprints, 1970), pp. 268-9.

61 Adam Smith, *The Theory of Moral Sentiments, The Works of Adam Smith*, 5 vols. (London: Cadell, 1812), 1: 345-6.

62 Blair, *Lectures*, p. 43.

63 Hutcheson, *An Inquiry Concerning Moral Good and Evil, Works*, 1: 214.

64 Friedrich Schiller, "Über die ästhetische Erziehung des Menschen in einer Reihe von Briefen," *Schillers Werke*, 20 vols. (Weimer: Herman Bohlaus, 1962), 20: 410-1.

65 La Tour, *L'Art de sentir*, 2: 87, 77.

66 Trublet, "Du goût," *Essais*, p. 283.

67 Crousaz, *Traité du beau*, p. 27.

68 Home, *Elements*, 1: 470.

2. THE FIGURE IN THE LANDSCAPE

1 References are to the following editions of Ann Radcliffe's works: *The Castles of Athlin and Dunbayne: A Highland Story*, foreword by Fred-

erick Schroyer, originally published 1789 (London, 1821; rep. New York: Arno Press, 1972); *A Sicilian Romance,* Foreword by Howard Mumford Jones, introduction by Devendra P. Varma, 2 vols. in 1, originally published 1790 (London: Jones, 1821; rep. New York: Arno Press, 1972); *The Romance of the Forest,* foreword by Frederick Barber, introduction by Devendra P. Varma, 3 vols., originally published 1791 (London: A. K. Newman, 1827; rep. New York: Arno Press, 1974); *The Mysteries of Udolpho: A Romance,* ed. with an introduction by Bonamy Dobrée, originally published 1794 (London: Oxford University Press, 1966); *A Journey Made in the Summer of 1794, through Holland to the Western Frontier of Germany,* etc., 2nd ed., 2 vols, originally published 1795 (London: Robinson, 1975); *The Italian, Or, The Confessional of the Black Penitents: A Romance,* ed. with an introduction by Frederick Garber, originally published 1797 (London: Oxford University Press, 1968); *Gaston de Blondeville: Or, The Court of Henry III Keeping Festival in Ardenne,* introduction by Devendra P. Varma, 3 vols. in 2, originally published 1826 (London, 1826; rep. New York: Arno Press, 1972).

2 Cf. Mary Poovey, "Ideology and 'The Mysteries of Udolpho,' " *Criticism* 21 (Fall 1979): 311: "Thus, in Radcliffe's romances, we have an excellent example of an ideology *in practice,* a testing of its images and values by one member of that class which had most at stake in it. In the tonal and structural dissonances, the competing ideas which characterize even Radcliffe's most successful novel, we see the conflicts within the ideology realized."

3 Cf. J. M. S. Tompkins, *The Popular Novel in England: 1770–1800* (London: Constable, 1932), p. 255: "The characters and conflicts of Emily and Montoni and Vivaldi and Adeline are not the centre of interest; the centre of interest is impersonal; it is the southern landscape, whose fullest effect is to be elicited by the happy musings of lovers or by their terror-stricken flight."

4 Robert Kiely, *The Romantic Novel in England* (Cambridge: Harvard University Press, 1972), p. 17. Also, cf. Devendra P. Varma, *The Gothic Flame* (New York: Russell and Russell, 1966), p. 117: "For Mrs. Radcliffe nature is a manifestation of Divine grandeur and her attitude contains all the germs of that philosophy of nature which was later so well expounded by the Romantic poets"; and Tompkins, *The Popular Novel,* p. 263: "From the divine order of nature the persecuted heroine draws fortitude, purifying her soul in the beauty of frequent dawns and sunsets."

5 Cf. Eino Railo's description of the actions of Radcliffe's characters at sentimental moments in *The Haunted Castle: A Study of the Elements of English Romanticism* (London: Routledge, 1927), p. 46: "Often, at such

moments, they touch the strings of their lutes and as it were unconsciously, and with astonishing prosodical skill, arrange their thoughts
in correct sonnet form, or still more frequently in an ode, the fashionable form of poetry in those days."

6 For descriptions of Radcliffe's borrowings, see Railo, *The Haunted Castle,*
p. 26; and Walter Francis Wright, *Sensibility in English Prose Fiction
1760–1814: A Reinterpretation,* Illinois Studies in Language and Literature vol. 22, nos. 3–4 (Urbana: University of Illinois Press, 1937), p.
82.

7 Similarly, it is significant that it is the corrupt marquis of *The Romance
of the Forest* who draws upon comparative anthropology and the behavior of animals in nature to argue against fixed standards of conduct
(*RF* 2: 248): "It is the first proof of a superior mind to liberate itself
from prejudices of country, or of education." Cf. Charlotte Dacre's
description of Fribourg in *Confessions of the Nun of St. Omer,* introduction by Devendra P. Varma, 2 vols. (London: Hughes, 1805; rep.
New York: Arno Press, 1972), 1: 166. This character's evil is also
specified in part by the way that he seeks to discredit religion and
conventional morality on the basis of a comparison of the variety of
attitudes in different countries.

8 See Radcliffe's description in the *Journey* (1: 232–3) of Bonn, in which
she sees the taste of its inhabitants as a direct consequence of their
laudable government; and Blanche's exclamation in *The Mysteries of
Udolpho,* p. 472: "How can the poor nuns and friars feel the full fer-
vour of devotion, if they never see the sun rise, or set? Never, till this
evening, did I know what true devotion is; for, never before did I see
the sun sink below the vast earth!"

9 For a comparable example of this idea of nature, which became a cliché
of Gothic and Romantic literature, see Eleanor Sleath, *The Orphan of
the Rhine,* The Northanger Set of Jane Austen Horrid Novels, 4 vols.
(London: Folio Press, 1968), 1: 61: "To the admirer of Nature every
object she presents becomes interesting. The variety of her charms
relieves the mind from satiety, and, in the enjoyment of her beauties,
the soul of the enthusiast becomes elevated above the narrow boundaries of the world: he sees the Creator in his works, and adores in
silence the perfection of the whole."

10 See Jane Austen, *Persuasion, The Novels of Jane Austen,* ed. R. W.
Chapman, 5 vols. (London: Oxford University Press, 1932–4), pp.
84–5, and my comments on this passage in Chapter 6.
 This contradiction also appears in William Godwin's *St. Leon; A
Tale of the Sixteenth Century,* foreword by Devendra P. Varma, introduction by Juliet Beckett (New York: Arno Press, 1972). At one point,
when St. Leon's family is poor, he writes, "The scenes of nature were

all our own; nor could wealth give them a more perfect, or a firmer, appropriation" (p. 6); but as soon as his family faces real, unromantic poverty, he feels quite differently: "It had destroyed all romance, I had almost said all dignity, in my mind for ever" (p. 130).

11 William Wordsworth, *Selected Poems and Prefaces,* ed. with an introduction and notes by Jack Stillinger (Boston: Houghton Mifflin, 1965), pp. 443, 463.

12 All quotes are taken from Wordsworth, "Resolution and Independence," *Selected Poems,* pp. 165–9.

13 For a passage by one of Radcliffe's imitators that epitomizes this aspect of her work, see Mary-Anne Radcliffe, *Manfroné: Or, the One-Handed Monk,* foreword by Devendra P. Varma, introduction by Coral Ann Howells, 2 vols. (London: Newman, 1828; rep. New York: Arno Press, 1972), pp. 166–7: "The path she had to tread in her weary pilgrimage was full of craggy rocks, precipices, and quicksands, where the least false step would consign her to destruction; the temple of happiness appeared far, far distant, and at times seemed but a cloud-formed fabric."

14 Cf. Poovey's argument that in contrast to *Clarissa, The Mysteries of Udolpho* shows an economic threat "endangering both the sexual *and* spiritual community." "Ideology and 'The Mysteries of Udolpho,' " p. 324n.

15 Cf. Kiely's description of how "the little she does see both repels and attracts" Emily when she confronts Montoni and his associates in *The Mysteries of Udolpho,* so that she "does not die a martyr's death nor become the whore of outlaws. Imprisoned midway between the two extremes, she suffers the fate of the prototypical romantic character: deprived of a cathartic experience, incapable of tragedy, she is periodically immobilized by the imperatives of an imagination which transforms the limitations of present reality into a limitless future." *The Romantic Novel,* pp. 75–6.

16 Cf. the comments on Radcliffe's use of obscurity in Tompkins, *The Popular Novel,* pp. 57–8; and James R. Foster, *History of the Pre-Romantic Novel in England* (New York: Modern Language Association; London: Oxford University Press, 1949), p. 263.

17 Cf. Louis I. Bredvold's analysis of "The Exaltation of Unhappiness," *The Natural History of Sensibility* (Detroit: Wayne State University Press, 1962), Ch. 3.

18 For examples of this conventional kind of description in other Gothic novelists, see Regina Maria Roche, *The Children of the Abbey; A Tale* (New York: Butler Brothers, 1888), p. 217: "Amanda looked thinner and paler than when he had seen her in Ireland – yet, if possible, more interesting from these circumstances"; Sleath, *The Nocturnal Minstrel:*

Or, The Spirit of the Wood, 2 vols. in 1 (London: Minerva Press, 1810; rep. New York: Arno Press, 1972), 2: 136: "Her beautiful face, to which a shade of sorrow had, without detracting from its loveliness, added a most affecting interest"; and Sleath, *The Orphan of the Rhine,* 1: 54: "The extreme agitation of her mind so seriously affected her health, that the rose had forsaken her cheek, though without considerably impairing her beauty, having left in its stead a bewitching softness of complexion, a kind of interesting dejection, which was infinitely more charming and attractive than the most striking animation of colour."

3. THE LABYRINTH OF DECORUM

1 See Lionel Trilling, "Mansfield Park," *The Opposing Self* (New York: Viking, 1955), p. 207: "We are quick, too quick, to understand that *Northanger Abbey* invites us into a smug conspiracy to disabuse the little heroine of the errors of her corrupted fancy – Catherine Morland, having become addicted to novels of terror, has accepted their inadmissible premise, she believes that life is violent and unpredictable. And that is exactly what life is shown to be by the events of the story: it is we who must be disabused of our belief that life is sane and orderly." Also, cf. Nelson C. Smith's analysis of Radcliffe's novels as works that reveal how, "far from being an advocate of sensibility, she, like Jane Austen two decades later, shows its weaknesses and flaws," in "Sense, Sensibility and Ann Radcliffe," *Studies in English Literature* 13 (Autumn 1973): 577.

2 For comparable examples of this situation, see Roche, *The Children of the Abbey,* p. 192: "Delicacy sealed the lips of Amanda and guarded her secret . . . But though she could command her words, she could not her feelings, and they were visibly expressed in her countenance." See also the speech Roche gives to Madeline in *Clairmont: A Tale,* The Northanger Set of Jane Austen Horrid Novels (London: Folio Press, 1968), p. 344: "Oh! let those tears, those agonies, plead for us! let them express the feelings which language cannot utter!"

3 Railo, *The Haunted Castle,* p. 43. Also, cf. Wright, *Sensibility in English Prose Fiction,* p. 105: "A special sensibility to terror was like the writing of sonnets, a manifestation of delicate sensibility."

4 Austen, *Northanger Abbey, The Novels of Jane Austen,* 5: 200.

5 Cf. my analysis in Chapter 4 of the way that Austen's heroines may not have the power of the negative, and the way that Scott consciously evokes Richardson's use of the Old Testament denial of power to a woman's word (Numbers 30: 2–15) in his Introduction to *The Bride of Lammermoor.*

Also, cf. Charlotte Dacre ("Rosa Matilda"), *The Libertine,* foreword by John Garrett, introduction by Devendra P. Varma, 4 vols. (London: Cadell, 1807; rep. New York: Arno Press, 1974), 59–60: "Thus is it with man – if a female wears the semblance of being virtuous, if even Calumny's self cannot prove her otherwise, then do they require some proof stronger even than truth itself; but if being not equally *wary* as *virtuous,* if unable to resist or circumvent various temptation and ceaseless manoeuvre, at length she fall, then do they despise her for her weakness, triumphantly and cruelly adducing it in confirmation of their assertion, that 'she could never have been virtuous.' " A slightly later comparison might be to that picture of a witch being drowned that so fascinates Maggie Tulliver in George Eliot's *The Mill on the Floss:* In that case, only a woman's death can prove her word.

6 Cf. the way that a series of characters are misidentified in Austen's *Sense and Sensibility* – Brandon for Willoughby, Willoughby for Brandon, Edward Ferrars for Brandon, Robert Ferrars for Edward, and so on.

7 Cf. Kiely's description of *The Mysteries of Udolpho* in *The Romantic Novel,* p. 71: "The properties of her novel . . . derive what interest they have from the shadow cast on them by the heroine's prolonged state of panic. She may preach prudence, moderation, and universal harmony, but the potential fertility of that irrational state remains the most original and convincing aspect of Mrs. Radcliffe's art."

8 The significance of this opinion is emphasized by the fact that it is twice described in the novel (*MU,* 510, 581) – an occurrence which, despite the formulaic nature of Radcliffe's work, is unusual.

9 Like Scott, who wrote one novel in which a ghostly figure was not rationalized away by the end of the narrative, Radcliffe wrote one novel, *Gaston de Blondeville,* in which a "real" ghost appears. However, the part of the novel in which this ghost appears is said to have been written by a credulous medieval monk; and thus this figure, like all the supernatural phenomena in Radcliffe's fiction, is rationalized as a product of ignorance. For the significance of Scott's one attempt to draw a "real" supernatural character, see Chapter 8.

10 This paranoia is liable to affect both villains and heroines in Radcliffe's work and in Gothic fiction generally. Cf. Matthew Lewis's description of Ambrosio on his way to ravish Antonia in *The Monk: A Romance,* ed. with an introduction by Howard Anderson (London: Oxford University Press, 1973), p. 299: "He looked round him every moment with apprehension and anxiety. He saw a Spy in every shadow, and heard a voice in every murmur of the night-breeze."

11 Cf. the description of a voice coming from behind a wall in Charles

Robert Maturin [Dennis Jasper Murphy], *The Fatal Revenge; Or, the Family of Montorio: A Romance,* foreword by Henry D. Hicks, introduction by Maurice Levy, 2 vols. (London: Longman, 1807; rep. New York: Arno Press, 1974), 2: 63–4: "I cannot tell you the effect of this cry . . . a sudden and inexpressible conviction, that the sounds I heard were not uttered by man . . . I felt all day like a man, upon whose peace some secret is preying. I looked in deep oppression around me, on the walls and windows, and dark corners of my room, as if they possessed a consciousness of what they had heard; as if they could pour out and unfold the terrible sounds they had swallowed."

12 Cf. Maturin, "Preface," *The Fatal Revenge,* 1: iv: "I question whether there be a source of emotion in the whole mental frame, so powerful or universal as *the fear arising from objects of invisible terror.* Perhaps there is no other that has been at some period or other of life, the predominant and indelible sensation of every mind, of every class, and under every circumstance. Love, supposed to be the most general of passions, has certainly been felt in its purity by very few, and by some not at all, even in its most indefinite and simple state."

13 See Trilling, "Mansfield Park," *The Opposing Self,* p. 228. Also, cf. the description of the heroine about to offer her hand to a man about whom she still has some questions in Roche, *Clairmont,* p. 98: "But delicacy, that celestial guardian of her sex, checked the rash impulse of romantic tenderness. She suddenly recollected herself, and recoiled, from the idea of the action she had been about committing, as if from a precipice."

14 Marc Bloch, *Feudal Society,* tr. L. A. Manyon, foreword by M. M. Postan (Chicago: University of Chicago Press, 1961), pp. 301–2.

15 For an analysis of the relation between Gothic fiction and the political upheavals of the French Revolution as well as social and religious turmoil in general, see Joel Porte, "In the Hands of an Angry God: Religious Terror in Gothic Fiction," *The Gothic Imagination: Essays in Dark Romanticism,* ed. G. R. Thompson (Pullman: Washington State University Press, 1974).

16 See Clara Reeve's reference to the incredible marvels of *The Castle of Otranto* in the Preface to the Second Edition, *The Old English Baron: A Gothic Story,* ed. with an introduction by James Trainer (London. Oxford University Press, 1967), p. 5: "When your expectation is wound up to the highest pitch, then circumstances take it down . . . destroy the work of imagination, and, instead of attention, excite laughter."

4. THE CONTROL OF MEANING

1 For an analysis of the various ways in which sexuality appears in Austen's work, including comments specifically relevant to my own dis-

cussion of motion and dancing, see Alice Chandler, " 'A Pair of Fine Eyes': Jane Austen's Treatment of Sex," *Studies in the Novel* 7 (Spring 1975).

2 Cf. the description of another scene in which Elinor, in a state that might be seen to be as erotic as it is compassionate, cannot drive Willoughby from her thoughts long enough to fall asleep, in Marvin Mudrick, *Jane Austen: Irony as Defense and Discovery* (Princeton: Princeton University Press, 1952), p. 84.

3 All quotations from Austen's works are taken from *The Novels of Jane Austen*, ed. R. W. Chapman, 5 vols. (London: Oxford University Press, 1932–4); and *Jane Austen's Letters*, ed. R. W. Chapman, 2 vols. (Oxford: Oxford University Press, 1932).

4 For the way in which eighteenth-century book reviewers were liable to use the writings of female authors as a basis for interpreting their characters in a particularly intimate and "unlicensed" way, see Mary Lascelles, *Jane Austen and Her Art* (London: Oxford University Press, 1939), pp. 127–9; and J. M. S. Tompkins, *The Popular Novel*, pp. 15–18, 22, 116–28.

5 Samuel Richardson, *The History of Sir Charles Grandison*, Shakespeare Head Edition, 6 vols. (Oxford: Blackwell, 1931), 1: 216.

6 Stuart M. Tave, *Some Words of Jane Austen* (Chicago: University of Chicago Press, 1973), p. 8. Also, cf. D. W. Harding, "Regulated Hatred: An Aspect of the Work of Jane Austen," in *Jane Austen: A Collection of Critical Essays*, ed. Ian Watt (Englewood Cliffs, N.J.: Prentice-Hall, 1963), p. 170: "Her object is not missionary; it is the more desperate one of merely finding some mode of existence for her critical attitudes"; and Tony Tanner, "Jane Austen and 'The Quiet Thing' – A Study of *Mansfield Park*," in *Critical Essays on Jane Austen*, ed. B. C. Southam (New York: Barnes and Noble, 1969), p. 158, for his comments on how Austen "never canvassed the idea of a flight from society into non-social freedom."

7 The three major works in this regard are Henrietta Ten Harmsel, *Jane Austen: A Study in Fictional Conventions*, Studies in English Literature 4 (The Hague: Mouton, 1964); Frank W. Bradbrook, *Jane Austen and Her Predecessors* (Cambridge: Cambridge University Press, 1966); and Kenneth L. Moler, *Jane Austen's Art of Illusion* (Lincoln: University of Nebraska Press, 1968). Harmsel goes so far as to say that "Jane Austen both reshapes and preserves the exaggerated Richardsonian conventions of late eighteenth-century fiction" (p. 36), but she, Bradbrook, and Moler generally speak of this preservation as a formal matter of fictional conventions without considering its social significance.

8 Scott refers to the same Old Testament law (Numbers 30: 3–15) in his introduction to *The Bride of Lammermoor* and within *The Heart of Mid-*

lothian. As in Richardson's use of this reference, Scott's use is not a light or purely formulaic one, and it provides an interesting contemporary context to Austen's work. Thus, in Scott's only novel set in contemporary times, *St. Ronan's Well*, which was explicitly patterned, in part, on the example of Austen, Clara asks a question virtually identical to that asked by Fanny Price in the passage I discuss in the text a few lines later. "Is it necessary," asks Clara, "that one must have actually some engagement or entanglement to make them unwilling to be given in marriage, or even to be pestered upon such a subject?" (p. 253) – and just as in *Mansfield Park*, Clara actually *does* have a previous commitment, so that this rule is accepted by the novel. (And explicit reference is made within the novel to the example of Richardson's heroines.) Also, in reference to this discussion of how Austen's women are not allowed the negative, one might instance Scott's comment in his Introduction to *Rob Roy* about the days of which he is writing, when "any woman who happened to please a man of spirit who had a good horse, and possessed a few chosen friends and a retreat in the mountains, was not permitted the alternative of saying him nay" (p. xlvi) – and his further comment that the women agreed with this practice. Quotations are taken from the 24 vol. Dryburgh Edition of Scott's novels (Edinburgh: Black, 1892).

9   Cf. Lloyd W. Brown's comment that Fanny "is also an actor, using moral judgments to mask her general loneliness and her jealousy of Mary Crawford," in *Bits of Ivory: Narrative Techniques in Jane Austen's Fiction* (Baton Rouge: Louisiana State University Press, 1973), p. 88.

10 Richardson, *Clarissa: Or, The History of a Young Lady,* Shakespeare Head Edition, 6 vols. (Oxford: Blackwell, 1930), 5: 228.

11 Frances Burney, *Camilla: Or, A Picture of Youth,* ed. with an introduction by Edward A. Bloom and Lillian D. Bloom (London: Oxford University Press, 1972), p. 359.

12 David Daiches, "Jane Austen, Karl Marx, and the Aristocratic Dance," *American Scholar* 17 (Summer 1948), p. 291.

13 Burney, *Evelina: Or, The History of a Young Lady's Entrance into the World,* ed. with an introduction by Edward A. Bloom, Oxford English Novels, ed. Herbert Davis (London: Oxford University Press, 1968), p. 83.

14 C. S. Lewis, "A Note on Jane Austen," in *Jane Austen: A Collection of Critical Essays,* p. 28. For some other disagreements with Lewis's opinion, see J. F. Burrows, *Jane Austen's "Emma,"* Sydney Studies in Literature, ed. G. A. Wilkes and A. P. Riemer (Sydney: Sydney University Press, 1968), pp. 11–12; E. Rubinstein, "Jane Austen's Novels: The Metaphor of Rank," in *Literary Monographs,* vol. 2, ed. Eric Rothstein and Richard N. Ringler (Madison: University of Wisconsin

Press, 1969), pp. 190–1; and D. D. Devlin, *Jane Austen and Education* (New York: Barnes and Noble, 1975), p. 20.

15 Richardson, *Clarissa*, 4: 133.

16 Cf. Mudrick's comment that Emma lacks "the customary vanity that springs from the desire to please a suitor or a lover" in *Jane Austen*, p. 186.

17 Joseph Wiesenfarth, *"Emma:* Point Counter Point," in *Jane Austen: Bicentenary Essays*, ed. John Halperin (Cambridge: Cambridge University Press, 1975), p. 217. A comparable comment is Lionel Trilling's claim that in *Pride and Prejudice* "a formal rhetoric, traditional and vigorous, must find a way to accommodate a female vivacity, which in turn must recognize the principled demands of the strict male syntax. The high moral import of the novel lies in the fact that the union of styles is accomplished without injury to either lover." "Mansfield Park," *The Opposing Self*, p. 222.

18 Alistair M. Duckworth notes that even laughter, *à la* Chesterfield's *Letters*, may be inappropriate. As he writes of Lydia Bennet, "Lydia's tendency to laughter, like her habits of running everywhere and speaking loudly and rudely at inappropriate times, marks her morally unrestrained conduct." "Prospects and Retrospects," in *Jane Austen Today*, ed. Joel Weinsheimer (Athens: University of Georgia Press, 1975), p. 7.

19 For another analysis of the importance of dance in Austen, see Barbara Hardy, *A Reading of Jane Austen* (London: Owen, 1975), Ch. 5, "Social Groups." Also, cf. the comments of Mr. Jenkinson in Thomas Love Peacock, *Headlong Hall, Headlong Hall and Nightmare Abbey*, ed. Ernest Rhys, introduction by Richard Garnett, Everyman's Library (London: Dent, 1908), p. 150: "There is certainly a great deal to be said against dancing! There is also a great deal to be said in its favour . . . I may venture to allege that no amusement seems more natural and more congenial to youth than this. It has the advantage of bringing young persons of both sexes together, in a manner which its publicity renders perfectly unexceptionable, enabling them to see and know each other better than, perhaps, any other mode of general association. Tête-à-têtes are dangerous things. Small family parties are too much under mutual observation. A ballroom appears to me almost the only scene uniting that degree of rational and innocent liberty of intercourse which it is desirable to promote as much as possible between young persons, with that scrupulous attention to the delicacy and propriety of female conduct, which I consider the fundamental basis of all our most valuable social relations."

20 Susan Morgan, "Intelligence in *Pride and Prejudice,*" *Modern Philology* 73 (August 1975), p. 55.

5. ATTACHMENTS AND SUPPLANTMENTS

1 Almost all of Austen's critics, of course, have described her satirical criticism of the excesses of sensibility represented by the sentimental novel of the late eighteenth century. Some important descriptions or comments upon the significance of circumstances in her work can be found in Reuben Arthur Brower, "Light and Bright and Sparkling: Irony and Fiction in 'Pride and Prejudice,' " *The Fields of Light: An Experiment in Critical Reading* (New York: Oxford University Press, 1951), esp. p. 172; Trilling, "Mansfield Park," *The Opposing Self,* esp. p. 207; Paul N. Zietlow, "Luck and Fortuitous Circumstance in *Persuasion:* Two Interpretations," *ELH* 32 (June 1963); Robert Alan Donovan, "*Mansfield Park* and Jane Austen's Moral Universe," *The Shaping Vision: Imagination in the English Novel from Defoe to Dickens* (Ithaca: Cornell University Press, 1966), esp. pp. 166–7; Joel Weinsheimer, "Chance and the Hierarchy of Marriages in *Pride and Prejudice,*" *ELH* 39 (September 1972); Jane Nardin, *Those Elegant Decorums: The Concept of Propriety in Jane Austen's Novels* (Albany: State University of New York Press, 1973), pp. 9, 33, 39; Darrel Mansell, *The Novels of Jane Austen: An Interpretation* (London: Macmillan, 1973), esp. p. 31; Tave, *Some Words of Jane Austen,* esp. p. 30; and Susan Morgan, "Polite Lies: The Veiled Heroine of *Sense and Sensibility,*" *Nineteenth-Century Fiction* 31 (September 1976), esp. p. 194.

2 For the dramatic and thematic significance of games in Austen's work, see Alistair M. Duckworth, " 'Spillikins, Paper Ships, Riddles, Conundrums, and Cards': Games in Jane Austen's Life and Fiction," *Jane Austen: Bicentenary Essays.* See also the comment on Emma by A. Walton Litz, *Jane Austen: A Study of Her Artistic Development* (New York: Oxford University Press, 1965), p. 138: "Ultimately she must realize that she has viewed life as a game in which she can display her imagination and powers of perception; it is no accident that Jane Austen uses Emma's fondness for conundrums, charades, and word-games to reveal her errors of imagination."

3 See the comments by Tompkins on the occurrence of this topic in late-eighteenth-century fiction in *The Popular Novel,* pp. 162–5. Also, see the reference to Mary Wollstonecraft's criticism of first impressions in Marian E. Fowler, "The Feminist Bias of *Pride and Prejudice,*" *Dalhousie Review* 57 (Spring 1977), p. 53. *First Impressions* was, of course, the title of an early version of *Pride and Prejudice.*

4 See Lawrence Lerner, *The Truthtellers: Jane Austen, George Eliot, D. H. Lawrence* (London: Chatto and Windus, 1967), p. 149: "I have never been able to find a convincing reason why Henry Crawford eloped with Maria."

5   Cf. Everett Zimmerman, "Admiring Pope No More than Is Proper: *Sense and Sensibility,*" *Jane Austen: Bicentenary Essays,* p. 120: "Decorum tends to become an independent force, separated from understanding and harnessed to no conceivable end."

6   Howard S. Babb, *Jane Austen's Novels: The Fabric of Dialogue* (Columbus, Ohio: Archon Books, 1967), p. 16.

7   Cf. Eric Rothstein, "The Lessons of *Northanger Abbey,*" *The University of Toronto Quarterly* 44 (Fall 1974), p. 25: "In this 'novel of manners,' manners express character and ethical values, but completely so only in retrospect, only in the shape of history or art, not life."

8   For the difficulty of interpreting people on the basis of their behavior, cf. G. Armour Craig, "Jane Austen's *Emma:* The Truths and Disguises of Human Disclosure," *In Defense of Reading: A Reader's Approach to Literary Criticism,* ed. Reuben A. Brower and Richard Poirier (New York: Dutton, 1962).

9   Brown, *Bits of Ivory,* p. 169. Also, cf. Tave, *Some Words of Jane Austen,* p. 17: "What seems to be more important than the sudden and fortunate event, however, because it precedes the ending again and again, in whatever manner the end is produced, is that the heroine is prepared to accept unhappiness."

10   Cf. Morgan, "Intelligence in *Pride and Prejudice,*" p. 55. Morgan is one of very few critics to argue against the idea that Austen's perspective "is one of social and national good": "We have been too eager to assume that Jane Austen's was a conclusive vision, a sort of apotheosis of the optimism of premodern fiction. Yet to understand *Pride and Prejudice* in terms of the ideal blend of the individual and the social is to speak of finalities about a writer who herself chooses to speak of the possible, the continuous, the incomplete."

11   Mudrick, *Jane Austen,* p. 15.

12   For an extensive analysis of the situation of social classes and the problem of rank in Austen's work, see Rubinstein, "Jane Austen's Novels: The Metaphor of Rank."

13   F. M. L. Thompson, *English Landed Society in the Nineteenth Century,* Studies in Social History, ed. Harold Perkin (London: Routledge and Kegan Paul, 1963), p. 70.

14   Alistair M. Duckworth, *The Improvement of the Estate: A Study of Jane Austen's Novels* (Baltimore: Johns Hopkins Press, 1971), pp. 125, 58.

15   See John Halperin, "The Victorian Novel and Jane Austen," *Egoism and Self-Discovery in the Victorian Novel: Studies in the Ordeal of Knowledge in the Nineteenth Century,* introduction by Walter Allen (New York: Burt Franklin, 1974).

16   Cf. Trilling's description of Austen as one who was "aware of the Terror which rules our moral situation, the ubiquitous anonymous

judgment to which we respond," in "Mansfield Park," *The Opposing Self,* p. 228.

17 Cf. Devlin, *Jane Austen and Education,* p. 18: "Fathers and mothers are roughly handled in these novels; they are either dead, absent, or disasters. They are not disposed of in order that Jane Austen may create Cinderella situations for the young women in her novels, but because she wishes to play down the importance of heredity in shaping the disposition of her heroines."

18 For comments on the importance of the entail and other legal considerations in Austen's fiction and in that of other novelists of her age, see Joseph Kastner, "Jane Austen: The Tradition of the English Romantic Novel, 1800–1832," *Wordsworth Circle* 7 (Autumn 1976), pp. 305–8.

19 A. N. Kaul, *The Action of English Comedy: Studies in the Encounter of Abstraction and Experience from Shakespeare to Shaw* (New Haven: Yale University Press, 1970), p. 225.

20 H. J. Habakkuk, "England," *The European Nobility in the Eighteenth Century: Studies in the Nobilities of the Major European States in the Pre-reform Era,* ed. A. Goodwin (London: Black, 1953), p. 2.

21 Cf. Francis R. Hart, "The Spaces of Privacy: Jane Austen," *Nineteenth-Century Fiction* 30 (December 1975).

22 In terms of the aforementioned conflicts in the transition from aristocratic to middle-class values, it is interesting to consider how much the quality of life in Austen's families resembles the traditional aristocratic family life even though these families also show some characteristics of the new "sentimental" family. For detailed descriptions of these two different family "styles," see Lawrence Stone, *The Family, Sex and Marriage in England: 1500–1800* (New York: Harper and Row, 1977).

Also, for some significant analyses of Austen's families, see F. G. Bornall, "Marriage, Property, and Romance in Jane Austen's Novels (1)," *The Hibbert Journal* 65 (Autumn 1966), and the conclusion of this article in *The Hibbert Journal* 66 (Autumn 1967); Lloyd W. Brown, "The Business of Marrying and Mothering," *Jane Austen's Achievement: Papers Delivered at the Jane Austen Bicentennial Conference at the University of Alberta,* ed. Juliet McMaster (New York: Barnes and Noble, 1976); Mark Shorer, "Fiction and the 'Analogical Matrix,' " *Critiques and Essays on Modern Fiction 1920–1951,* ed. John W. Aldridge, foreword by Mark Shorer (New York: Ronald Press, 1952); Harrison R. Steeves, *Before Jane Austen: The Shaping of the English Novel in the Eighteenth Century* (New York: Holt, Rinehart and Winston, 1965), pp. 377–8; and Frederick R. Karl, *A Reader's Guide to the Nineteenth-*

Century British Novel (New York: Noonday Press, 1965), pp. 28–9 and 42–4.

See also R. W. Chapman's quaint but perceptive comment about how ill-matched the members of Austen's families are – in "defiance of the probabilities of heredity" – in *Jane Austen: Facts and Problems* (Oxford: Oxford University Press, 1948), p. 184.

23 Richardson, *Sir Charles Grandison*, 3: 74.

24 Richard Simpson, "Review," *Jane Austen: The Critical Heritage*, ed. B. C. Southam, The Critical Heritage Series, ed. B. C. Southam (London: Routledge and Kegan Paul, 1968), p. 244. For an example of the persistence of this type of reading in contemporary criticism, see Juliet McMaster, "Love and Pedagogy," in Weinsheimer, ed., *Jane Austen Today*.

25 Samuel Johnson, *The Adventurer, The Yale Edition of the Works of Samuel Johnson* (New Haven: Yale University Press, 1958–), 2: 456.

26 Mandeville, *The Fable of the Bees*, 1: 68.

27 The only critic I have found who treats this as a complex passage in which Henry's voice is not necessarily dominant is Donald D. Stone, "Sense and Semantics in Jane Austen," *Nineteenth-Century Fiction* 25 (June 1970), pp. 38–9.

28 Cf. Mark Shorer, "The Humiliation of Emma Woodhouse," *The Literary Review* 2 (Summer 1959); and Alison G. Sulloway, "Emma Woodhouse and *A Vindication of the Rights of Women*," *Wordsworth Circle* 7 (Autumn 1976). For a differing analysis of this process of education in Austen's fiction that relates it more to literary than social traditions, see George Levine, "Translating the Monstrous: *Northanger Abbey*," *Nineteenth-Century Fiction* 30 (December 1975).

6. READING THE WORD OF NATURE

1 C. S. Lewis, "A Note on Jane Austen," in Watt, ed., *Jane Austen: A Collection of Critical Essays*, p. 28; Andrew H. Wright, *Jane Austen's Novels: A Study in Structure* (London: Chatto and Windus, 1953), pp. 36–82; Bradbrook, *Jane Austen and Her Predecessors*, p. 46; Burrows, *Jane Austen's "Emma,"* pp. 11–12, 40–9; Rubinstein, "Jane Austen's Novels: The Metaphor of Rank," pp. 190–1; K. C. Phillips, *Jane Austen's English* (London: Deutsch, 1970), pp. 37–40; Norman Page, *The Language of Jane Austen* (Oxford: Blackwell, 1972), p. 22; Nardin, *Those Elegant Decorums*, p. 9; Tave, *Some Words of Jane Austen*, p. 30; Mansell, *The Novels of Jane Austen*, p. 31; Brown, *Bits of Ivory*, pp. 15–51; Devlin, *Jane Austen and Education*, p. 20; Alistair M. Duckworth, "Prospects and Retrospects," p. 14.

2   David Daiches, "Austen, Marx, and the Aristocratic Dance," p. 296.

3   Possible exceptions are D. W. Harding, "Regulated Hatred," especially in his comment (p. 171) that under Austen's treatment "one can never say where caricature leaves off and the claim to serious portraiture begins"; Sulloway, "Emma Woodhouse and *A Vindication of the Rights of Women*"; and Morgan, "Intelligence in *Pride and Prejudice.*"

4   Henry James, "The Lesson of Balzac," *The Future of the Novel: Essays on the Art of Fiction,* ed. with an introduction by Leon Edel (New York: Vintage Books, 1956), p. 100.

5   W. A. Craik, *Jane Austen: The Six Novels* (London: Methuen, 1965), p. 3.

6   See Marvin Mudrick, *Jane Austen,* pp. 34–5, 51, 85, 91.

7   Lionel Trilling, "*Emma* and the Legend of Jane Austen" in *Jane Austen: Emma,* ed. David Lodge, Casebook Series (London: Macmillan, 1968), p. 150.

8   Arthur O. Lovejoy, "Some Meanings of 'Nature,' " in George Boas and Arthur O. Lovejoy, *Primitivism and Related Ideas in Antiquity,* with supplementary essays by W. F. Albright and P .E. Dumont (New York: Octagon Books, 1973).

9   See, for example, Carl L. Becker, *The Heavenly City of the Eighteenth-Century Philosophers* (New Haven: Yale University Press, 1932), pp. 51–4; and Paul Hazard, *European Thought in the Eighteenth Century: From Montesquieu to Lessing,* tr. J. Lewis May (London: Hollis and Carter, 1954), pp. 284–350.

10 Voltaire, "Essai sur la poésie épique," *Oeuvres,* 8: 312.

11 Cf. Brown, "The Business of Marrying and Mothering," *Jane Austen's Achievement,* p. 41: "It is important to note that the happy marriage of the hero and the heroine is one of the comically self-conscious mechanics of Austen's happy endings. In elaborating on the contrived inevitability of her happy endings Austen is able to emphasize in a comic way the superiority of her art to the more transparent artifices of popular fiction while at the same time conceding the essential artifices (including the happy ending) of her own fictive realism." One might add that this concession shows deference to a power that is not just that of fictional convention but also of social suasion.

12 Virginia Woolf, "Jane Austen," in *The Common Reader* (New York: Harcourt, Brace, 1925).

13 Steele, *The Spectator,* 1: No. 11.

7. BLIND ROADS

1   George Lukács, *The Historical Novel,* tr. Hannah Mitchell and Stanley Mitchell (London: Merlin Press, 1962), p. 54.

2 Donald Davie, *"Waverley,"* in *Walter Scott: Modern Judgments,* ed.
   D. D. Devlin (London: Macmillan, 1968), p. 91.
3 D. D. Devlin, *The Author of Waverley: A Critical Study of Walter Scott*
   (London: Macmillan, 1971), p. 47.
4 Allan Frazer, ed., *Sir Walter Scott 1771–1832: An Edinburgh Keepsake*
   (Edinburgh: Edinburgh University Press, 1971).
5 All references to Scott's novels are to the authoritative 24-volume
   Dryburgh Edition (Edinburgh: Black, 1892).
6 David Daiches, "Scott and Scotland," in *Scott Bicentenary Essays: Selected Papers Read at the Sir Walter Scott Bicentenary Conference,* ed. Alan
   Bell (Edinburgh: Scottish Academic Press, 1973), p. 57.
7 The exceptions are *The Bride of Lammermoor, Kenilworth, The Highland
   Widow, St. Ronan's Well,* and *The Surgeon's Daughter.*
8 Robert C. Gordon, *Under Which King?: A Study of the Scottish Waverley
   Novels* (Edinburgh: Oliver and Boyd, 1969), p. 109.
9 *The Spectator,* 3:568.
10 Essential works for a description of this transition are the historical
   studies of Lawrence Stone, especially *The Crisis of the Aristocracy: 1558–
   1641* (Oxford: Oxford University Press, 1965), and *The Family, Sex
   and Marriage in England: 1500–1800* (New York: Harper and Row,
   1977).
11 Avrom Fleishman, *The English Historical Novel: Walter Scott to Virginia
   Woolf* (Baltimore: Johns Hopkins Press, 1971), p. 38.
12 See Mario Praz, *The Hero in Eclipse in Victorian Fiction,* tr. Angus Da-
   vidson (London: Oxford University Press, 1969), pp. 54–64.
13 For an overview of the conflicts between feudal and commercial codes
   in Scott's fiction, see Laurence Poston, III, "The Commercial Motif
   of the Waverley Novels," *ELH* 42 (Spring 1975), pp. 62–87.
14 Cf. P. D. Garside, "Scott, the Romantic Past and the Nineteenth Century," *The Review of English Studies* 23 (May 1972), p. 155: "Scott
   gives few signs of believing that an age of pure chivalry ever existed."

8. SUPERSTITION AND THE ENCHANTED READER

1 For an extensive discussion of the varieties of superstition used by
   Scott and for their historical background, see Coleman O. Parsons,
   Witchcraft and Demonology in Scott's Fiction (Edinburgh: Oliver and Boyd,
   1964).
2 Angus Calder and Jenni Calder, *Scott,* Literature in Perspective, ed.
   Kenneth H. Grose (London: Evans Brothers, 1969), p. 57.
3 Alexander Welsh, *The Hero of the Waverley Novels* (New Haven: Yale
   University Press, 1963), p. 156.
4 Some notable examples of modern Scott criticism related to this tradition

are Welsh, *The Hero of the Waverley Novels;* Francis R. Hart, *Scott's Novels: The Plotting of Historical Survival* (Charlottesville: University Press of Virginia, 1966); Joseph E. Duncan's "The Anti-Romantic in *Ivanhoe,"* David Daiches's "Scott's *Redgauntlet,"* and Donald Davie's *"Waverley"* in *Walter Scott: Modern Judgments;* Gordon, *Under Which King?;* Devlin, *The Author of Waverley;* David Daiches, "Scott's Achievement as a Novelist," *Scott's Mind and Art,* ed. A. Norman Jeffares (New York: Barnes and Noble, 1970); Garside, "Scott, the Romantic Past and the Nineteenth Century"; Robin Mayhead, *Walter Scott* (Cambridge: Cambridge University Press, 1973).

5 It is curious that the three most famous nineteenth-century critics of Scott – Carlyle, Hazlitt, and Bagehot – all commented on the fitness of his novels for the sickbed. See Thomas Carlyle, "Sir Walter Scott," *Critical and Miscellaneous Essays,* 5 vols. (London: Chapman and Hall, 1899), 4: 22–87; William Hazlitt, *The Spirit of the Age, The Complete Works of William Hazlitt,* ed. P. P. Howe, Centenary Edition, 21 vols. (London: Dent, 1932), 11: 57–68; Walter Bagehot, "The Waverley Novels," *The Collected Works of Walter Bagehot,* ed. Norman St. John-Stevas, 8 vols. (Cambridge: Harvard University Press, 1965), 2: 44–75.

6 For another example of this recognition, see Charles Robert Maturin, *The Albigenses: A Romance,* foreword by James Gray, introduction by Dale Kramer, 3 vols. (London: Hurst, Robinson, 1824; rep. New York: Arno Press, 1974), 1: 420: "The belief in the power of witchcraft, and its influence as connected with that belief, were during the dark ages in a state of fluctuation and obscurity, equally puzzling to the historian and the writer of romances.

   "The art was denounced as unlawful and damnable, yet often resorted to by those who reviled it most. It was at once disclaimed and confided in, forbidden, and employed."

7 Cf. Stone, *The Crisis of the Aristocracy,* p. 21: "In fact as late as 1870 England was basically aristocratic in tone, taking its moral standards, its hierarchy of social values, and its political system from the landed classes."

8 Lukács, *The Historical Novel,* p. 48.

9 Mario Praz, *The Hero in Eclipse in Victorian Fiction,* p. 54.

10 Ibid., p. 56.

11 Lukács, *The Historical Novel,* p. 54.

12 Ibid., p. 31.

13 All quotations are from *The Complete Poetical Works of Samuel Taylor Coleridge,* ed. with textual and bibliographical notes by Ernest Hartley Coleridge, 2 vols. (Oxford: Oxford University Press, 1912).

14 Lukács, *The Historical Novel*, p. 55.

15 Cf. the description of Harry as one impressed by the values of chivalry that Scott places at the beginning of the novel (*FMP*, 46–7).

16 Mark Twain, *Life on the Mississippi, The Complete Travel Books of Mark Twain*, ed. Charles Neider, 2 vols. (Garden City: Doubleday, 1967), 2: 576–7.

9. VIOLENCE AND LAW

1 For Scott's attitude toward history and the constants within that attitude, see Avrom Fleishman's comparison of his ideas to those of the philosopher Adam Ferguson in *The English Historical Novel: Walter Scott to Virginia Woolf* (Baltimore: Johns Hopkins Press, 1971), pp. 38–44.

2 Karl Kroeber, *Romantic Narrative Art* (Madison: University of Wisconsin Press, 1960), p. 185.

3 Stone, *The Crisis of the Aristocracy*, esp. p. 240.

4 Cf. Godwin's description of a tournament in which "the stiffness of unwieldy form was laid aside, and the heart of man expanded itself with generosity and confidence," in *St. Leon*, p. 6.

5 Cf. Lars Hartveit's similar comment that in *Guy Mannering* " 'Extralegal' agents are required to effect . . . a restoration of rights." *Dream within a Dream: A Thematic Approach to Scott's Vision of Fictional Reality*, Norwegian Studies in English No. 18 (New York: Humanities Press, 1974), p. 137.

6 Cf. Edgar Johnson, *Sir Walter Scott: The Great Unknown*, 2 vols. (New York: Macmillan, 1970), 1: 192, for the reaction of James Hogg's mother to Scott's publication of her old ballads: "There war never ane o' my songs prentit till ye prentit them yoursel', an' ye hae spoilt them awthegither. They were made for singin' an' no for readin'; but ye hae broke the charm noo, an' they'll never be sung mair."

7 Hart, *Scott's Novels*, p. 81.

8 Cf. *Quentin Durward*, Introduction, p. xxiii: "I gradually sipped and smoked myself into a certain degree of acquaintance with *un homme comme il faut*, one of the few fine old specimens of nobility who are still to be found in France, who, like mutilated statues of an antiquated and obsolete worship, still command a certain portion of awe and estimation in the eyes even of those by whom neither one nor other are voluntarily rendered."

9 See Basil Willey, *The Eighteenth Century Background: Studies in the Idea of Nature in the Thought of the Period* (New York: Columbia University Press, 1941), pp. 49–50.

10 Cf. Fleishman, *The English Historical Novel,* p. 84: "The large number of royal intercessions into a legal system that was widely recognized as excessively severe built aristocratic *noblesse oblige* into the institutional structure of the law."

INDEX

∽

Index

Index